Jack and Rochelle

Jack and Rochelle

A HOLOCAUST STORY

OF LOVE AND RESISTANCE

BY JACK AND ROCHELLE SUTIN

EDITED BY LAWRENCE SUTIN

GRAYWOLF PRESS

Publication of this volume is made possible in part by a grant provided by the Minnesota State Arts Board, through an appropriation by the Minnesota State Legislature; a grant from the Wells Fargo Foundation Minnesota; and a grant from the National Endowment for the Arts, which believes that a great nation deserves great art. Significant support has also been provided by the Bush Foundation; Target; the McKnight Foundation; and other generous contributions from foundations, corporations, and individuals. To these organizations and individuals we offer our heartfelt thanks.

Published by Graywolf Press
2402 University Avenue, Suite 203
Saint Paul, Minnesota 55114
All rights reserved.

www.graywolfpress.org

Published in the United States of America

ISBN 978-1-55597-224-0 (cloth edition)
ISBN 978-1-55597-243-1 (previous paperback edition)

ISBN 978-1-55597-503-6

2 4 6 8 9 7 5 3

Library of Congress Control Number: 2007940218

Cover design: Jeenee Lee Design

Cover photograph: Courtesy of Jack and Rochelle Sutin

Contents

Preface   IX

Principal Locations in the Narrative, 1939–1945   XI

I   Family Roots and Coming of Age   1

II   Life Under Soviet Rule   21

III   Onset of the Nazi Horror   33

IV   Jack Escapes from the Mir Ghetto   57

V   Rochelle Escapes from the Stolpce Ghetto   71

VI   Courtship in the Woods   87

VII   From the Bunker to the Atrad   109

VIII   Nazi Assault on the Nalibocka Forest   129

IX   Under the Soviet Yoke Again   149

X   From Germany to America   173

XI   Life in America   193

An Afterword on the "Second Generation"   205

Notes and Acknowledgments   219

For the grandchildren—
David, Danny, and Sarah

Preface

The narrative you are about to read is true. It has been assembled from numerous interview sessions between myself and my parents, Jack and Rochelle Sutin. They have pored over every word of this book, determined that it be an accurate account of their lives.

There were dilemmas posed for all Holocaust survivors who started families in the postwar years. What should they say of their experiences? When? Was there a risk of traumatizing the young? Would silence create a gulf of unease between parents and children?

My parents chose to speak openly of their experiences to us—to my sister Cecilia and myself. I cannot remember at what age I first began to hear their Holocaust stories. But they were part of my childhood, and they did not harm me. This is not to deny that they were painful in the extreme. Nor is it to deny that the pain has left its mark upon me. But none of us escape suffering. And I always felt, as far back as I can remember, that it was a necessary pain.

Silence—a refusal to entrust us with the truth—would have been far worse. Unbearable.

The pain extended beyond the content of the stories themselves. Watching the faces of my parents as they spoke was the hardest part. Seeing my parents cry was a grief, a humiliation, an agony to sit through.

Early on, my parents would say to us, "We know you won't be able to believe these things. They don't happen in the world you know here in America." But we did believe them. And we were encouraged to ask all the questions that came to our minds. These story sessions became the occasions when we spoke most openly with our parents. To learn about the Holocaust is to learn about life as well as death.

It needs to be said that there were times, while telling these stories, that *none* of us in the room were sad. We were laughing, fascinated by the stories of their very different childhoods in the Polish towns of Stolpce and Mir, and delighted in hearing—again and again—how our father and mother had fallen in love in the Polish woods while hiding from the Nazis and fighting for the Jewish partisans.

Let it also be said that we were never such fools as to believe that our parents' survival had to do with any moral or other superiority on their part. Death in the Holocaust was omnipresent; the millions of Jews who died and the small living remnant of survivors are One, but for the accidents of fate.

There are two voices intertwined in the narrative: those of Jack and Rochelle. Now and then they interrupt each other. That is the way they have told these stories for the past fifty years: side by side, listening intently each to the other, at the ready to speak up lest a single detail be lost. These stories are their lives—the testament of their survival and their love for each other. LAWRENCE SUTIN

PRINCIPAL LOCATIONS
IN THE NARRATIVE
1939 - 1945

Jack and Rochelle

I

Family Roots and Coming of Age

ROCHELLE
My mother and father met just after the end of World War I. It was a chance event, and perhaps an unfortunate one.

My mother Cila was born in 1900 and grew up in the Russian city of Minsk. Her maiden name was Benienson. Her family was upper-class, well-educated, cultured. Her father was in the timber business and her mother ran the household and was devoted to her children—a son and five daughters, including Cila.

It was an unusual family for the time in that all of the daughters were encouraged to pursue a university education. Cila graduated with a dental diploma from the University of Charkow, while another one of her sisters, Rachel, trained as a lawyer and moved to Warsaw to practice. Rachel was not fated to have a long life. She married and had a son, but then died in childbirth. It was, indirectly, through her death that my parents would meet.

Cila travelled from Minsk to Warsaw to attend her sister's funeral. It was a somewhat complicated journey, as it involved changing trains at the border between Poland and Russia. On her way home, Stolpce was the changing point—the last town on the Polish side. Stolpce is located in the region of Belorussia (White Russia), which had been in Russian hands until the end of World War I, when Poland gained back the lands on its eastern frontier that it had not held for over a century. Stolpce had a talent, you can see, for being always in the path of conquering armies. That talent would continue on into my own lifetime.

But when my mother stepped off the train at Stolpce that day, everything was peaceful. She was very young then, and quite beautiful. Her hair was a rich dark black, and she had large and probing blue eyes. You could see that she was a sensitive one—she registered what happened around her. And she had an air of kindness. Because of the train schedules, she was going to have to wait in Stolpce for two days for the next train to Minsk.

On that very day when Cila arrived, my father, Lazar Schleiff, was working at the train station, supervising the loading of turpentine and tar into railroad cars. That was the Schleiff family business—*smolarne* (refined lumber products) as well as coal. It had been founded by my grandfather, but he had died not long before and control had passed to two of his sons, Lazar and his younger brother Oscar.

My mother caught Lazar's eye on that day as she waited on the platform, checking the schedule for the train to Minsk. Lazar was twelve years older than Cila. He was a handsome man with a strong brow and dominating eyes. And he must have been quite a talker, because he managed to convince Cila to stay on in Stolpce for the next two nights in a guest bedroom in the Schleiff family home. Lazar immediately began to court Cila with every means at his disposal, promising her his devotion and the comforts of his wealth. To lessen her desire to return to Minsk, Lazar warned her that life would not fare well for educated professionals under the new Communist regime in Russia.

As it turned out, Cila never took the train to Minsk. In fact, she never saw her family again. To be perfectly honest, I'm not sure why that was the case. Cila corresponded regularly with her family for many years, and sent them money and food packages as well. I would hear her say, from time to time, that she missed them. But they didn't come to the wedding, and there were never any visits. That may have been due to the difficulty of travel between Poland and Russia once the new Soviet regime set up its rules and regulations. Under both Lenin and Stalin—especially under Stalin—contacts with the non-Communist West—including, at that time, Poland— were viewed with extreme suspicion. In 1933, Cila's mother wrote her to say that she would have to break off further correspondence—to continue would be to place herself and the rest of the family under threat of arrest.

For their first three years of married life, Cila and Lazar lived with the rest of the Schleiff family. It was a large house that included not only Lazar's mother, Ethel Schleiff, but also his eight sisters. Living together as an extended family was much more common in those days in Poland than it is in America today. Even so, there were fierce tensions that made Cila's life miserable.

You must understand that, amongst Polish Jews of that time, there was a kind of unwritten law: the brothers of a family had to wait until their sisters married before they themselves got married. It didn't matter if there were substantial age differences between the siblings—that's the way it was. The important thing was that the brothers should assist in providing each of the sisters with as large a dowry as possible. The larger the dowry, you see, the better the match that could be made for them. Since Lazar's father had died, it was especially important that Lazar oversee his eight sisters' marriages.

Lazar could see that there would be no end to this business, and so he broke the rule. He had fallen so hard for Cila that he could not wait to marry her. And then he dared to bring her into the family home!

All of the sisters resented Cila. The primary reason was that Lazar had married her out of turn. And now that Lazar was married, he was less motivated to provide for his sisters, since his thoughts had turned to preparing for the family he planned to have with Cila. But even beyond these factors, the sisters hated Cila because they could not help but see her as in a class above themselves. Cila was educated and articulate. They were neither. But rather than admit their jealousy, they insisted on acting as if Cila was a snob who took pleasure in treating them badly.

My father Lazar resembled his sisters in many basic ways. Like them, he had been raised in Stolpce, an isolated and provincial town. As a boy, he had received a basic Jewish education and had spent a brief amount of time in high school during the period of Russian rule. But Lazar never wanted to attend a university. My father was all business—a very ambitious, high-strung man. Not only was there the lumber-products company, but on the family estate they raised horses, cows, chickens. . . . They made money from everything. My mother, by comparison, came from a big city—Minsk. She liked to read, to play the piano. She didn't know how to milk a cow or tend to laying chickens. The sisters despised her for her ignorance. As for Lazar, he was pleased with himself for having won a cultured woman as his wife.

I was the first child, born during the fourth year of their marriage. I have very few memories of life in the Schleiff family house, however, because we moved out when I was three years old. My father, who was growing steadily more prosperous, decided to build a *bigger* house for his wife and his child and the children to come. And he built it far away—on the other side of town. Perhaps he felt sorry for my mother. And perhaps he was himself tired of living under the eyes of his family. But he made up his mind to outdo the old family house, and he succeeded.

What a house it was! By the standards of Stolpce, it was luxurious beyond compare. Everyone in town used outhouses. But we had flushing indoor toilets! And while some of the better houses in town had indoor running water, it was cold water only. If you wanted hot water, you heated it up on your stove. But in our house, we had indoor copper-pipe plumbing. When we used our stove for cooking, the copper pipes heated the water tank in the attic. So we had hot baths, hot showers, simply by turning on the faucet. Unheard of! Of course, all of the rooms and furnishings were deluxe, and the surrounding yard was vast. It was a very comfortable house, a palace.

As you can imagine, the move to that new house did nothing to improve relations between my mother and the Schleiff family. And the hostilities spilled out onto myself and my sisters, even though all of Lazar's sisters did eventually marry and were provided with large dowries on each occasion. I always used to feel that I and my two younger sisters, Sofka and Miriam, were treated as *Tzila's kinder* (Cila's children)—the least favorite of all the grandchildren. I was more sensitive to this than Sofka was—she was a happy-go-lucky type. Miriam was so young that their behavior did not make an impact upon her before the war came.

My mother tried to heal the wounds over time, but no matter what she did, somehow it was counted against her. For example, Cila always liked to dress with style—to look "put-together," you would call it. And the family, instead of saying, "How nice she looks!" would mutter, "What does she care? Lazar makes the money and she spends it!" Eventually, my mother stopped paying visits to the family house altogether, as did her children. My father would go there by himself.

As the years went on, things did not go so smoothly between my father and my mother. Looking back now, I can see that it wasn't a good marriage. But, as a child, I did not pass judgment. It was different back then, in Poland, than it is today in America, where so many children become involved in the private details of their parents' marriages by way of family counselling or divorce proceedings. My generation did not question—or even wonder about—the relationship between their parents. But I do remember how it was between them.

When my father first planned our new house, he had two rooms built at the very front to serve as a lobby and a treatment office for my mother, so that she could continue with her dental practice. But she did not continue for long. I was born, and then Sofka was born, and even though we had a nanny and a maid, my father did not want her to practice dentistry anymore. He wanted her to focus on the children. She loved being home with us, and in truth it was no great sorrow for her to give up her work. Her dental-practice rooms were rented out as an apartment unit. The house was so big that ultimately all the rooms on the second floor were let out as well. Only well-to-do citizens of the town could afford them.

But the real problem for me at that time did not come from the tension between my parents. It was from the hatred felt by the majority of Poles for the Jews. From the time I started school, I was always called a "dirty Jew." Sometimes I was beaten up by my classmates. Sometimes they threw stones at me as I was walking home. Not far from us there lived a Polish family with a girl my age. We used to play together. She would tell me the stories about Jews that her mother had told her: that if she was a bad girl, the Jews would come and kill her; that Jews kill Christian children to get the blood they need to make their Passover matzoh. All of those stories you can still hear today, not only in Eastern Europe but in America as well.

During holidays such as Christmas or Easter, the Christian residents of Stolpce used to have processions through the streets. Jews didn't dare appear in public then. We had to close all the windows and pull the curtains. If they saw you outside, they would throw stones. If they caught you, they would beat you. There were always threats about full-scale pogroms [attacks en masse against a Jewish community]. There was a tiny marketplace in which the Jewish businesses of the town were located. A Polish policeman named Schultz, who worked that neighborhood beat, received bribes regularly from members of the Jewish community, including my father. In exchange for those bribes, Schultz would alert us—some of the time, at least—to planned lootings and attacks.

My father was not a devoutly religious man, and yet he involved himself with the Jewish community in important ways. As a matter of practical assistance, he served on the board of a bank founded by Jews to serve other Jewish businessmen, because it was nearly impossible for Jews to obtain loans from Polish-run banks. But my father also placed value on certain Jewish rituals for their own sake. He was the voluntary head of the local *Chevre Kaddishe* [Brotherhood of the Kaddish—the kaddish being the Jewish prayer of mourning], an organization that devoted itself to fulfilling the Jewish burial laws. If someone in the community died, my father would be summoned to the home of the deceased. With his fellow brethren, he would wash the body, prepare a shroud for it, and take care of the funeral details.

My father set the religious tone for the household. He wasn't a regular worshipper at the synagogue, but he always attended on the major Jewish holidays—Rosh Hashanah, Yom Kippur, Passover and others—and so did we. We lit the Sabbath candles every Friday night, but we didn't keep the Sabbath in any strict sense. By American standards, we came within the category of "conservative" Judaism. I was taught enough Hebrew to recite with understanding the basic blessings and prayers. I grew up believing in the Jewish faith and the Jewish God, as they were presented to me by my father.

To some extent, my father's loyalty to the Jewish community carried over into the way he ran his business. The managers of my father's factories were always Jews. The workers were drawn from the local Polish population. As for the basic raw materials used for processing—the large root systems of old trees—they came from wooded lands leased from the Polish gentry, who also leased farmlands to the Polish peasants. It was the Polish gentry who had the real power in the region.

In the conduct of his business, my father was generous only to himself and to his family. His younger brother Oscar was more of a field man, weighing the roots for payment and overseeing the factory workers. But Lazar was what you would call the CEO or chief decision maker. He took care of long-range planning, financing, billing. And he was not softhearted. I remember that one of his Jewish managers developed a severe case of rheumatism in his hip. It was hard for him. He had been advised by his doctor to go to a mineral bath spa in southern Poland, but he couldn't afford it. My mother would plead with my father, "Give him a raise. Send him there, send him there." But my father was as tough as nuts. "It's not your affair," he would tell her. "You take care of the family. The business is mine."

He was the same way with his workers. In every one of the factories, there was a little provisions store that sold the basics, such as salt, salt pork, sugar, and kerosene. The kerosene was for their lamps, as their homes had no electricity. Shopping at this factory store saved them a trip into town, but the prices were high. My father made a considerable profit from these stores. So he was making money on anything and everything. And he paid very little in official taxes. If you had connections with the right Polish officials—and bribed them heavily enough—you were basically taken care of. Lazar was not the only one who took advantage of this; bribery was a way of life in Poland, for Jews and Poles alike. But he did know how to handle it smoothly, wining and dining officials and sending them exorbitant gifts.

But there were limits to what even Lazar's riches could buy. As it happened, one of the tenants in our house was a Polish woman who held the post of director of the local Polish *gymnasium* [a school corresponding to the American grades seven through twelve; admission was dependent on the passage of rigorous examinations]. She had chosen to rent with us because the apartment we offered her—the two rooms that were to have served my mother's dental practice—was far and away the nicest one available in little Stolpce. She shared our kitchen and even our shower, but there was no communication between her and our family. She was very standoffish.

When I turned twelve years old, and it was time for me to go to the *gymnasium,* I took and passed the entrance exam. But that wasn't enough for a Jew to enter the Polish schools— not with the strict quotas in effect. My father decided to make a large financial contribution to the Stolpce *gymnasium* that year, and I was admitted—but with extreme reluctance, even with the director living in our home! And two years later, when it came my sister Sofka's turn, she was refused even though she too had passed the exam. The director told us point-blank: two Jews from the same house in which she lived would make her look very bad. There was no donation, no bribe, that my father could offer that would make it worth her while to appear sympathetic to Jews. So my father made plans, the following year, to send Sofka to a special Jewish *gymnasium* in nearby Baranowicze.

I may have been admitted to the Stolpce *gymnasium,* but my classmates made it clear to me that I didn't belong there. They would say to me, "Just wait! Hitler is coming and he'll cut off the heads of all you Jews." I used to answer them, "What are you so happy about? The Germans might cut off my head, but your independence will be gone. Poland won't be Poland anymore!" They would tell me that it was worth losing their independence just to get rid of the Jews.

Within our house, life was very comfortable. But we had

heard of dark things going on in Germany. Not as bad as what would ultimately take place, of course. But Cila, my mother, could see the clouds gathering on the horizon. I still have a letter that she sent to an aunt in America, in which she wrote: *"Mir kenen leben, ober mi lost nit."* ["We could live, but they won't let us."]

My father was aware both of the political situation in Germany and of the vicious anti-Semitism in Poland. But his very success in business blinded him to the implications. My mother would urge him to take advantage of the fact that, as a wealthy capitalist, he could take his family to virtually any country on earth and be welcomed, since he would pose no financial burden to the host country. She begged him to leave Poland. But my father would tell her, "We lived through the Russian Cossacks and we lived through World War I. With money you can always survive by bribing whatever new regime comes into power. And if there is a war, well, there's always been war." No one understood the horror that was coming— not my father, not even my mother. It was beyond imagining at that point in history.

America was always the first alternative that Cila would put forward to Lazar. America was the *goldineh medinah* [golden land]. But a visit paid by my uncle Oscar to America in 1938 put a real damper on that possibility. Oscar had gone to visit Herman, the youngest brother, who had left home as a teenager and emigrated to America, because he had been unhappy with his family. Nonetheless, relations had improved enough so that Oscar paid him a visit. And when Oscar came back, he had nothing very glowing to say about America. He told us, *"Kinder* [children; here used as an intimate colloquialism for all family members], we have here in Poland a Garden of Eden. Over in America they work like horses. It's not nearly as easy there to earn a living. There's no place like home."

Jews used to come to us asking for money on behalf of the Jewish settlements in Israel. The money my father was happy to give. But when they asked Lazar if he was interested in buying land there, he refused. Israel—or Palestine as it was then, an undeveloped British colony—was too primitive, too rough.

He would say, "I'm not going to go there, my children aren't going to go there, so here's your contribution and that's it!" All the same, my father was interested in the founding of a Jewish state. Nearly all the Jews in Poland had a position of some sort with respect to the various Zionist parties and philosophies. My father sided with the more militant right wing, Beitar, led by Vladimir Jabotinsky.

My mother would have gone to Israel or to anywhere else. But my father didn't listen and that was that.

My father was a prosperous man, and we lived well as a result. In the winter we could escape the worst of the cold by vacationing in Zakopane, in the Carpathian Mountains to the south. And in the summer, we stayed in posh resort towns like Druskeniki and Ciechocinek.

But even with these luxuries, my father was not an easy man to grow up with. As he was in business, so he was with his family. Very strict.

I remember that dinner was at six o'clock sharp. If I wasn't there at six, I had better have a good explanation of why not. If I was late, he would make me stand in the corner—it was a big dining room—and watch them eat dinner while keeping my arms against my sides. I was not to say a word, and I would not be given my dinner that night. If I didn't respect the rules of the family, that was my fitting punishment.

We had a bellpull over the table to ring the maid. She would carry the food from the kitchen on beautiful platters. We children would be served heaping portions. If I did not finish what was on my plate, he would tell me how, when he was my age, he was living through World War I and was grateful to have even a hard crust of bread to eat.

Sometimes, if I left too much my plate, my father would—instead of just telling a story from his childhood—slap me pretty good on the hands and make me eat it. On the underside of our large, wooden dining-room table, there were pouches for storing napkins and the like. So I decided that, when I couldn't finish my portion, I would only chew it up and then secretly spit it in my hand and hide it in one of those pouches. Later I would come back and clean up the mess. But once I forgot to do that. So the mess got moldy and started to smell. No one could figure out what the horrible odor in the house was! And then they found my mess. I got a real good slap on the hands for that. . . . I never did it again!

My mother did not like the harsh streak in my father—not with his employees, and especially not with his children. But for the most part, my father was well content to leave our upbringing in our mother's hands. If we needed help with homework, or just needed to talk, we turned to my mother. My father was making money.

I wanted to please my parents, but especially I wanted to please my mother. Before we children would go to sleep, my mother would kiss us all good night. But if she was mad at me, she wouldn't kiss me good night. When that happened, I would sit up in my bed and sometimes fall asleep in a sitting position. But I would try not to let myself fall asleep until she came and kissed me—forgave me. Sometimes she would wait an hour before she came back. Sometimes she wouldn't come back at all. It drove me crazy! I hated for her to be angry at me.

When Miriam, the youngest, was born in 1933, it devastated my father. Three daughters! He had always wanted a son, a *kaddishl,* a male child who could say kaddish for him when he died, because that was something that the Jewish tradition forbade girls to do.

Within a half a year of Miriam's birth, my father fell ill. The one doctor in town, Srkin, was good friends with my family. He and my father played poker together with some regular cronies a couple of nights a week. But Srkin was no medical genius. He diagnosed my father's condition as leukemia. My father wanted a second opinion, so he travelled to Warsaw, which was very difficult for him. It was winter. I remember seeing my father, as he set off, in a dark fur coat with a very high collar to protect his neck from the cold, because his lymph nodes were inflamed. He was pale. Large boils had been breaking out under his arms. The eminent Warsaw specialist told him that he had Hodgkin's disease and that, with good care, he could live for another ten years.

He used to have flare-ups. He would feel better, then worse. All the medications . . . a nurse would come and give him a shot when his white-blood-cell count went especially high. They would tell him to drink lots of egg yolks to boost his red-cell count. He was in and out of the hospital.

In the midst of all this, my father began to mellow a bit, because he saw that money couldn't buy you health or happiness. He was gentler after he fell ill. Not a saint, but gentler. He still continued to focus as much as he could on the business, even though it was hard for him. Money was still money. Even with his illness, he still believed that it could buffer the worst that life had to offer.

On 1 September 1939, the invasion of Poland began—the Germans on one front, the Russians on the other. The Hitler-Stalin pact called for Germany and Russia to split Poland in two. The Germans took the western sector. We lived in the eastern sector. That delayed—for us—the coming of the Nazi murderers for nearly two years.

JACK

My grandfather Isaac was a rabbi. He and his wife Miriam lived in a little Russian town called Puchowicze. I never met either of my grandparents. My father Julius did not like to talk about his relationship with them.

Basically, Julius could not see eye-to-eye with his father about a suitable profession. His father hoped Julius would follow in his footsteps as a rabbi, but Julius was not the religious type. He was far more modern, you might say, in outlook than his father. And Julius loved the full flavor of life. So things were difficult between them. Julius also had three brothers, but he was not particularly close to them.

As a young man, Julius moved from Puchowicze to Warsaw, the Polish capital, to avoid being drafted by the Russian army. But he was also happy to get away from his father's orthodox ways. In Warsaw, he first opened a leather-goods store. His father helped him out financially in that enterprise, but it was not a success. Julius then enrolled in some art-school painting classes with dreams of becoming an artist. There is a strange kind of pattern here, because a cousin of his, a member of his same generation (though they never met), also moved away from Russia to become a painter. But he moved to Paris, not Warsaw, and he persisted, as Julius never did. That was Chaim Soutine, who is now regarded as one of the great painters of the century. Soutine is the French spelling of our family name.

In Warsaw, Julius was introduced to Sarah, my mother, through a mutual friend. Sarah was then studying to become a dentist—yes, just like Cila. Julius and Sarah were quite different personalities. Julius was a good man, but easygoing. He was short, but well-knit and lively, and he had a beautiful smile that you saw often. Sarah was serious. She had a round face framed by short, light brown hair. Her eyes were hazel, and she could seem very sad and dreamy. Maybe that was what drew my father to her at first. And maybe it was his happier outlook that drew Sarah to Julius.

Early on, Julius was very impressed by Sarah's professional ambitions, and he decided to give up art school and instead study to become a dental technician. After they married, they opened a dental practice together. From Warsaw they moved to a small Polish town, Rubizewicze. From there, a short time later, they went to Stolpce, Rochelle's hometown. So our mothers were the two female dentists in town! But they never knew each other. And shortly after I was born we moved some miles away to Mir.

Both of my grandparents on my mother's side died before I was born. I never got a chance to meet them. She had three sisters and two brothers, but they were not nearby. Two of the sisters and one of the brothers were killed by the Nazis.

In Mir, my parents were very successful. My mother was the only dentist in a town of some 4,000 people. The Jewish population in Mir comprised roughly 25 percent of that total, but it included the students and teachers of a very famous yeshiva [Jewish religious school that trained both laymen and rabbis]. The Mir yeshiva was known all over the world. Students came there not only from Eastern Europe, but also from America and Africa. The Jewish families in Mir could rent out rooms in their homes and make quite a nice income, as most of the Mir students were well-to-do.

Life was pleasant in Mir. The Jewish community was a close-knit and friendly one. There was a good relationship between the orthodox and the less religious Jews. Actually, there were virtually no Jews in Mir, or elsewhere in eastern Poland, whom you could call nonreligious. We all used to go to *shul* [synagogue] for the holidays. On Succot we would all build *succahs* [ritual outdoor huts to celebrate the harvest and the successful observance of the New Year]. We all contributed to the support of the rabbi and the *shammes* [all-purpose assistant to the rabbi] and the *shochet* [kosher butcher]. We always ate kosher meat because there wasn't any other meat to buy, unless you went well out of your way.

I did not attend the yeshiva, but I did go to grade school in Mir. The teachers—and most of the students—in that school made things difficult for the minority of Jews who attended. There were maybe twelve other Jewish students in my particular class. The school day began with a Catholic prayer, and the Jewish students were instructed to stand up and then to remain absolutely silent while the rest of the students recited this prayer. It made us feel awkward, singled out. As for school work, if we failed to complete an assignment or to pass a test, we were singled out for special criticism, well beyond what a Polish student would receive. "What's the matter, Jew?" the teacher would ask us. "Can't keep up?"

During recess, a small percentage of the Polish students would be willing to include Jews in their games. Most would not. All the same, I managed to make a number of friends, mainly Jews, but also some non-Jews. I was relatively outgoing, but I was also very careful. Only after I saw that a boy or a girl was an honest and decent person would I begin a friendship with them. With the students I didn't like, especially the anti-Semites amongst them, I tried to avoid confrontations, even when remarks were directed at me. I knew that, in that environment, once I started something—anything—the confrontations would go on forever.

In addition to the grade-school education, my parents hired

a tutor from the yeshiva to prepare me for my bar mitzvah. He taught me Hebrew, *Chumash* [the five books of the Torah], and *Tanach* [prophetic and other biblical writings]. I was fairly good at these studies. Our family was not very religious, but we did observe the Jewish holidays and we always prepared a special meal and recited the blessings on the Sabbath. I believed in God, but it wasn't in a way that conformed closely to Jewish orthodoxy. It was a very personal belief—a sense that there was an guiding meaning to things, no more formal or detailed than that. My most important Jewish involvement was with a Zionist youth organization called *Hashomer Hatzair* [Young Guard]. It was labor-oriented, left-wing. Its basic credo was that Palestine was to be settled by Jewish youth collectively working the land, as was already taking place. There was no tension then, in Poland, between Zionists and orthodox Jews, many of whom today deny the validity—according to the Torah—of the state of Israel. Back then, there was too much pressure on the Jewish community from the outside to allow us to split up into separate and opposing groups. You had to remain united to survive.

You should understand that in those days you couldn't just pick up and move from Poland to Israel. There were immigration quotas set by the British mandate government, and there was strong resistance to Jewish settlement from the Palestinian Arabs. If you were wealthy, you could go and establish yourself, but my family was not wealthy. But there was another alternative—you could emigrate by way of attending a school in Palestine. That was my long-range plan. Jewish girls as well as boys yearned to leave Poland for Palestine. Through *Hashomer Hatzair* and other organizations, it was sometimes arranged for these girls to enter into purely "paper" marriages with Jewish boys who would come from Palestine to Poland for that purpose. Legally, the woman could follow the man. In many cases, Jewish youths would simply smuggle themselves into Palestine. They would stay in a kibbutz as a guest for a time, then make their way into the life of the land, disappearing from the authorities.

Yes, we knew that Palestine was a difficult place in which to live. But we also knew that there was no freedom, no future. for us in Poland.

Did I have a *sense* that Jews were hated in Poland? You didn't need to have a *sense* of it. I *knew* it from the time I was two, three years old. By that age, you knew that you were not the same as all the other kids, that you were discriminated against in the subtlest ways, as well as in the most overt and painful ways. I remember once, while I was a young student, I boarded a crowded train. I went through several cars and finally found a passenger compartment with a single empty seat. But the man sitting next to it stared at me and then spat out the words, "No Jews allowed!" I remember that moment because it made me realize, more than anything that had come before, that in Poland I would never be allowed to live a normal and peaceful life.

The hatred was built into the society throughout. You couldn't count on attending a university because of the small quotas. And even if you were admitted, you weren't allowed to sit during classes. Jews stood in the back. It was very difficult to establish a business unless your parents were wealthy and could give you financial backing. So that left becoming a merchant, or a shoemaker, or a tailor, something small-scale and nonthreatening to the Poles.

So we dreamed of Israel. We followed the news there through Jewish newspapers published in Poland and, occasionally, magazines sent directly from Israel. Radio we could listen to only at night, because in Mir there was electricity only at night. If there was a special crisis in Israel—a violent attack on a Jewish kibbutz, or something equally grim—the Polish radio would include mention of it in their news of the world. We collected money for the settlements there through the *Keren Kayemet* [Zionist fund-raising agency]. We bought special stamps to pay for the planting of trees, for the purchase of land from the Arabs, for the building of new kibbutzim.

When I was age eight, something very painful happened. My parents separated. It was, for that time, an unusual sort of separation in that, in many ways, the family was still intact. We ate together often and celebrated holidays together. My mother and father were friendly with each other—there was no anger between them, at least not on the surface. Their behavior was meant to make things easier for me. But it also confused me, because I could see that the separation was serious business. After all, my life had changed significantly: I was living with my mother in our original home, but also shuttling back and forth to the little apartment that my father had rented just half a block away.

Why did they separate? Why did they never file for a formal, legal divorce? I don't know the answers to these questions. I was too young to understand. And I never asked these questions of either of my parents—not even of my father, who survived the war and lived with me until his death at age ninety. Not in all those years to come did I ask. It wasn't my place to ask. It would have been painful to go into it.

My parents both genuinely loved me, but back in those days they often would fall into fighting—quietly—for my love. Each would question me about the other—what did your mother say? what did your father give you? and so on. It became a minor issue, for example, as to which one of them would pick out and pay for my school clothes and shoes. Neither wanted to fall behind the other in gift-giving. So I tried to be careful about what I said, what I didn't say, in order to please them both. I was a young boy, but I behaved like a diplomat.

At some point, my mother Sarah began to see how hard it was on me. And as a result she did a wonderful thing. She took me aside one day and told me that, even though the two of them were not living under the same roof, my father was still my father and my mother was still my mother. They both loved me as their one and only child—and they would love me forever. My father was my father and it was natural that he should want to give me the best things in life. And it was equally natural that my mother should feel the same way.

This talk did succeed in taking some of the pressure off me. But I still kept thinking that, since my mother and my father were good people, and good to each other, maybe I could make things right between them. So I would do things like arrange for them to have dinner together—which they would agree to because they wanted to make me happy. And I would hope that somehow things would suddenly be all right—that we would be a unified family again—a child's dream.

It came time for me to enter a *gymnasium.* Stolpce was closest, but Rochelle has already told you about the Jewish quota there. So I went to the special Jewish *gymnasium* in Baranowicze, which was a larger town than I had ever lived in before. From the time I was twelve years old, I was living away from home. Financially, I was supported by my parents, but in terms of practical daily life, I was on my own.

Going to school in Baranowicze was definitely what you would call a "mixed blessing." On the one hand, I was delighted to be in a setting in which all the teachers and the students were Jewish—the hazings and hatreds of the Mir grade school were behind me at last. But on the other hand, I was leaving my parents behind. My efforts at bringing them together would have to come to an end. I finally had to face the fact that the separation would be permanent.

I rented a room from a Jewish family in Baranowicze, went to school by myself, and came back at night and prepared dinner and studied on my own. As for studies, don't forget that we didn't have five or six subjects to learn, like American students do. There were a total of fifteen mandatory subjects for us, including Latin, Polish, Jewish religion, geography, physics, chemistry, history, psychology, on and on. Three failing grades and you were expelled.

All of that was not easy for me at first, but soon enough I became comfortable with my independence. I kept up my studies, made friends easily, went out with six or seven girlfriends. I only went out with Jewish girls, and usually they were two or three years older than me. I was bigger than most of my friends, more mature. The older girls liked me and I liked them. Baranowicze was bigger than Mir, but still it was a little town. So on dates there were not many options. Usually we would go to a coffee shop and have lots of pastries with coffee. Sometimes I would skip dinner and just live on the pastry. Or we would go to the movies—usually American films with subtitles. Or we would take a walk. It didn't matter much what

we did. We would behave ourselves, but by the time I was thir-
teen I had done some serious experimenting. By the time I was
fourteen I could write a book. I was not unique in that; I would
say with most of my friends it was the same.

Through all of my independent living, I developed confidence. I became used to fending for myself, thinking on my
feet. It may have helped me survive what was to come.

I did still see my parents fairly regularly, what with winter
and spring school breaks and the summer vacations. During
my return visits to Mir, I continued to shuttle back and forth
between my parents' separate homes. And even though they
questioned me less, each one continued to try to outdo the
other in giving me gifts, treats, and special foods.

Always, at meals with my family—this was true even before
the divorce—I was encouraged to eat all the rich foods I could
swallow, and to drink not merely milk, but cream! When we
went on vacation to a nice resort, if I did not gain five or six
pounds during our stay, it was considered a waste of money.
This attitude toward food was not unique to my family, or even
to Jews. In Poland, at that time, if you were gaining weight
or pleasantly plump, you were considered healthy. If you were
just average weight, or, even worse, skinny, people would
ask what was wrong with you. If you went to a butcher, you
asked for a chicken with lots of fat. No one wanted lean meat.
A chicken without a good amount of fat was called a *padleh*
[sick chicken]. Food was not as plentiful in Poland as it is in
America. When you were plump and rosy-cheeked, that was
a sign that you were well-off. The poor man was skinny, while
the rich man showed his riches on his body.

During my second year at Baranowicze, I came home for an
extended visit to celebrate my bar mitzvah. Lots of friends and
family came—it was a big celebration. But one of the gifts was
a violin, and I had to start taking lessons. I hated the violin. I
was lousy at it—even my teacher said that there was no future
for me there, but my mother insisted. A pain in the tush!

I was still intent on moving to Palestine someday. In fact, if
it weren't for the war, I would have gone and probably would
still be there today. Six months before the invasion of Poland,

a *shaliach* [Zionist leader] came to Mir and recruited young boys and girls to attend an agricultural school in Israel. The Zionist movement treated boys and girls very much alike—a very different approach than the orthodox tradition. I signed on for the school because I wanted to emigrate to Palestine. So I filled out the applications and my mother sent in a deposit; she and my father planned eventually to come and join me. I was supposed to go with two of my friends. But they received their papers two months before the war. And they left Poland.

Then the world was turned upside down. And my papers never arrived.

II

Life Under Soviet Rule

JACK
The invasion of Poland, which began on 1 September 1939, was over with quickly. The Polish army was overwhelmed from the start. There was no serious resistance. Within a month, the two conquerors were already setting up their respective regimes in the western and eastern sectors.

There is no question that things were far better for the Jews in the east. Amongst the Russian people there were, of course, a considerable number of anti-Semites, and Stalin himself—as history shows—held a deep and violent hatred of Jews. But the official Soviet policy was that discrimination on the basis of ethnic or religious groupings was illegal and intolerable as it cut against the formation of a unified socialist society. So there was no such thing as Pole or Jew or Belorussian—only members of the state.

Mir, where my parents lived, was so close to the Russian border that the Soviet troops arrived and took control literally a day or two after the invasion began. I remember that they came around noon, and that the first vehicles to arrive were not tanks but open trucks full of Russian soldiers. The people of Mir were very confused as to what they should do . . . go in the house and hide, or go outside and wave. The trucks were parked and the soldiers were basically waiting there. Finally, they came down from the trucks and began giving away candy, cigarettes. They seemed to be friendly so the people began opening their windows, coming out of their homes, even inviting the Russian soldiers inside for dinner.

As Jews, we learned that we were lucky that it was the Russians, not the Germans, who had arrived. We didn't hear about the atrocities in the western section of Poland for three or more months, when a very few of the Jews from that section managed to sneak over to our side. Those Jews were called *byegentses* [refugees]. In some cases they managed it by bribing the border guards. Anyway, they started to let us in on what was going on. We had no idea of the extent of what was to come—we didn't know, for example, about the concentration camps. But we understood what to expect—that many Jews would suffer and die. We heard that the Germans were seizing Jewish houses and possessions and putting all the Jews into ghettos, which were always in the most run-down sections of a town. The refugees told us that, when entering the ghettos, each Jew was allowed to carry one suitcase with only basic clothing items. If you were caught trying to smuggle in furs, gold, even a nice warm coat that a German or a Pole might want, you were immediately shot. Jews had to wear the yellow star patches, which symbolized that they were less than human, with no legal rights, no right to attend school or receive medical aid or even adequate food—there were strict rations for items such as stale bread and watery soup with fish bones. We heard that the younger Jews were being put to work while the older ones and the very young children and the babies were somehow disappearing.

None of that information was ever officially acknowledged by the Russian occupiers. Either they were uninformed, or, more likely, they had decided not to discuss it. Perhaps they did not wish to cast a bad light on their German allies, or perhaps they did not want to deal with the unrest that the news might have caused if it reached the Jewish population as a whole. But the net effect was that the Russians ignored the "Jewish problem."

Please understand that we were not so foolish as to think that the Russians had brought Paradise with them. As time went on, we discovered that there were many Jews amongst the soldiers and officers of the occupying Soviet army. They would stay for a few weeks in Mir and become friendly with the local Jews so that we could talk straight with one another. They told us of the horrors that were going on in

Russia—horrors affecting the entire population. Remember that, beginning in the thirties, Stalin had begun his internal program of liquidating literally millions of Russians whom he suspected of opposing him and the Soviet ideology. Overnight disappearances of family, friends, and neighbors was commonplace. If you were lucky, your life was spared and you were exiled to Siberia for years, maybe decades. And even if they left you alone, you knew that you were under surveillance. You couldn't buy what you wanted—it wasn't available. (That was why so many of the Russian soldiers, as soon as they arrived in Poland, tried to buy watches from the conquered civilians. They were crazy for watches.) In Russia, you had to be afraid of what you said, how you looked, whether you seemed to be eating better than others around you. So the Russian soldiers warned us not to feel too happy about our new rulers.

The same kind of brutality that went on in Russia extended to conquered Poland soon enough. In Mir, there were maybe a dozen or so Polish patriots who were opposed to the Russian occupation. Within the first month they disappeared—they were picked up in the middle of the night, and the next day we realized that they were gone. But you didn't have to be a Polish patriot to be in trouble. If you were viewed as bourgeois—that is, as having money—or intellectual, the future was grim for you. There was no room for expressing—or even so much as *thinking*—ideas that varied in any respect from the official Soviet line. One of the first things the Russians did in Mir was to close down the famous yeshiva—which had functioned for centuries—and to convert the building into a people's social hall. Every weekend there was Russian music, Russian dances, and lots of propaganda speeches.

ROCHELLE

I'll tell you how I felt when the Russians came to Stolpce.

I remember that it was early one morning when I heard a rumbling. I ran out of the house and looked down the street. There was a Russian tank with a red flag coming toward me. I thought it was so exciting! The tank was moving slowly, and the soldiers riding on it were very friendly, saying hello to everybody, giving candy to the kids. They were shouting to us, "We came to liberate you from the Polish kulak [the wealthy class]."

I ran back into the house thinking that this was going to be terrific! My mother could see how excited I was, and she looked at me sadly and said, "My dear child, you have no idea what is happening. Your life, the way you know it, is coming to an end. You just wait and see what is going to happen to us!" I thought to myself, what the hell is she talking about? The Russian soldiers seemed so friendly and kind.

As one of the wealthiest men in town, my father was singled out as a special target by the Russians. Very shortly after they arrived, they not only stripped him of control of his business, but also requisitioned most of our home to house KGB officials. The KGB was the first wave of Russian occupiers to arrive. They were in charge of setting up the political and social regime just they way they wanted it—without opposition of any kind from the Poles. We learned to be afraid of the KGB. Just like that, they could have you killed or sent into exile. Later, when the "regular" Russian people came—the teachers and other functionaries—you could relax a little bit in their presence. They would tell you nicely what you could and could not do if you wanted to get along.

But it was the KGB officials—with their wives—who lived in our very own home. They took over nearly all of it—the house that my father had built for his family. Our former Polish tenants—including the director of the Stolpce *gymnasium* who had turned down my sister Sofka—were arrested immediately, because they were members of the Polish ruling elite. That director was told to pack a single suitcase. She left all of her furniture and possessions behind. And she disappeared. The KGB left us with two bedrooms. The kitchen was for common use. That was a dangerous situation because we were afraid to cook anything that might seem in any way better than what the KGB had to eat. So it was either don't cook it, or offer it to them first. The tension spread through our entire home life. We were afraid of offending in what we said, how we dressed. We lived in constant terror.

All of this severely depressed and upset my father. He had a heart attack. When he went to the Soviet-run medical center, they barely bothered with him, just gave him some drops and told him to stay in bed. This all came on top of the Hodgkin's disease. He recovered somewhat from the heart attack, but he was just not the same man. Everything that he had worked for in his life had been taken from him. He even went so far as to go to the Russians and offer to work as an *employee* in his former business, just so he could have a hand in things and show himself to be of value to them. But they didn't want him.

We knew how much danger we were in by how miserable they made my father's life. He was called into the KGB offices for interrogation at least a couple of times each week. The pattern was always the same. They would come for him unannounced around two in the morning, waking us all up in the process. They would roust him out of bed and he would go with them and not come back until maybe five or six A.M. When he came home, he would be as white as a sheet. When we asked him what the questioning was all about, he would say, "Don't ask!" He was forbidden by the KGB to say anything about it. His friends and neighbors weren't even to know that he was being taken for these nightly questionings. Just once he let us in a little about what happened during those sessions. The KGB would ask him about his friends, his fellow kulaks. The KGB wanted to know how much money they had, what their capitalistic views were, if they were disloyal to the Communist state. And on other nights, they would call in my father's friends and ask them about him. So everyone was being played off everyone else. You could not trust your friends. You could hardly dare to speak to them.

From the pattern and tone of these interrogations, it seemed likely that the KGB would come one night and send our entire family to Siberia. So my father tried to do something to prepare for that crisis. All the money he had kept in the bank before the Soviets arrived was gone, of course. But he had privately hidden a number of foreign gold coins—Russian rubles, English pounds, American dollars. We put the coins in glass jars, then melted pork fat over them to hide them from view.

The plan was that when the Russians came at night and gave us fifteen minutes to pack—as was their method—we could grab at least some of these jars and have in them not only the coins but also the pork fat to help keep us alive. Because we had been told that in Siberia you needed a lot of fat to give you the energy to survive the cold. My father hid these jars all around the house and drilled us children on how to find them. "Don't forget," he would say, "this one is hidden in the corner, this one is in the bush alongside the tree."

So, in that way, we lived with the Russians. We wondered from day to day what was going to happen to us.

JACK

The Soviet policy was to even out all social and economic distinctions from the start—and, at the same time, to take what they wanted and needed for Stalin and for the war effort. Within the first week of the occupation, the Russians posted a notice: you must turn in *all* of your Polish zlotys. And in return, no matter how many zlotys you had turned in, you received *exactly* 100 Russian rubles, in paper bills. So your former savings were automatically nil. We all became poor in a week. No one had any money to buy anything. Most of the stores closed.

My family was prosperous—both my mother and my father were educated professionals. They had wealthy friends who were deported at once to Siberia. And the longer the Russians stayed, the worse it became for persons who had lived a "bourgeois" life under the former Polish rule. Within the first few months, most of the "bourgeois" persons were deported to Siberia.

But, thank God, we had some luck early on. My mother was the only dentist in Mir, and the Russians needed a dentist there not only for the local population, but also to work on their own teeth. As for my father, he found work as a book-keeper for one of the Russian agencies. Because he was working for them, he was able to obtain special food rations, which was a great benefit given the wartime shortages. We also had some privileges for obtaining consumer goods, but supplies were so chaotic that it did us little good. You might be able to obtain razors, but not blades, or vice versa. Meanwhile, my mother was able to bring home chickens, peas, cheese, butter, and bread because that was how she was paid by the peasant farmers who came to her for dental work. It was a barter system, no one had any money.

But even though we could eat, we had to be cautious because if you seemed to be living too well, you attracted the suspicion of the Soviet authorities. Very early on, my parents were forced to move from their nice house to a shabbier location because their house was allocated to a Soviet official. My mother practiced dentistry out of this house. Party members would be coming in and out for appointments, which meant that we had to careful to hide not only our food but also any nice thing we had. Because if a Soviet official saw, for example, a crystal dish that you owned, and if the official so much as said, "Isn't that nice," then you had to give it to them as a present at once—to save your life!

Because of the official Soviet policy of nondiscrimination toward Jews, it was no longer necessary for me to attend the Jewish *gymnasium* in Baranowicze. The Stolpce *gymnasium* was now a Soviet school. They called it a *djeschiletka*—it had ten grades, was open to all students, and the curriculum was very different. The Russian teachers who had arrived stressed the Soviet constitution, Communist philosophy, Russian geography and history. But I was happy to go to school in Stolpce because I was closer now to my family. The studies were less rigorous than they had been under the Poles. And if you knew how to handle yourself, how to say the right thing at the right time, and how otherwise to keep your mouth shut, it wasn't difficult to get along with the Soviets.

They organized chess tournaments in town, and I won one of those and received a chess set with pieces that looked like ivory, though I doubt it was ivory. I was also on the editorial staff of the school newspaper. But one of the best things I did was to take training to become a first-aid instructor. Even with their treaty with Germany, the Russians somehow suspected that there might be future warfare with the Nazis, and so they were keen on everyone learning first aid. So I took a class, and then I was suddenly teaching the younger children in our school first aid. Imagine! I barely knew a thing. But when you graduated from the course, you received a specially designed Russian medal. Once, after I became an instructor, I was invited to go to a convention on first aid in Baranowicze. I had a really good time there and met a Russian girl, a party member. She was very well built and four or five years older than I was. Oh, this Russian girl, she was really friendly!

One of the things the Russian girl advised me to do was to join the Communist party. This I did not want. And even if I had filled out an application, they would probably not have accepted me. My parents were bourgeois. But if the Russians had remained long enough, I would have been forced to join somehow in order to survive.

Do you know who was in my first-aid class? Rochelle's younger sister Sofka. And as for Rochelle herself, I once gave her first-aid treatment! The Soviets emphasized physical fitness as part of the school curriculum, so all of the students had to run long races—something like the marathons in America. At the finish line, I gave first aid to those who needed it. I had no medications, not even salt tablets. What I had was cold water. And I gave some to Rochelle.

I was interested in her. I would have dated her if I could. I saw her—from a distance—fairly often, because a girlfriend of hers, Ashke Prass, lived in the same Stolpce boarding house as I did. At that time, when I was dating, I would often take out two or three girls at the same time. We would go and indulge ourselves at the pastry shops, talk and laugh over coffee. There was a friendly atmosphere among us, without jealousy. So once I mentioned to one of the girls I dated—who knew Rochelle—that I would like to ask out Rochelle some time. But that girl said, "No, you can't do that. Rochelle is not a girl who goes out on dates with boys yet."

Still, I had my eye on her. I used to go to the post office in Stolpce often. Few of the houses in Stolpce had telephones, and so you went to the post office to make your calls. I had a girlfriend in another town with whom I liked to stay in touch. On my way to the post office I would see Rochelle standing in her yard and I would say hello to her. But she never invited me to come and visit with her. It would have been nice to have a chance to meet her parents—I never so much as saw them.

ROCHELLE

There was no question of inviting Jack for a visit. You need to understand that my life was very different from Jack's at that time. I was under strict parental supervision, like most of my girlfriends who had grown up in Stolpce. Maybe if I had gone away to school in a strange town where no one in the community knew me, I would have loosened up like Jack and his friends. But in Stolpce, there was no way that I could feel free to go out with boys.

I remember once, on a cold day, being told by my parents to be sure to wear a scarf to school. I always used to get sore throats, and my parents were very concerned. On the way to school I undid my scarf, so that it was just hanging down over my coat. When I came home that day, wouldn't you know, the first thing my parents asked me was why I didn't keep my scarf wrapped around my neck. I asked them, "How did you know?" Someone in town had seen me and told them. If I sneezed in one part of town, they would say "Gesundheit!" in the other.

Still, I can remember my friends telling me, "You should go out with that Izik [Jack's Yiddish name] Sutin. He always has a lot of money, and he doesn't mind taking out a couple of girls at once."

JACK

There was a school dance that was attended by all of the Stolpce students, including Rochelle. So I saw her and asked her to dance. You might call it a magic moment.

ROCHELLE

I was wearing a new pair of navy blue suede shoes. Jack started dancing with me and all I can remember is that he kept stepping on my toes. He was scraping my new shoes to the bare leather! I couldn't wait to be rid of him. He was an unbeliev-able klutz. After that dance, for the rest of the evening, if I saw him approaching, I hid myself within my group of friends.

JACK
That was the closest we came to having a date during the two years of Soviet rule.

ROCHELLE
In the new Russian school in Stolpce, I felt like an outcast. They called me a "kulak's daughter." I had to be very quiet, and I had to be better at my studies than anyone else in the class to do at all well with my Russian teachers. This was not so hard for me, because my mother Cila had been raised and educated in Russia and not only spoke Russian to us children but also read us stories in that language. One thing I must say—while I was in trouble for being from the wealthy class, I no longer had to worry about being threatened or beaten because I was a Jew. Unofficially, amongst my fellow Polish students, a dirty Jew was still a dirty Jew. But if any of them called you a "dirty Jew" or raised the issue in any way, they would be sent to the principal and severely punished. All of a sudden, they all shut up.

In the Russian school, there were not only the principal and the teachers, but also *politruks* [political advisors]. They were supposed to indoctrinate all of the students into the Soviet ideology and to mobilize us into *comsomoles* [young Communist pioneer groups]. Of course, I didn't bother to try to join one of these groups, because I knew that they would never take me. The *politruks* were the eyes and ears of the school. Every activity came under their scrutiny. If there was a school assembly of any kind, large photographs were dis-played of the dozen or so members of the Soviet politburo: Stalin, Molotov, Beria, and the rest. All of the students would have to rise and chant, "Long live *Tovarish* [Beloved Leader] Stalin" and so on for the whole list of names. During the en-tire chant we had to be clapping our hands with joy.

Once I was standing in assembly with my sister Sofka and

a couple of other friends. We were reciting the chant for the second or third name, and suddenly it all struck me as funny. I started laughing hysterically! I couldn't stop myself.

My sister and my friends started pulling at me, even pinching me. They were saying, "What are you doing? You're going to bring down not only yourself, but your entire family!" But it did no good.

As soon as the assembly was over, the *politruks* led me to the principal's office. They questioned me at length. What was so funny? Didn't I like Comrade Stalin? Didn't I like the other Soviet leaders? I made up a story that I had been thinking of something funny that had happened to me that day—and that when that memory had come suddenly to my mind, I burst out laughing. It had nothing to do with the names of the great Soviet leaders! They kept at me with questions for hours. But somehow, my story saved me from serious punishment.

That evening, when my parents found out what had happened, they were furious with me. My father was in enough trouble already. He didn't need his daughter drawing suspicion on him through her crazy behavior.

JACK

During the final stage of the Soviet occupation, maybe three months before the German invasion of eastern Poland in June 1941, my family heard some frightening news.

One of my mother's patients was a Soviet prosecutor who had trouble with his teeth. He came to the house often. Once he came a little bit drunk. He said to my mother, "I like you. So I want you to know that during our last few planning meetings, we have decided that, as a matter of Soviet policy, we are going to bring in our own Russian doctors and dentists to Mir." That would probably have meant that not only my mother, but also my father, as a fellow bourgeois, and myself, as their son, would have been sent straight off to Siberia.

In retrospect, that might have been a good thing. We might all have survived—most of the Jews sent to Siberia before the Germans came did survive. My mother might have lived a full life.

ROCHELLE

My father was in such despair over the Russians that he actually believed that things would be better if the Germans invaded eastern Poland and drove the Communists out. He didn't understand who the Nazis were, what they believed. When Lazar thought of Germany, he thought of World War I, when his father was still alive and was able to do business with the kaiser's army. "With the Communists you can't do anything," my father would say to us in private. "But if the Germans come, I'll get back to producing turpentine and tar. They'll need it to build roads. With money I'll be able to bribe them and avoid any problems." As I have said, my father had no idea what was coming. His illness and depression during the Soviet occupation made him blinder than ever.

III

Onset of the Nazi Horror

ROCHELLE

In June 1941, the Germans invaded eastern Poland—and were clearly on their way to Russia. The Russians may have had their suspicions about the long-term durability of their alliance with Hitler, but they were definitely caught by surprise by the Nazi blitzkrieg. There was little effective resistance by the Soviet army. We were close to the Russian border, and within two or three days of the invasion, we watched a stream of Soviet troop trucks retreating to their homeland.

When we heard that the Germans were on the way, we wanted to flee to the east, to Russia. Even my father agreed that this would have been wise, if only it was possible. Many Jews would have fled to Russia if they could. But only a few succeeded in doing so. Everything conspired against it.

Officially, the Soviet borders were not open to Jews or any other refugees from Poland. The Russians were suspicious of the Polish population—they suspected that there might be subversives or spies amongst the refugees. So during the first days of the German attack, only Soviet officials and Soviet troops were allowed through the checkpoints. It was only in the final days of the German onslaught, when the border was no longer maintained by the Russians because the entire region was in bloody chaos, that some Polish civilians, including some Jews, managed to slip through. Most of them pretended to be Russians. Meanwhile, in Poland, thousands of Soviet troops were left behind, so rapid was the German advance, and so sloppy and hasty was the Russian retreat. The Germans pushed some two hundred miles into Russia, all the way to Minsk, very early on. Their strategy was a pincer movement to encircle the tens of thousands of Soviet troops who were stranded in Poland without supplies and without any immediate prospect of help. Several thousand Russian soldiers were taken as prisoners of war. And many of them were shot almost immediately by the Germans, who were not interested in maintaining POW camps during their push into Russia. In the camps that were set up, many of the Russian soldiers were starved to death. We later found out that hundreds of Russian soldiers were hiding on Polish farms, burying their uniforms and offering labor to the Polish farmers in exchange for their lives.

There were also many groups of Russian soldiers who were hiding in the woods and forming into armed bands to obtain food. Many of them later evolved into partisan groups, but at that point in time they were taking no serious military action against the Germans. Their goal was simply to stay alive. These men were armed and trained soldiers, unlike the Jews, who were unarmed, untrained, and had old and young family members to consider.

Even if we had decided to leave Stolpce and take to the road, there was no guarantee that we would make it alive to the Russian border, much less into Russia itself. Don't imagine that there were family automobiles in Stolpce! My father, a wealthy man, had constructed not a garage, but a large barn in our backyard to house the horses to pull the wagons we used. Many Jews did take to the roads, sometimes with horses, or horse-drawn wagons, but more often on foot. The trains had stopped running. The roads were filled with would-be Jewish refugees, as well as Poles and Soviet troops. If you took the back roads, which were difficult for any kind of travel, you had a slim chance. But the German Luftwaffe kept the main roads east under constant surveillance—and the machine gun strafings of those main roads by the Luftwaffe fighter planes spared no one. They fired on soldiers, they fired on children. The dead were piled along the roads, and bombed-out troop trucks blocked the way for those who came after.

When my family realized that the Germans would soon be in Stolpce, we packed our most important clothing, as well as the jars of gold coins covered with fat. And then we went as fast as we could to one of my father's factories in a little town nearby called Kruglice. We stayed in the home of the Jewish factory supervisor until we could find out what was happening in Stolpce. Our major fear at that point was the bombing by the Luftwaffe, which, we had learned, had levelled many of the small Polish towns to the west. Remember, nearly all the homes were little and made of wood. They could not withstand explosions, and fires could spread quickly. So we did not wish to risk sitting in our house during the saturation bombings of Stolpce.

Even so, once the Germans had occupied Stolpce, we had no idea if our house was still standing or not. The only way to find out was to go and look. My father was too ill to undertake such a trip, which was fourteen kilometers each way and would have to be done on foot and in stealth. My mother needed to take care of my younger sisters. So it was decided that I would go to Stolpce and see if there was anything to return to. I waited until the Germans had been there for a week. On my way, I kept to the woods as much as I could. When I did follow the road, I saw dead Russian soldiers. It was the first time that I had seen dead bodies. The flies were crawling into their eyes and mouths.

When I got to the edge of Stolpce, and hid near the Niemen River, I could see that many of the buildings had gone up in smoke. It looked like a completely different town. But fortunately, I knew my way well enough to follow the streets, even when the structures around them were rubble. I came to our house and found it still standing. It was already filled up with desperate Jews who had taken shelter there, because their own homes were gone. In our barn in the backyard, there was a large storage area that contained barrels of flour, sugar, peas, and the like. I opened up the barrels and distributed the food to them. Everyone was very hungry. I slept in the house that night, and I told them, "Hey, my family is coming back, so leave room for us."

The Germans saw me while I was in town, but I wasn't as conspicuous with all the people around me as I would have been if I was spotted alone on the road. Also, at that point, the German presence was still primarily that of an advancing army. It was chaos, a no-man's-land. They didn't yet look at you as a Jew or a non-Jew. The Nazi SS personnel would arrive shortly—and that's when the organized actions against the Jews would begin. But this I did not yet understand.

The next day, I made the journey back to my parents. They cried when they saw me. They thought I had been killed because I had been gone three days—a little longer than we had planned. I told them the situation and we decided to go back to our own home. The Jews who were already there were very friendly to us, as we were to them. There were no arguments about property rights. Everyone understood, from previous stories told to us by Jewish refugees, that we were in a desperate situation—that we would be moved out of the house and into a ghetto soon enough. When we returned, we took one of the rooms in the house for our own family. And then we waited.

Two weeks later, the SS arrived. It was the SS that really established the German presence in Stolpce. Within a few days, they had linked up with the local Polish police, who were happy—delighted—to cooperate with the Nazis. Right off, they made up a list of prominent persons . . . mostly Jews, but also some Poles who might effectively organize against them. So seven or so of these persons were killed almost at once. At first, the Germans tried to cover up the killings. They told us that the persons had been taken to a special camp somewhere. But later we found out that they had been taken to a barren spot some seven miles outside of Stolpce. And there they were forced to dig their own mass grave.

My father Lazar was one of them. The Nazis came for him, accompanied by some of the collaborating Polish police. They forced him out of bed and ordered him to get dressed quickly—so fast that he wasn't allowed time to put on his shoes. He left in his leather slippers and a thin jacket. My mother told them that my father needed medication to live. They said to her, "Don't worry, he'll be back soon." Their explanation was that they were going to keep my father and other prominent citizens as hostages, to make sure that there were no attacks on German soldiers by the local population.

But what happened, as I have said, is that they were murdered immediately. After they dug their mass grave, they were killed by stoning. Only a few bullets were found in the bodies; the Germans did not want to waste their ammunition. In 1945, when the war was over, the Stolpce police—who were operating under Soviet rule again—dug up the mass gravesite as part of their investigation of Nazi crimes. My father's slippers were still on his feet.

A few days after they took my father away, one of the German officers returned to our house to tell us that he was doing fine. The officer said that he would take the needed medication to my father. The officer also suggested that we pack up all of my father's best and warmest clothes, as my father would need them with winter coming. Before the officer left, we all thanked him again and again for coming. All this and my father was already dead! But this was a way for the officer to have his pick of fine clothing without the bother of searching through the house. For the time being, the Germans preferred to do things in secrecy, or by means of polite lies. The threat of death was there, but it was veiled—thinly veiled.

The next step followed in this pattern of polite lies. The Jews of Stolpce were told to select a committee of six or so persons to serve as a *Judenrat,* a governing body—under Nazi control— for the local Jewish population. The German military and the Polish police would use the *Judenrat* to convey their orders. One of the first of these orders was to prepare and to sew onto our clothing—on the left side in the front and in the center on the back—the yellow stars with the imprint *Jude* [Jew] on them. They told the *Judenrat* that any Jew caught without these stars would be shot.

Even before these stars, however, there was almost no chance that a Jew might pass as a Pole and evade the persecutions that way. It wasn't that Jews were so obviously recognizable as a physical type. Often times, a German could not tell, by sight, the difference between a Pole and a Jew. But here they had the help of the Polish police. You must realize that, in many ways, the collaborating Poles were worse than the Germans. The Poles knew very well who the Jews were—in many cases, the Jews were kids with whom they had grown up. It was a chance to settle scores and grudges that had festered for years.

The Poles knew which Jews had money and valuables, and could extort them whenever they wished. More than that, they now had carte blanche to inflict whatever terror on Jews they liked—breaking into their homes, beating them up, raping the women, taking whatever they wanted.

It was not only the Polish police. Virtually all of the Polish population of Stolpce—even those people you thought were friends—were happy to cooperate with the Nazi actions. Any harm they could do to you, they did it. And if you tried to do anything outside the Nazi regulations, they would report you. These were our neighbors, our schoolmates.

Early on, the Germans put us to work. Jews were their forced labor to clean up the mess they had made in conquering Poland. They used the young Jewish girls and boys, but also all Jewish adults who were still able to move. Only the old people—mainly old women—were left to care for the babies and toddlers. We cleaned up the rubble in the streets from all the bombing. My mother and my younger sister Sofka and I worked together. Miriam was too young.

The Germans oversaw our labor early on; later they transferred this duty to the Poles. We knew the Germans hated us, but we didn't yet believe that they would shoot us on the spot. I was kind of a cocky little kid—I dared to speak up to them. One day, as we were clearing, the Germans kept shouting at us, "You dirty Jews! Work harder!" And then they started to complain that they had gone to war because of us. So finally I said to them, "What are you talking about? We didn't come to you! You came to us! How can you say we started the war?"

One of the German officers reached for his leather whip and then grabbed me with one hand. With the other, he whipped my back again and again. It went on for five or ten minutes. As he whipped me, he said, "Now you'll know who started the war, you dirty Jew." My mother and my sister didn't dare to look up—they didn't want to see, and they were afraid that they too would be beaten if they lifted their heads. As soon as the beating was over, I was forced to go back to work picking up the rubble. My back was swollen and bloody from the whip. When I came home that night, I saw that I was striped like a zebra. I couldn't move without pain for weeks. But I had to work every day.

After we were finished with the roads, they had us clean up the building that had been our high school. They were using it to house German troops. I was in a group of girls assigned to wash the floors and the bathroom areas. We would be washing the toilets and the SS officers would come in and piss on our hands. And laugh.

There were SS officers staying in our own home in those opening weeks. We still kept our single room, but the other Stolpce refugees had been moved out. The ghetto for the Jews was not created until two months after the Germans arrived. So there we were, living for some weeks with an SS officer upstairs and some regular German army officers downstairs. The regular officers were not so bad. They were heading toward the Russian front and were more worried about what was going to happen to them there than they were about the Jews. Those officers even shared some of their rations with us. I remember that one of them said to us one day, "I look at you and I feel sorry for you, because I know what's coming." We asked him what he meant, but he said he couldn't tell us.

After we were done at the school, we were set to work cleaning the *Kommandantur*—the command building where the local head of the SS had his office. It had been one month since my father was taken away, and I wanted badly to find out how he was doing. For some reason, I decided that I would knock on the door of the chief SS officer and ask! There I was, a Jewish girl, grimy from my work, explaining what had happened to my father and asking if he had gotten the clothes we had sent along to him. The German officer who had taken those clothes had promised that we would hear from my father—but we hadn't. I told the chief SS officer that I knew he was a big man in town. Could he find out about my father and then let me know?

The SS officer looked at me as if he thought something was wrong with my mind. But I think he also felt sorry for me. After all, he could have had me beaten or killed. But he didn't even holler at me. He said, "I don't know anything about your father. But if I find out, I'll let you know."

When I came home and told my mother what I had done, she nearly became hysterical. She couldn't believe it. She kept saying over and over, "You could have been shot on the spot!"

About two months after the initial occupation, the actions against the Jews were intensified. The SS gave orders to the *Judenrat* and the *Judenrat* passed on the orders to us. First, we were told to turn in all our gold and jewelry. We kept two jars of gold coins that we had buried, but we turned in all our other remaining valuables. My mother gave up her wedding ring. She had no choice. If you were caught with any jewelry at all, you were shot. The next order required us to turn in all fur coats. They were more common in Poland than they are today in America. They were for warmth, not show. Finally, when everything of value was gone, they told us to pack what we could carry and move into the ghetto. We could no longer live in our own homes—they were turned over to the German officers or to cooperative Poles.

The ghetto was located in the worst part of town. The Germans surrounded it with thick barbed wire, leaving only a single large gate for both entrance and exit. The gate was always guarded by the German SS and the local Polish police. Every time a Jew walked in or out he was searched.

Shortly after we were moved into the ghetto, nearly all the remaining young and middle-aged men were taken away. That included my uncles and nephews. We were told that they were being sent to a labor camp. Primarily women and children and old men remained in the ghetto. There was nobody left to organize anything.

It was just the four of us then—my mother and her three daughters. By that time, we had all given up hope that the Germans were really keeping my father alive as a hostage. Too many Jews were disappearing, too many stories were circulating about mass murders of Jews in other ghettos. We understood that the Germans did not need my father as a hostage. All the Jews in Stolpce—in *all* the ghettos—were hostages of the Nazis. It was terrible, after so many lies from the Germans, to realize the truth that our father had been murdered. And then we had to live with that truth while the murderers walked about us in triumph, in control of Poland, in control of all our lives. For my mother, it was hell. For myself and for Sofka as well. Miriam was so young, she was blessed to have no real understanding of it.

When we first moved into the ghetto, we were assigned to live in an old meeting hall where the Baptists in town used to pray. They brought in some old furniture and jammed in dozens of Jewish families. You had only as much space as you needed to sleep. There were two woodstoves that everyone used for cooking and for warming themselves. There was not much to cook—we were on minimal food rations, stale bread or worse. There was no place to bathe, so you couldn't keep clean. At night you couldn't sleep well, no matter how tired you were, because the mattresses were filled with bedbugs that sucked the blood out of you. When you woke up in the morning, your sheets were red with blood from the bugs you had squashed while rolling over in your sleep. During the day, the lice took the bedbugs' place. They were in our hair, in every crevice of our bodies. We itched, we had rashes that were as red and thick as welts.

My mother was very frail. It was now up to me to make sure that the family was provided for. We were assigned to work in a sawmill. My mother started to work there with me, but she couldn't keep up the pace. It was too hard for her to carry the big boxes of sawdust. So she remained in the ghetto—the Germans allowed older people and very young children to stay back because they were earmarked for death soon enough in any event. My younger sister Sofka was in good enough physical condition to work. We had both been chubby prior to the German invasion, and even though we had lost a great deal of weight, we still had our strength. But Sofka refused to go to the sawmill. She was in despair and would say, "Why should I work until I freeze? They're going to kill us anyway." As for Miriam, who had just turned nine, she had been frail from the beginning. In the ghetto, she became very thin and weak. She couldn't walk without support—we almost had to carry her. Miriam was disintegrating in front of our eyes.

So the three of them stayed behind in the ghetto and I

worked with other young girls in the sawmill on the outskirts of Stolpce. It was the winter of 1941–42. My job had two parts. I would sweep the sawdust into boxes and then dump the sawdust into the basement furnace to fuel the sawing machines, which ran by steam. And I also ran the machine that cut the bark off the raw boards. When the cutting was done, I would load the boards onto carts and wheel them outside and then load them onto the customers' wagons. During the day you froze, but you weren't allowed even to warm your hands. The Germans did allow us to bring as much bark as we wanted back into the ghetto. Bark was garbage to them, waste material, but we could use it as fuel for the woodstove. It burned wet and smoky, but we could get some heat from it and cook on the metal stovetop. Our staple was a flour-and-water paste from which we sometimes made a kind of pancake; other times we boiled it up into a thin soup. I remember a special meal we had in the fall of 1941, just after Yom Kippur. My mother had somehow obtained a small quantity of milk from a Jew who had smuggled it into the ghetto. Milk was a rarity, a delicacy. My mother put some into our flour-and-water soup, and we ate it as if it was the traditional meal to break the Yom Kippur fast. It tasted unbelievably good.

I remember an incident from that time that tells you how little, as a general rule, we could count upon our neighbors to help us. There was a Belorussian man named Schekele who used to sell pork to my father's factory-supply stores. Supposedly, he and my father were good friends. So before we were moved into the ghetto, my mother and I had gone to Schekele and asked him to take some of our nice living-room furniture and keep it in his own house. The idea was that, if we somehow managed to live through the German occupation, we could come back for our belongings. And in the meantime, Schekele could help us out with some food here and there if we were starving.

One day, while I was working at the mill, I saw Schekele. He had come with a big load of cut trees to be made into boards. We were being watched carefully as we worked, and the rule was that we were not supposed to speak to any Polish civilians and they were not to speak to us. But somehow I managed to sneak near to Schekele and beg him to bring me some food for my family—a loaf of bread, anything. Immediately, Schekele started to cry that he himself didn't have anything to eat. There he was, nicely dressed and doing business with the Germans, and he was telling me he was starving. Two days later, when Schekele came back with another load of trees, he slipped me a small jar of honey. That was all he could give, he told me. I had to smuggle this jar back into the ghetto by hiding it in a load of bark. At least it was something I could give to my mother, and that she could give to her daughters as a rare sweet taste on the tongue.

In the spring of 1942, around Passover, my grandmother Ethel Schleiff died. She was already in her seventies, and she came down with a cold that turned into pneumonia. In the ghetto, if you got sick, that was it. No doctors would come to treat a Jew. She had been living with her daughters—my father's sisters—and some of her other grandchildren, all of them crowded into a single room. I was not her favorite, but still there was contact between us, and I remember that I stopped by one morning on the way to being taken to the sawmill. Her daughters had laid out her body on the floor; she had died during the night. My little nephews and nieces were frantically running around her. I remember that one of them was pulling open her eyelids and yelling, "Grandma, wake up!"

Finally, the remnants of the *Chevre Kaddishe* in the ghetto—the old men who belonged to the burial organization that my father Lazar had devoted himself to—took Lazar's mother's body and buried her in the Jewish cemetary not far from the sawmill. And everyone talked about how lucky Ethel Schleiff was to have died a natural death with her grandchildren around her, given the alternatives. Ethel must have been a *tzaddik* [righteous one] to have deserved such good fortune! Besides, in Jewish tradition, if you died around Passover it was a sign that you were going straight to heaven.

By that point everyone in the ghetto understood clearly that our days were numbered. During the spring, the Germans had already started in on wholesale *shchitim* [slaughters] of Jews

43

in the neighboring towns, including Mir. Often, not all of the Jews were killed in the first *shchite*—there were always a few who happened, by chance, to be on the road or in the fields. A few others hid themselves away. So there were always two or three subsequent "cleanings"—the Nazi term was *Judenrein* [clean of Jews]. The killing was a constant. We heard about it in the ghetto through word of mouth. And there was no place to run away, no safe territory.

The summer passed. Every time I left for work in the morning, I would think to myself that maybe my mother and sisters would not be there when I came back. But, in my thoughts, I would not include myself with them in that fate. I had a premonition that it would happen to them and not to me. I would wonder to myself, "Why do I think that *they're* going to die and *I* am not?" I couldn't explain it then. I can't explain it now.

I never told my family about this. But I always thought it. It was not a happiness to me. It was not even what you would call hope. It was just a sense within me.

Then came the autumn of 1942. The day after Yom Kippur— a year from the time of our delicious milk-and-flour soup—I woke up in the morning to go to work as usual. The procedure was that we were marched to work in a group guarded by a German soldier and a local Polish policeman. So we were used to an armed presence.

But that morning I looked out the window and saw that the ghetto was surrounded by German troops and Polish police armed with machine guns. It was like a siege! All of it had been set up during the night while we were sleeping.

Everybody started crying, screaming. We didn't know what to do. Someone asked one of the Germans if they were still taking out Jews for labor duties that morning. The answer was yes. I ran to the main gate of the ghetto and saw that it was so. Then I came running back to our room. As for my youngest sister Miriam, it was impossible—she was so weak she could hardly walk, much less do labor. But I begged my mother and my sister Sofka to come with me to the sawmill that day. I pleaded with them, "Come with me! Maybe they won't notice that there are two more people in the labor group. You have nothing to lose! Come!" But Sofka said that she didn't want to go and my mother Cila said that she wouldn't leave Miriam to die all by herself. She just hugged Miriam and said, "Whatever happens to her is going to happen to me."

I walked out and I knew that I would never see them again. I joined up with the labor group and we were led out of the ghetto to the sawmill. And within two or three hours we heard screaming like we'd never heard before. Remember, the sawmill was not an enclosed building—there was only a roof on top of an open frame to cover the equipment. Not far from the sawmill was the site on the outskirts of town the Germans had chosen for a mass grave. As we worked, we could look out and see military trucks filled with Jewish women and children passing by on the road. They were being guarded by German SS officers and Polish police. The screams were coming from these trucks.

The screams. . . . If there is a God upstairs, he didn't hear those women and children.

We could see not only the trucks passing, but the local population of Stolpce gathered on both sides of the road, as if they had come to see a parade. And every time the trucks went by—especially the empty ones going back to town—these people would all clap their hands!

I was sure that they had killed my mother and sisters that day. I was in shock. Something snapped inside me. I couldn't talk or move. I couldn't cry. It was such a hell that I can't find the words to describe what my state of mind was like. It is not something that most people will ever have to experience, and for that they should thank God.

The Germans didn't take the Jewish workers back to the ghetto that night. We were herded into an empty room not far from the German army barracks. That was where we were to be kept for a week, while the Germans finished their butchery in the ghetto.

The Jews with whom I worked realized that, in my mental state, I wouldn't be able to stand up to forced labor the next day. My mind had literally stopped working. So they took a risk—a *great* risk, which could have meant death for them. They hid me for a couple of days inside of a large woodpile next to our sleeping hut. Inside there, they hoped, I would somehow snap out of it. For those two days, I didn't eat or drink. Probably I slept for twenty-four hours straight at some point. Honestly, I don't know what happened, what I thought, how I existed. The Polish police who oversaw our workforce didn't keep count of us closely enough to notice my absence. If a Jew was missing at the beginning of the day, they figured that it was probably because the Jew had died overnight from starvation or illness.

At last, when I felt able, I crawled out from under the woodpile and went back to work.

Meanwhile, the Germans were going through the ghetto room by room with police dogs, searching for any Jews who had tried to hide. When they were finished with the killing, they let the Polish population in to take anything they wanted from the ghetto . . . clothing, sheets, pillows, pots, pans. That was a way to gain support with the locals, but the Germans had first seen to it that nothing valuable was left.

We knew that after they had finished cleaning up the ghetto—making it *Judenrein*—they would finish us off as well.

A week went by. I was back to working at the sawmill, though my state of mind was barely adequate to make it through the day. Then one day I saw a Polish boy who had been a classmate of mine at the *gymnasium*. His name was Dmitri Zarutsky. He had had a small crush on me, and would occasionally ask me out to see a movie. My family would never have allowed us to date, but we did become friends—he used to come by the house for visits. He even understood Yiddish a little bit. Dmitri was standing in a barn not far from the sawmill, motioning for me to come over and talk to him. I hesitated as to whether or not to go. I could have been beaten for leaving my workstation, and besides that, I had no idea what he could want from me at that point in time.

I decided to go over and talk with him. Dmitri spoke to me quickly—he didn't want to be seen speaking to a Jew. He said, "Listen. I just walked by the ghetto and the Germans are gathering up the last of the Jews who were found hidden away. Your whole family . . . your mother, your sisters, your aunts and your cousins are all sitting together in a single group. They're being guarded by the SS and the Polish police."

As I learned later, it was common practice in the ghetto liquidations for the rounded-up Jews to be guarded all day and then taken to the mass graves for killing at dusk. The rationale behind this was that it allowed the Germans to spend all day hunting out and gathering Jews together, and then to murder them all at the same time, rather than having to bother with lots of smaller-volume killings throughout the day.

When Dmitri was walking by the ghetto, my mother recognized him. She yelled to him to come nearer and take a message. She had to yell for him to hear, but apparently the guards didn't care, as her death and the death of the others was certain. Dmitri was to find out where I was working and to tell me that they were all going to be killed on that day. She explained to Dmitri that they had been hiding for the past week in a hiding place that my uncles had prepared before they were taken away and killed. There was a sofa in the room assigned to them. They had cut out a piece of the wooden floor beneath the sofa, dug a hole deep into the earth underneath, then covered up the hole with the wooden floor piece. My mother and my sisters had hidden themselves with the rest of the family in that hole. For a week, I had been sure that they were already dead.

So when Dmitri let me know that my family was still alive, I just said, "Thanks for telling me." There was nothing else I could think of to say. Hearing the news, it was for me as if they had died twice.

There was one more thing that Dmitri let me know. My mother had screamed at him to tell me that I should take *nekome*—revenge.

JACK

When I understood that the Germans were on their way, I left Stolpce to rejoin my parents in Mir. I knew that life would be very different than it had been under the Soviets. Enough stories about the German handling of the Jews in western Poland had reached me. I knew that I had to be with my family.

In Mir, as elsewhere, there was a *Judenrat* established. There were roughly 2,000 Jews still living in the town when the Germans arrived; remember that the yeshiva had been disbanded two years previously. So out of this population, there were six or seven persons chosen for the *Judenrat*. They were older men, elders of the community. One of the first instructions given to the *Judenrat* by the Germans was to assemble a list of all the young Jewish people from ages sixteen to thirty or so. All of those young people—I was one of them, of course—were to report to work to fix up the roads, clean the homes of the German officers, take care of the stables the officers had seized. If any German—or any of the Polish police—disapproved of the behavior of any one of us, we could be severely beaten. Or shot immediately. And then the rest of the work group would be told to dig a grave and bury their dead comrade.

One of the next steps was to require the *Judenrat* to register all Jews over the age of fifty. That was so they could be rounded up and killed more efficiently, as the Germans considered that age group useless for work purposes.

After two weeks or so of hard labor, we were told that we would be moving into a special ghetto area that would be the home for all the Jews of Mir. The Polish population occupying those few blocks were moved out and then transferred into the better Jewish homes left vacant. They took over all the furnishings and clothing that we were required to leave behind. It was a happy occasion for those Poles.

My mother Sarah was the only dentist in Mir, and the Germans needed a dentist, so they allowed her to continue her practice. They gave her a room in a house in the Mir ghetto reserved for professionals and skilled laborers—one doctor, one pharmacist, some shoemakers and tailors—who would do work for the Germans. That was the section into which we were originally placed. My father was placed in that house as a dental technician—he and my mother were working together again.

My main job was to repair the main highways for the benefit of the German military. I was part of a large Jewish work crew. Sometimes, as we worked, some German troop trucks would pass by and the soldiers in them would start shooting. Sometimes they would shoot in the air, just to scare us. Sometimes they would kill a few of us, just for the thrill of it. It went on for quite a while. Every day there were casualties—if not in our road work crew, then elsewhere in the ghetto. It was casual killing—no investigations, no special orders required. They were killing babies, old people, anyone who was reported for any sort of transgression of the German regulations, however minor.

The ghetto was very congested. There were usually six or so Jewish families packed into each of the small houses. In each room, five or six people slept. Your bed space was your only private space. There were no showers, no toilets, just outhouses. We kept hearing rumors about Jews being rounded up in the neighboring towns and killed. The only ones who were spared were professionals or skilled laborers whom the Germans regarded as useful—a small percentage of the Jewish population. The Germans had promised my mother that they would keep her alive because they needed dentists. So it didn't seem to us that she was in real danger. But as the days went on and it became clear, from all the rumors we heard, that the mass killings would come to Mir, my father—who as a technician was not valued as highly as my mother—and I realized that we needed to find hiding places. This was in the autumn of 1941.

We found a place for my father in the attic of a Christian family in Mir. The family members were all dental patients of my mother, and their son was a friend of mine from school. They promised that they would keep my father's presence a secret and provide him with enough food to live.

As for me, it was decided that I would run away to a farmhouse some six kilometers outside of Mir. The farmhouse was owned by the Kurluta family, all of whom had also been patients of my mother. When the troubles started with first the Russians and then the Germans, my parents had given them some of our belongings for safekeeping, and they had been honest in acknowledging this throughout all the horrors. By contrast, there were many Polish houses that took Jewish possessions on in that way and then later denied any such dealings, even if the Jewish owner somehow survived and came to their door. The Kurluta farm was in a wooded area, but to make doubly sure that I did not stand out they dressed me as a farmhand and I worked in the fields.

Both of these families were very good to us, but obviously there was danger in the entire situation. Could we be certain they would not betray us? The answer is that we had no choice but to trust people.

In early November, after I had been on the farm for a few days, I found out that the Germans and the Polish police—including police sent for from a neighboring town to assist in the killing—had surrounded the Mir ghetto. Then they had marched all of the Jews they could find—group after group—out of town and forced them to dig their own mass grave at gunpoint. The killings went on for two days. The first casualties were the chief Mir rabbi and the most orthodox Jews. After that, it was group by group, random murder. And while this went on, they searched through the ghetto for hiding places. Most of the Polish population of Mir assisted them—if they knew of any Jews in concealment, or trying to pass as Poles, they pointed them out. Only the useful Jews were spared—roughly 800 in number.

While the news of the killings had reached me at the farm, I was still in complete ignorance as to the fate of my parents. This tore at me. After a few days, when things had quieted down a bit, the farmer who was hiding me went into Mir and made some discreet inquiries. When he came back, he told me that my mother Sarah had been killed. . . . I found out later that the Germans had planned to keep her alive, but the Polish police came into her room, robbed her, and killed her with great pleasure.

I loved my mother very much. She had been murdered by senseless butchers, and there was no immediate way for me to fight back, to avenge her. It was an agony—the worst agony of my life.

Thank God, I also learned from the farmer that my father

had survived in his attic hiding place. The fact that my father was still alive and might need my help convinced me to leave the farm and go back to Mir. In addition, the wave of killings had made it plain that the farmer and his family were in mortal danger so long as I continued to stay on with them. He was a good man, but he could not bring himself to protect me at the possible cost of his own life and those of his wife and children.

At that point, most of the Jews still living in Mir were either skilled laborers, or those who tended the horses and gardens of the German officers, or those who were still needed for road repair. There were also a certain number of Jews, such as my father and myself, who had managed to hide themselves outside the ghetto. The attitude of the Germans toward those few Jews who had concealed themselves was surprisingly casual. The Germans knew that we had no place to go—the Polish population would not hide us. So we went back to the ghetto, to rejoin our fellow Jews, and they let us do so without hindrance for the time being, for the sake of the labor we could provide. There would be another wave of killings when it suited them.

But because of our reduced numbers, they moved us in May 1942 out of the original ghetto, which was then deemed too large for our needs. As it happened, there was a old structure, the Mirski Castle—in Polish, the Mir *zamek*—on the outskirts of Mir. It had been built in the eighteenth century, and was in total disrepair—no heat, crumbling inner walls, filth and rubble everywhere. A Polish landowner who had been living in it had been killed by the Russians shortly after their arrival in 1939, and the castle had remained empty ever since. It was into that *zamek* that the Germans decided to herd the remaining Jews of Mir. The *zamek* had an eery atmosphere—there were old dungeons in the basement with rusted iron bars. Its thick outer stone wall had a single gate, as well as a number of small windowlike openings that were high above the ground. The Germans ringed the top of the walls with barbed wire. What few bathroom facilities there were in the *zamek* were totally inadequate for the 800 some Jews crammed within it.

It was during that summer in the *zamek* that roughly forty of us younger persons—many of whom had gotten to know one another in the *Hashomer Hatzair* [the labor-oriented Zionist youth organization]—began to attempt to organize some sort of resistance. We ranged in age from roughly sixteen to thirty. The majority were men, but there were some women as well. In any ordinary sense, our situation was completely hopeless. We had no weapons except for rocks, bottles, and a few knives. We were completely outnumbered and surrounded by a trained German military force supported loyally by the local population. But then again, we had no expectation that we would live beyond the next few weeks or months. Why not resist when the alternative was death at a time and a place chosen by the Nazis? Desperation was what drove us, along with the desire for revenge. Our families had been butchered and piled into nameless graves. The thought of taking at least a few German lives in return was a powerful incentive.

And so our early planning consisted in thinking out strategies by which the *zamek*—which was, after all, an old fortress—could be defended for a time. A very brief time.

But then an opportunity arose for us that seemed altogether unbelievable and impossible. We learned that there was a Jew in Mir who had managed to infiltrate the ranks of the German military police. This Jew was willing, at the risk of his own life, to pass information and, later, armaments to the Jews of the Mir ghetto, in the hope of saving at least a few of our lives.

The name of this Jew was Oswald Rufeisen. Rufeisen had grown up in the countryside in western Poland, not far from Germany itself. In fact, Rufeisen's father had served in the Austro-German army during World War I and had been decorated for bravery. Some of Rufeisen's early school classes had been conducted in German, so he was fluent in both Polish and German, although—and this was unusual for a Polish Jew—he couldn't speak Yiddish. All the same, he had participated in Zionist youth movements and felt close to the Jewish people.

After the Germans invaded western Poland, Rufeisen fled east and ultimately wound up in the vicinity of Mir, where he posed as a citizen of dual Polish and German ancestry. Through a series of accidents and chance opportunities, Rufeisen was asked to become an officer in the German police and serve as a translator, because of his fluency in German and Polish. That was a job that he could not turn down without attracting undue suspicion. It sickened him to be working for the Germans, but Rufeisen was determined to find an opportunity to save Jewish lives in the process.

Early in 1942, Rufeisen took the risk of making personal contact with one of the Jewish residents of Mir. This particular Jew was Dov Resnik, a young man who, like Rufeisen, had lived in Vilna before the war. In fact, Resnik and Rufeisen had met briefly on a couple of occasions through their participation in different Zionist youth groups.

One day Resnik was marched into the Mir police station to do some repair work. Rufeisen recognized him, just as Resnik recognized Rufeisen. They spoke briefly, in secret, on that day, and managed to arrange for a second meeting in a remote part of town that evening. It was extremely dangerous for both of them. For an officer of the German police to be seen talking on a casual basis with a Jew would attract immediate suspicion to them both. There was the possibility of informers from either the Polish or Jewish sides who would be anxious to obtain favor from the German authorities. Still, Rufeisen promised Resnik that he would help the Jews of Mir as much as he could. No concrete plans were made, but they would work out a means— through a limited number of Jewish intermediaries—by which they could maintain contact. Resnik promised Rufeisen that he would only tell two other young men in the Mir ghetto the truth as to Rufeisen's Jewish identity—that was necessary to gain their trust in Rufeisen as an ally. For the rest, Rufeisen would be described as a sympathetic German officer. That was how I first heard of him, although later in the summer I would learn the full truth. I never spoke at any length with Rufeisen during this time, though we would exchange curt hellos in the street, with myself playing the part of the respectful Jew and Rufeisen that of the firm Nazi officer.

Even before we had any concrete assistance from Rufeisen, there was an underground resistance effort underway within the Mir *zamek*, as I have described. But we had no weapons, which meant that any plans we could make would be a matter of pure desperation. But with Rufeisen's help, we managed to accumulate a small number of pistols, rifles, grenades, and ammunition. He would usually obtain the firearms from the storehouse of captured weapons kept by the German police. Rufeisen had risen to the rank of an assistant police chief for the town of Mir, although he was still under orders from the German commandant of the gendarmerie, Polizei Meister Reinhold Hein. Hein held Rufeisen in great affection and respect, and that helped Rufeisen maintain a position of official power through which he could help us. Of course, he had to act "tough" toward Jews in public. But he employed no violence and tried to mitigate the actions of the German police and their Polish henchmen.

A transfer of weapons would frequently go like this: Rufeisen, in his role of police chief, would come up to a small group of Jews standing about in an out-of-the-way place, maybe next to some bushes, and he would yell at them for not working hard enough. At the same time he would leave a few weapons in those bushes. Other times Rufeisen would simply make "drops" that were picked up by members of the Jewish underground later that day. On one occasion I made a pick-up of some hand grenades. It wasn't easy. Because I seemed to be dawdling in the area where Rufeisen had hidden the grenades, a German policeman came up and slapped me hard and told me to get back to work. I had to circle back later to make the pick-up.

One of the most difficult hurdles was how to get the weapons back into the ghetto *zamek* without being searched. The penalty for possessing any kind of weapons was immediate death. In my own case, I was able to smuggle in the grenades through one of the *zamek* windows. Rufeisen was sometimes able to help us in his official capacity by taking us back to the ghetto under his own "guard." He also promised us that he would let us know in advance of any plans the Germans might have for *shchitim* [slaughters].

There was some difference of opinion, early on, as to whether we should use the arms to make a stand in the *zamek,* or instead to make an escape to the woods and try to join up with the Russian partisans, of whose activities we had heard vague rumors. Relatively quickly, we decided on the escape option, because our position in the *zamek* left us with no real possibility other than quick destruction. We would also be endangering our families, the elderly, the women, and the young children. There was no possibility of discussing the matter with the ghetto population as a whole—the possibility of a leak, of betrayal, was too great. And even if we had done so, there was no likelihood of consensus to carry on an armed resistance within the *zamek*. In the minds of many of the *Judenrat* members, there was still hope of keeping the Jewish community alive by fulfilling the work commands of the Germans. This was understandable. It is difficult to imagine the worst that can be imagined. And also, for the elderly, for the women with children, there was no real option. It was all but impossible for them to imagine themselves surviving in the woods. And to attempt to escape in large numbers—including old people and infants—would have endangered the chances of any of us getting away.

For those of us who were planning to escape, it was a horror to think of leaving family members behind. But there was, in our minds, no way of avoiding the conclusion that they would die whether we ran or stayed. We were certain that the Nazis intended to liquidate the Mir ghetto just as they had all the ghettos around us. And in that belief, we were proven right. I say this without any sense of pride. But we recognized the hell we were living in—we could not but recognize it.

IV

Jack Escapes from the Mir Ghetto

JACK

Rufeisen learned in June 1942 that the liquidation of the Mir ghetto under the command of Polizei Meister Hein was set for 13 August. He conveyed the information to us a short time later. The risks were tremendous on all sides. If news got out that the Jewish population knew what was coming and when, Hein would have recognized that Rufeisen had betrayed him, because Rufeisen was the only person other than Hein who knew the exact 13 August date in advance. At the same time, it was necessary to warn the Jewish population, so that those who wished to run would have the chance. The date was revealed to some of the members of the *Judenrat* a week or so in advance. There were a variety of reactions. Some felt that the information must be false—the Germans could be fended off through a combination of bribes and labor. Some claimed that the information provided by Rufeisen must be a trap—how could you trust a German officer? It was due to the latter opinion that the truth of Rufeisen's Jewish identity was revealed to the *Judenrat* at some point in the very last days. Rumors of the Jew posing as a German circulated quickly throughout the *zamek*.

Our plan was to escape on the night of 9 August—a Sunday night—four days before the 13 August liquidation date. Things were very tense in the *zamek* over that weekend. It was necessary for people to make a choice—to run or stay. We made it known that Sunday would be the night for everyone who wanted to run. For on that night, Rufeisen had informed us, he would lead the German and Polish police forces of the town off in the opposite direction, on the basis of an alleged tip that there were Russian partisans nearby who could be entrapped and destroyed. There was a great fear at that time that the Russian partisans might arise in Poland and hinder the German advance into Russia by breaking up German supply and communication lines. So any opportunity to crush the Russian partisans was hotly pursued. For Rufeisen, the risk of taking the police on a wild-goose chase was relatively low, because tips as to Russian partisan locations were notoriously unreliable. There would be only a handful of police left in Mir on that evening, and no guards whatsoever at the main entries of the *zamek*. As the Germans had no idea that we knew the massacre was coming, or that we knew of their plans to leave town on that Sunday evening, they had no real reason to fear that we would attempt a mass escape.

There was a core group of us—the forty or so underground members—who planned to make our escape in groups of five or six, to increase our chances of at least some of us getting away and perhaps making contact with the Russian partisans. There was some intention of regrouping once we reached the woods, but that never came about. The weapons were distributed amongst the groups—there were barely enough arms to go around. But merely to possess them was a vital advantage because, as we understood it, there was a much better chance of a Jew being taken into a Russian partisan group if that Jew was armed.

We tried to explain to the older Jews in the *zamek* that, once we younger ones had run away, if they started to hear any rumors about a final liquidation, they should try to run away to certain areas in the country that we described to them. There were areas that Rufeisen had told us would be safest—that he himself would try to keep the German and Polish police forces away from those places once the search was underway for escaping Jews. If they managed to do so, we said that we would try to find and help them. If they refused to believe the rumors, if they still hoped that the Jews in the Mir *zamek* ghetto would be left to live, there was nothing that we could do.

My father Julius had no such hopes. That is how he came to survive. He was well into his middle age by this point, but he was still in good physical health. He possessed a great determination to live and an ability to be patient with the most hellish conditions. He made his escape, with another Jewish man, on 10 August, the day after our main group. For roughly a week, Julius and the other man lived in a hole they dug in the side of a hill not far from a couple of farms. During the day they would stay hidden in the hole. At night they would take turns going out and scavenging for food in the fields and the barns. I was able to learn of his location from another Jewish escapee and to come and fetch him so that he could join our group in the woods. I cannot tell you how happy I was to find my father still alive.

Julius was not alone in making his escape the day after we left. There were others—older persons, women, and children— who ran and survived. All told, there were some 300 Jews who ran away on the days of 9 August and 10 August, before the German and Polish police returned from their wild-goose chase and reestablished close guard on the Mir ghetto. Not all of those people survived, of course. But at least they had a chance.

As I remember it, there were plans for our reuniting with Rufeisen if we managed to get away safely to the woods. Rufeisen would, of course, take a major role in the police search for the runaways. So he would be able to lead them to a certain place in the woods where we would be waiting for the police forces and could ambush them—kill as many as we could, seize their ammunition and supplies, and manage for Rufeisen to transfer over to our side during the fighting and remain with us. By that plan, there would be a twofold victory: we would manage to reward Rufeisen for his help to us and enable him to escape his dangerous position with the German police. And we would also be taking revenge—an armed attack by Jews against the butchers who had killed our families.

But that plan never came about, because, after we ran away but before the final 13 August liquidation, Rufeisen was betrayed—his identity as a Jew who had helped us was revealed to Meister Hein by a Jew from the Mir *zamek* ghetto named Stanislawski, who worked in the stables of the German gendarmerie. Stanislawski probably hoped to save his life by informing. He had no wife or children, only himself to care about. He succeeded in gaining one extra day of life—Meister Hein had him shot on 14 August, the day after the mass murder of the remaining Jews in the *zamek*.

If Rufeisen had not been betrayed, think what would have been different. Our ambush would have been a unique event in the history of the Holocaust. Perhaps the life of the Mir ghetto itself could have been prolonged by wiping out the gendarmerie stationed in the town. But instead, the traitor Stanislawski brought ruin upon himself and the entire ghetto.

What happened to Rufeisen is a story in itself. For Rufeisen was not shot by the Germans, although by all odds he should have been. He managed to escape, because Meister Hein, who cared for Rufeisen like a son, refused to take immediate punitive action against him, even after he learned that Rufeisen was a Jew who had supplied arms to the ghetto. There could be no greater betrayal of Hein's plans than this! But Hein allowed Rufeisen to live, even invited him to eat with the other German officers while he deliberated on what Rufeisen's fate should be. During the meal—it must have been with Hein's tacit understanding—Rufeisen slipped away and hid himself in a wheat field outside Mir. Soon enough the German police were searching for him—it was as if Hein had given Rufeisen a chance to live or to die, and to leave the final result up to fate.

Within a few days, Rufeisen found a place to hide—a Catholic convent in Mir, located near the offices of the German gendarmerie. During the remaining war years, Rufeisen not only served in a Russian partisan unit but also converted to the Catholic faith. After the war, he moved to Israel—still feeling himself a Zionist—and took vows as a priest and a Carmelite monk. His new name as a monk is Father Daniel and he calls himself a Christian Jew and works to improve relations between Christians and Jews in Israel. He has also maintained friendly relations with the survivors of the Mir ghetto. I am grateful that, in the summer of 1944, after the Russian liberation of Poland, I had a chance to meet briefly with Rufeisen and to thank him for risking his life to help us. During a visit

Rochelle and I made to Israel in the 1970s, I was again able to pay a visit to Rufeisen—who was by now Father Daniel—and to express my gratitude.

Rufeisen's fate became known to me much later, of course. On the night of 9 August, as I made my escape with my fellow underground comrades, we knew very little beyond that we should run to the woods and hope for the best. Even with the police out of town and no guards standing at the main entrance of the *zamek,* we dared not simply walk—or run—out of the main entrance. Instead, we used a window that opened out onto rubble and a long open field with the woods at the other end. We left in groups of five.

I remember how fast I ran when it came to be my turn. When I had played soccer, I was pretty good at going up and down the field at full speed. But running in pure terror was new to me. My head was spinning. I was so afraid, so excited, that I wasn't myself at all. I felt like someone watching myself from above racing for my life.

We all made it into the woods that night, thanks to Rufeisen. As I mentioned, our original plans called for us to try to regroup once we made it to safety. But then news reached us from a later escapee that Rufeisen had been betrayed and captured. That killed any hope of an ambush, and made us feel far more insecure about our position. So we broke up into small groups and set about trying to survive in the woods. Our hope at that point was still to join up with the Russian partisans, but as yet we had no idea where they were.

In the early weeks of our escape, the five young men in my group hid out in the woods, not too far from a main road. We dug a shallow underground shelter, about five feet wide, ten feet long, and six feet deep. We made a cover for it out of branches and evergreens. We were about a mile away from a farmer named Kurluta—the same farmer with whom I had hidden as a farmhand earlier in the summer. Kurluta was very friendly to us. He gave us food. He also gave me a rifle and a pistol, at a time when any working weapons were a treasure to us. We gathered enough rifles to go around. One problem we faced was that we couldn't keep getting food just from Kurluta—not only was that too great a burden for him, but it would also endanger both him and us, as it would make our movements too predictable. We didn't want to walk into a German trap.

So twice a week, during the evening, we went out to the unfriendly farmers who were cooperating with the Germans. We asked them for food and we would take it on our own if they didn't give it to us. If we found some Jewish memorabilia in their homes, like menorahs [ritual candelabra] or other items that were clearly stolen from the homes of the Jews of Mir, we got mad and smashed up everything in their houses. Sometimes, we beat those jerks up a little.

Because of those visits, food was not a big problem as we moved into autumn in the woods. At first we cooked by making a small wood fire, but then we got smarter. We found some bricks and built a little fire pit, burning the wood between the bricks and cooking up whatever food we had on metal wires we used as spits over the flames. We cooked late at night, to avoid having our fire spotted by Germans patrolling the woods, or by Polish passersby who might inform on us. Most of the time we ate potatoes, sometimes with mushrooms. Less often we had sausages or other kinds of meat. We could get bread from the farms fairly often, and now and then we could obtain milk, but what we mostly drank was water from the streams.

As the summer came to an end, our small group joined up for a brief time with a larger group of partisans—some fifty to sixty in number. Those people—roughly 60 percent Jews, 40 percent Belorussians—came from various towns in the region: Mir, Stolpce, Nieswierz, Turec, and Horodej. We had heard of the group from other Jewish runaways we met in the woods. There was no question of constructing an underground bunker for so many people. We kept constantly on the move and slept on the ground in thickly wooded areas.

One of the members of the group was a Russian soldier who claimed to have been left behind the lines during the German advance through eastern Poland. He was a *politruk* [political advisor], someone who was supposed to be trained to keep a Soviet presence amongst the Polish people and organize resistance against the Nazis.

The *politruk* suggested to us that we launch a surprise attack on a German police station just outside of Nieswierz. We had rifles, a good supply of ammunition, even a few automatic weapons. To demolish a police station was a tempting dream for us. So we spent a long evening in discussion, working out a plan. And then we headed toward Nieswierz, which was no easy matter—the march was roughly sixteen miles long, and it took us a full two days and two nights. Remember, we had to be in constant hiding, to move in darkness. The plan was that once we were within striking distance, we would rest for a day. Then, at four A.M. of the following morning, we would move out, surround the police station, and attack. We would throw some grenades—we had only a few—and keep up a steady rifle fire. If all went well, we would burn the station building to the ground, kill a good many police, and maybe even take two or three as hostages. From the hostages we hoped to obtain information about any plans the Germans had to sweep through the woods and hunt out Jewish groups. There had also been some talk in our camp, especially by the boys from Nieswierz, that we could take revenge on the hostages for what had been done to our families.

But nothing that we had planned came into being. As the time neared for our four A.M. assault, we noticed that our *politruk* was suddenly missing—a terrible and frightening blow. We figured that, most likely, the *politruk* was a German spy who had run off to rejoin his bosses. But we weren't sure. Maybe he had just gone off to scout out the station and the surrounding terrain. So what were we supposed to do now? If the *politruk* was a spy and if we went on with the attack as planned, the Germans would surely be waiting for us and we would be killed. On the other hand, our chances of a safe retreat were less than good.

We waited to see if the *politruk* might come back on his own. But by daylight he was nowhere to be seen. So we started to gather our things and to pull back as fast as we could.

Before we could make any start at a retreat, we were hit by intense automatic weapon fire—whether it was Germans or Polish police or both we couldn't be sure. Bullets were flying over my head, all around me. There were screams. I remember one boy from Nieswierz. He was carrying a machine gun, and when the police opened fire he moved closer to the direction of the shooting and fired back for ten, maybe fifteen seconds. God knows what had happened to his family. But he fought back very bravely. Very soon his body was covered with blood, and he was dead, with maybe six or eight bullets in him.

There was no hope of waging a real battle with them. We decided to run for our lives. Once I started to run it seemed that my feet barely touched the ground. Bushes and branches would loom ahead of me and I would jump and fly over them like a bird. There were bullets hitting the trees on either side of me. There were bodies falling. I kept running for maybe an hour, never stopping, not tiring until the very end. Whoever was left from our group had completely dispersed. I was on my own.

I remember that I crossed a road and then went into a deep stretch of woods. I found a secluded place to lie down. I needed to rest and plan how to get back to our camp. While I was lying there, I heard footsteps coming toward me through the woods. I thought it would be a German who had somehow followed me. But instead it was one of my fellow Mir runaways who had joined the *politruk*'s group at the same time I had. He too had survived the ambush. It was a happy occasion for both of us to meet in the woods. We were both relieved at no longer being alone or surrounded by the enemy.

It took us three days to get back to the camp. We were very careful, because the *politruk* would have told the Germans the location of the camp, and it was possible that they would launch a follow-up attack. As it turned out, there had been a few other survivors from the ambush who had reached camp ahead of us and broken the news to the others. As a result, everyone had scattered off into small groups. Thank God, my father was still waiting for me. The Germans must have decided that the ambush was successful enough that a full-scale counterattack on our camp would have been a waste of time and supplies.

My father and I became part of a small group, five or so of us at first. We knew that winter was coming on, that we would have to dig a larger bunker in which to live, and that we could not take the risk of remaining close to the road. We also decided that our chances for survival would increase if we could link up with other Jews in hiding and form a larger group. So we merged with another small band of Jews whom we had seen coming and going in the woods. The wilderness region in which we were living was called Miranke—basically a swampland with trees on the higher patches of land.

Now there were fourteen of us, including three women, one of whom was a doctor who had run away with her husband. There were eight young men who could go out and obtain food and, if need be, engage in skirmishes with the German or Polish police. My father stayed behind and helped with the cooking and other camp chores, as did the women.

Together we started to dig a new bunker for winter deep in the woods. It was a difficult task, given as many people as we had in the group. It wasn't possible to do anything too extensive, because the larger it was, the harder it would be to conceal.

We found a small hill, more a mound than a hill. Then we dug down into the ground and created an underground hole roughly five feet deep and fifteen feet by twelve feet in length and width. In the four corners of the bunker, we set the trunks of four small trees as support poles. We also lined the dirt walls with saplings, to prevent the earth from crumbling down on us. Over the top we constructed a cover of intertwined branches covered first by earth and then by small standing evergreen shrubs. After the first lasting snowfall, the bunker looked just like a little mound with evergreens.

The entrance to the bunker, which took up one of its sides, was a sloping passageway that you went down like a children's slide. Only one person at a time could slide in or climb out. On two of the sides within there were sleeping bunks made out of saplings and branches. They weren't comfortable, but they kept our bodies from touching the cold earth directly. On one of the sleeping sides there was also a food-storage area. We ate what we could scavenge and what would keep in those underground conditions—mainly flour, potatoes, and roots.

The fourth and final side was reserved as a cooking area.

We made a tiny hole in the cover of our shelter, to which we rigged up a piece of metal pipe we had scavenged. It served as a chimney for the little fire we kept going through the nights in a small brick fire pit we had set up in the center of the bunker. We used the fire both for cooking and for warmth, though we were always cold, given what little clothing we had. We had managed to take some blankets from the farms, but they weren't enough to keep the winter from sinking into our bones. And the fire was for nighttime only—because during the day, especially in the winter sky, any smoke could be clearly seen for a mile or more. At night, under cover of the dark, we could only hope that the farmers would be sleeping.

Our schedule was to start cooking at two A.M., eat in the middle of the night, and sleep during the day. We set a pail on top of the bricks of our firepit, and in this pail we would cook our staple main dish. Here was the recipe:

We started with water. Next to our firepit we dug a deeper hole that served as a kind of well into which the underground swamp water would seep. It did not take much digging to strike water—brackish water, brown like strong beer. And it stank of the swamp. We would drink it through pieces of rag. And on the other side of the rag, as we drank, things would be crawling. It was unbelievable at first, to live this way. If on a particular night we could use melted snow instead of the strained swamp water, it was a gourmet dish! When the water came to a boil we poured some flour in it, so that it came to look like thick clay. That was it—our basic soup, a clay to eat with spoons we had stolen from the farms. We didn't even have salt for seasoning. We called the soup *zacierke*. For a different dish with the same ingredients, we would replace the pail with a flat piece of scrap metal and then pour the flour-water clay into little patties that we baked on both sides. That was our bread. Now and then we boiled a big pailful of potatoes.

We couldn't relieve ourselves outside, because any farmers passing through the woods would have noticed the human waste. So we dug a second hole alongside of our bunker, and dug a small window opening between the two. Then we would relieve ourselves in small pots and empty the pots into that second hole through the window, which we stopped up with rags when it was not in use. That was our toilet-flushing system.

We didn't dare go outside unless there was a big snowstorm. Our tracks would disappear right away if the snowfall was heavy enough. We could take walks, make expeditions for food. But if the snowfalls didn't come, we could be trapped inside the bunker for days on end. Naturally, that meant the numbers of visits we could pay to neighboring farms was dramatically reduced, and our diet suffered as a result. Still, there were times, even when the snow was not falling, that we had to go out and get ourselves food from the farms. We had to worry about tracks, about being followed. Our hiding place never felt fully secure. We just hoped that we would not be trapped inside by a surprise ambush, without the chance to wage a fight.

So during this winter of 1942–43, we basically lived like squirrels, hiding in a hole. As you can imagine, the air in the bunker stank like hell. On nights when it was snowing or otherwise very dark, we would lift open the cover of the bunker a bit. Otherwise, we would sit in our hole.

We were doing our best to survive, even to resist, but no one in our group expected to come out alive from that hell. The main thing was not to be taken alive by the Germans, not to submit to their questions, their torture, and a passive death at their hands. We were always armed and had an understanding that if we were ambushed, we would fight until we were killed. If need be, we would shoot one another rather than be captured. It was inevitable that we would die—but death would come on our terms.

Once I became used to that idea, I became extremely brave. I don't say this to boast, but only to describe the state of mind I was in. I wasn't afraid of death any longer. I established myself as the leader of the group and always went out on food raids from the farmers in the region. I took huge risks. I would pick farms that were owned by Nazi sympathizers and were situated only two miles from German police headquarters. We would break into the houses and steal lots of food and clothing. Then we would smash the windows and the furniture. We killed their dogs when they bit us.

It came to the point that the Germans already knew me by name. I found out from some of the farmers that the German police had placed a price on my head! This was an honor at a time when Jewish life came very cheap.

I should tell you that something happened to me during that time—in August or September 1942. It was a dream, a very powerful dream—one that I believed in completely, without logic or reason.

A voice—I think it was my mother's voice—told me that I would meet Rochelle in the woods and that we would come together and remain together. I don't remember seeing the face that was speaking to me in the dream. It was just a voice coming toward me. But I did see Rochelle's face very clearly.

When I woke up I started to think. Yes, Rochelle and I had known each other in Stolpce before the war, but we hadn't dated or even had a close relationship. Why would she come into my dream? I didn't even know if she was still alive. The chances were that she had died in the liquidation of the Stolpce ghetto. And even if she had survived that ordeal, the chances of her running to the same place in the woods where I was hiding were not even one in a million.

But I believed in the dream, as I have said. I took it so seriously that, while we were digging out our winter bunker—roughly a month after the dream—I insisted that we construct one extra space next to my own to be saved especially for Rochelle.

When I told the members of the group that Rochelle would be coming, they all thought I was going crazy. I'm sure they were laughing and joking about it behind my back. But I was a very effective leader on the food raids and they needed me. So they tried to reason with me, because space was at a premium in the bunker. "How can you know she is going to come?" they would ask. "Maybe she's dead, maybe she's a hundred miles away!"

I didn't want to tell them about the dream. In fact, I didn't give them any explanation at all. I said only, "Don't any of you worry about it. I just want a space ready for her when she comes."

Jack Escapes from the Mir Ghetto

So matters stood in November 1942, roughly three months since the dream had come to me. I was sitting in the bunker. Outside we had two young men standing guard at two different observation posts, to make sure we weren't taken by surprise. One of the lookouts came back to me to report that there were three Jewish women coming toward our shelter. The guard had stopped them, and they told him they wanted to speak to me. I had no idea who the women were—the guard hadn't gotten their names. So I went out to meet them.

Rochelle was standing out there. It was unbelievable! She was alongside a friend of hers, Tanya, and they were being led by a girl from my hometown of Mir, named Fania, who was in a little partisan group of her own in a nearby part of the woods. Even in Fania's group, they had heard the story about how this crazy Izik Sutin wanted to save a place in the bunker for a girl he hadn't seen for years and knew nothing about. In fact, that's how Fania knew to take Rochelle to our bunker. She had heard the story, and when she ran into Rochelle she decided to bring her to me.

Well, there she was.

What I felt when I first saw Rochelle standing there was that my dream had not lied to me. Someone, something, was watching over us. Rochelle and I had been fated to meet.

How else could she have arrived at the same small hole in the woods in which I was hiding? How else could I have known to prepare for her arrival?

All this is something of what I felt at that moment. The rest—and there is more—I cannot find the words to tell.

V

Rochelle Escapes from the Stolpce Ghetto

ROCHELLE

A former schoolmate whispered in my ear, and suddenly I was an orphan.

My mother's last message to me was to take *nekome,* revenge. On a certain abstract level, I could understand. I wanted it myself. But, at the same time, it was incomprehensible to me. I was alone, a girl without weapons or power, surrounded by a world that had shown me nothing but hate.

People use the word "trauma" to describe how they feel when something very bad happens to them, something they know will have a lasting effect. To me, the word is not strong enough to convey what the first days—after learning of the death of my mother and sisters—were like.

One thing I know I did *not* feel at that time—a sense of fear over what might happen to me. In truth, the worst I could imagine had already happened. The Nazi murderers had conquered without much effort and now they were doing their work without hindrance. I was a slave in their hands, one who worked in the local sawmill to produce the lumber demanded by the German war machine. What was left to fear?

In fact, as my head started to clear, I even began to feel a crazy sense of freedom. I had been helping my mother care for my younger sisters—watching over them, scavenging bits of wood from the sawmill to serve as fuel for the stove. But now they were gone. And so now there was nothing to prevent me from doing whatever I had to do. My life was my own to give up, so to speak.

The night after I had resumed my labor, I returned to the cold, bare ghetto room in which my mother and sisters and

I had been living for the past few months. I found a couple of photos on the floor—my mother, my sisters, their faces before me again. I picked up the photos and put them in my brassiere. I still have them.

I knew then. . . . I had made up my mind.

There was nothing left for me but escape. It wasn't a matter of wanting to survive. At that point, I did not even know that there was such a thing as a Jewish resistance effort. There was no media, no communications network to let those of us trapped in the ghetto know that there were Jewish partisans in the woods. Under the Nazis, those Jews who lived at all lived in total isolation. But I would not let them strip me naked in front of the German police and the Polish people I had gone to school with. They were not going to take me on a truck to the grave. I was not going to wait for that. I decided that I would die running!

At the sawmill, I worked alongside another Jewish girl named Tanya. We had both grown up in Stolpce, though we were never close friends. Our job was to catch and pile the bark as it was sawed off the raw boards, and then to stack the boards. The boards kept coming all day—we had to move constantly.

Physically, Tanya and I resembled each other: we both had brown wavy hair and we were both buxom. Tanya was a very sweet and friendly girl. So I confided in her. I said, "Listen, they're going to kill us in a couple of weeks anyway. Right now they're just organizing us into groups to see how many they have to liquidate. I'm going to make a break for it. Let them shoot me in the back as I try to escape."

Tanya decided to go along with me. Her parents and her siblings had all been killed. For Tanya, life had become a sorrow. She was willing to try to escape, I did not have to work to persuade her. There was a Jewish man and his wife who worked alongside us as well. The man's name, I remember, was Mottel. He was a tall, gangly man in his twenties. He and his wife had been sweethearts since high school, and they had a five-year-old son together. We decided that we were going to try to escape together—all at once. For Mottel and his wife, it was an awful decision, because they knew that if they took their son with them he would never survive. It would be a death they would have to watch. So, on the morning we had planned for our escape, they left him in the ghetto. They said good-bye to him and left him with the older Jewish women with whom they were packed together in a room. They were saying good-bye knowing their son would die. There were no good choices, there were only ways of dying.

The sawmill was located on the Niemen River. Right across the Niemen was a forest. We would try to swim across the river and then head for the woods. Why as a group? Only because it gave us an extra bit of courage to die together. There was no plan beyond that. We never even talked about what we would do if we reached the woods. We didn't expect to live that long. We just decided that we didn't want to be killed the way the Nazis planned—slowly, as it suited their purposes, and after we had worked ourselves to near death. We could die with some dignity. We would try to get away, they would shoot us with their machine guns, and that would be it.

There was a chance element that played a role—the local terrain. Because there was a forest across the Niemen River, we had a very slim chance of success that somehow helped us to take the risk, even though none of us really believed that we would survive. Without the forest, it would have been a joint suicide pact, pure and simple.

We decided to wait for an especially foggy morning. Such a morning came toward the end of September, 1942. Our plan called for making a break just after we had been marched by the Nazis, in the early dawn, from the ghetto to the sawmill for our daylong labor. There were two outhouses that stood at the very end of the sawmill, not far from the river. The German routine called for allowing the Jewish workers, upon arrival, five or so free minutes for stretching and physical needs before we had to go to our machines.

And so we began our escape by moving casually toward the outhouses. I was wearing clothing that the Nazis had decided was not worth confiscating. It was my high-school uniform—a pleated skirt and a top, shoes, and a jacket.

The four of us first crawled under some loose barbed wire that had been set up by the Germans, and then we ran roughly fifty yards to the river just before the bell rang that called the Jews to our machines. Once we reached the river, we dove in, still clothed, and started swimming as hard and as fast as we could.

Within a minute we could hear the German police raising a cry. But they didn't have cars or motorcycles—those were too valuable for the large-scale liquidation and military operations to be wasted on a ragged Jewish work crew. And so the German police who chased us had only bicycles. But they were fully armed. The machine guns were loud . . . rat tat tat tat. We heard the bullets hit the water all around us and we thought *that* was what we wanted: to die at any minute.

But somehow, I don't know how, we managed to swim all the way across the river to the other side. Then we ran for the woods. The machine guns were still going. You could hear the bullets striking the trees and ripping the leaves that were still left on the branches. Mottel and his wife must have run in another direction, because I didn't see them again for a long time. But Tanya and I ran together. Meanwhile, between swimming and running, I had lost my shoes, so I was barefooted. And I had thrown away my jacket just before diving into the river because it would have been too hard to swim in it. So I was just in my pleated school skirt and blouse.

We ran and ran. But still we heard the machine guns and at times the shooting was intense—bursts of fire in specific areas. I remember thinking that they must have caught and killed Mottel and his wife. And I was certain that they would follow Tanya and me until we dropped from exhaustion. We ran all day like that. We went deep into the woods and finally had to sit down—collapse!—and rest. Looking back, I can only guess that the German police decided that it didn't pay for them to run so hard after two Jewish girls. It was autumn already. The cold would take care of us.

In late September, during the day, it was still fairly warm. But after dusk it was frosty. So during the night, while we were trying to doze off—which we could only do in fits and starts—

our wet clothes became frozen. And my feet, from running, were scratched and bloody. I was very sore. Tanya and I both sat like that through the night, through hours of cold and misery. Our clothes grew so stiff that, when dawn finally came and we wanted to get up and stretch, we couldn't. It was as if we were in metal armor. At last, by making small and difficult movements, we reached a tiny clearing in the woods where the sun was shining. It took what seemed like hours, but our clothes finally began to soften up. Even so, we could barely walk at first.

Amazingly, we weren't hungry. Adrenaline was still working overtime within us. As we talked about what to do next, we still weren't thinking about surviving in the long term. It was only that, now that we had achieved it, we wanted to make something of our escape—just so the Germans didn't find us right off and shoot us. Our main goal was to get farther away from Stolpce. But after our clothes had thawed out, we decided to stay in that same hiding place for another day and night, to avoid being spotted if there was any sweeping search for us underway. When we didn't hear any shooting during that time, we figured that they had given up on us for the time being.

As we talked, Tanya came up with a suggestion. While we were at the sawmill, she had learned from a fellow laborer—a Belorussian who had worked there for years, and who felt sorry for the young Jews who now served as slaves around him—that there were Russian partisans hiding out in the woods. Those partisans were small bands of Russian troops who had been caught by surprise by the Nazi blitzkrieg invasion of eastern Poland. The Belorussian laborer had given Tanya the name and location of his uncle, a farmer who lived some ten miles from the sawmill. The farmer was friendly to the Russian partisans and knew how to contact them.

According to Tanya, if we could make it to the farm, there was a possibility that we could somehow join the Russian resistance efforts against the Nazis. It seemed remote, but what other possibilities did we have? Besides, the thought of helping out the Russian partisans and then, after we had proven ourselves, being given guns with which to fight—this was as big a dream as either of us could imagine, under the circumstances.

Unfortunately, our information about the Russian partisans was seriously lacking in details. What was missing was the knowledge that most of the Russian partisan groups treated Jewish escapees not as allies, as potential fellow fighters, but rather as enemies on a par with the Nazis themselves. Imagine that—at the very time that the Nazis were invading the Russian homeland!

We started walking—hoping that, even though neither of us knew the countryside well, we could somehow find this farm and join up with the Russians.

There was another chance factor that helped us, like there being a forest across the Niemen River. In the prewar years, there had been reasonably good relations between Belorussians and Jews, as opposed to Poles and Jews. That was because the Belorussians were a minority ethnic group in eastern Poland. Most of their people lived across the border, in the Soviet Union. Many Belorussians had welcomed the Soviet troops who had been occupying eastern Poland up until the Nazi invasion. The majority of the Jews in eastern Poland had welcomed the Soviet troops as well—for the obvious reason that the alternative would have been falling into the hands of the Nazis.

Most of the Belorussians were peasant farmers scattered throughout the northeastern Polish countryside. That was the region in which my hometown of Stolpce was situated. Not all Belorussian farmers were friendly to the Jews, of course.

But some were. As it turned out, while the assistance the friendly Belorussian farmers offered was minimal, it was enough to make a difference.

Somehow, toward the end of the first day after leaving our hiding place in the woods, we arrived at the farm we were looking for. We didn't go up to the house, but we saw the Belorussian—his name, I remember, was Usik—working in the field. So we decided to approach him—what else could we do under the circumstances? He knew who we were, he didn't have to ask. We told him we were hungry, we asked if he could give us something to eat. He told us that he didn't have any food to spare—all he could give us was a couple of eggs from his chicken. He gave each of us a little egg, and we made a hole and sipped the yolks out, just like you would drink water. We felt that at least we had something in us.

Then we asked the farmer if he knew of any Russian partisans hiding out nearby. He told us that he had heard of some, but he didn't know exactly where they were. He suggested that we go on several miles more to another Belorussian farmer—maybe he would have clearer information.

It was hard for us to make our way—we were new to the woods, and so we wandered in circles and wasted all of one day. We were still barefooted. But still, in a couple of days, we got to the farm the first farmer had described.

The second farmer gave us something to eat—our first food since the eggs two days before. We asked him if there were any Russian resistance fighters we could join. He said, "Yeah, some Russians may come by today. Stick around here, and when they come, you can ask them if they'll take you."

A few hours later, he gave us a signal that some Russian partisans were coming. There were a couple of them. They were unshaven, in filthy uniforms, but they were armed to the teeth. And there we were—two teenage Jewish girls in ragged clothing. We must have looked like animals after our days and nights in the woods. But we talked to them. We begged them to let us join them. We told them we'd do anything . . . cook, clean, wash, whatever was needed for the resistance effort. They felt sorry for us and agreed to take us in.

Their group consisted of roughly forty to fifty soldiers. Some of them had been accidentally caught behind the Nazi lines. But others were simply deserters with no choice but to band together with their former comrades. The leader of the group was one Sorokin; he had earned his position by virtue of being the highest-ranking Soviet officer amongst them. But there was nothing like military discipline in the group. Its goal was sheer survival, rather than determined resistance. There were other Russian partisan groups in the area who did undertake effective action against the German military during that period. But that particular band, although well-armed, conducted raids only for the food and supplies it needed to hold out in concealment in the woods.

The two partisans who had brought us in had some sympathy for us. The rest did not. They started in with . . . we should cook for them, look for dry wood for the fire, bring water from God knows where. All these things, however, we had *expected* to do. We wanted to contribute, to play a part in helping to fight back against the Germans.

Tanya and I were barefooted, so they gave us some boots from dead Russian soldiers. But there were no matching pairs. I had two left boots, with no laces and no socks. Still, Tanya and I were glad to have boots in any condition, because our feet were so sore. They had accumulated tents, blankets, old army coats. None were given to us. We had nothing with which to cover ourselves. During the nights we sat so close to the fire that we almost burned our toes.

In the group we met a Jewish girl named Sonia. She was living amongst them with a Belorussian boy from a local farm who had joined the Russian partisans. Sonia was his "girl" and was somewhat protected from abuse for that reason. When she first saw Tanya and me, we were freezing cold, dressed in our torn clothing, with nothing to keep us warm. The partisans always kept a fire going, and Sonia was cooking up for them whatever they brought back from their raids. Sonia took pity on us and gave us some clothing. She also tried to help us whenever she could and to teach us what we needed to know to survive in the midst of the partisans.

It was October, and the cold weather was fast approaching. Misery of a whole new kind opened up for Tanya and for me. The demands started to increase, and labor was no longer the issue. They said, "You want better boots? You want a jacket, a blanket? Then sleep with me! Otherwise, you can sit by the fire all night." When we refused, they would say, "You Jewish sluts! You were sleeping with the Germans! Now you come to the Russian partisans, we let you live, and you don't want to sleep with us!" It was what you call a "no-win" situation. What are you going to answer them?

The charge that we had slept with Nazi soldiers was particularly difficult for Tanya and me to bear. We kept quiet. We were afraid of argument, of seeming to contradict them. We also knew that no matter how much we might insist that we were telling the truth, it would have done nothing to convince the partisans. They were intent upon their lust.

The truth went beyond the fact that we would never have slept with the Nazis. Here was the tangled insanity of the Nazi mind—even the worst of the Nazis would not have been eager to try to sleep with us. From our time in the ghetto, we knew of the rules and limits placed upon Nazi soldiers: they were permitted any and all violent atrocities against Jewish men and women alike, not to mention Jewish children, Jewish babies. But they would have been immediately shot for raping a Jewish woman. The reason was the Nazi fear of polluting the master "Aryan" race. The crime of intercourse with a Jew was called *Rassenschande* [race defilement].

But the Russian partisans who now governed our lives knew nothing of *Rassenschande*. For them, we were women, we were Jews, and so we were fit for nothing more than filthy labor and filthy sex.

Sonia knew what was going on. That's why she was sleeping with her guy—she had no choice. Sonia said, "Listen, I hate to be the one to tell you this. But sooner or later, it comes down to sex or your life. A lot of the partisans are mad that you're even here. They feel that you don't earn your keep. They're going to kill you."

But then Sonia talked to her "husband." He was a pretty nice boy, and he said, "Okay, let them sleep in our tent for a while." So Sonia brought us into their tent and gave us some of their blankets. We felt that we were in Heaven . . . that we had a protector. But then Sonia said, "Don't feel too safe. He's not happy protecting you two against the wishes of the others. He won't keep you for long. He's just being nice because I begged him to help you."

Shortly afterwards, Sonia came into the tent and told us that she had bad news. Her "husband" had told her that a few of the more bitter partisans had decided to get rid of us—they didn't need us. Sonia explained the plot, "These partisans plan to start the rumor that you brought in venereal disease, that the Germans sent you specifically into the woods to infect them all. They'll say that before you arrived in this camp, you slept with another Russian partisan group and that all of those partisans came down with disease. There will be a quick trial and they'll kill you." Never mind that the accusations made no sense: why would they be constantly asking to sleep with us if they really believed we had venereal disease? Those men were sure to be believed over Jewish girls who had wandered in from the forest.

A few days later, Tanya and I were cooking a meal at the campfire. It was dawn. The partisans who were plotting against us had just returned after having been out all night. They were drunk and laughing and they came to sit by the fire. They told us that they had ambushed and killed some young Jews on the road leading from Minsk to the east. They said that they had killed the boys right off and had been raping the girls all night long. When they were finished, they shot the Jewish "sluts."

We sat by the fire and waited. They taunted us, "Are you cold? You want a blanket, come in my tent!" We were certain that they would rape and kill us. But somehow, that morning, the partisans only threatened us. Maybe they had had enough for one night.

But things grew much, much worse in the days that followed. . . .

The Russian partisans began to say to us, "Why did you come to us? We hate you as much as the Germans do!" I thought, "Is this the reason I escaped from the sawmill? If this is survival, then I don't care much for survival, either." Remember, when Tanya and I had first escaped, our idea had been to run so that we would be shot in the back. We had wanted to be killed so that we wouldn't be taken alive to our graves. So now we saw what we had survived for—to be tormented and treated like dirt. But then again, I didn't think we would survive much longer in that partisan camp. The only thing that stopped them from killing us outright was that they were afraid of witnesses—such as Sonia's "husband"— later testifying against them to the Soviet military authorities.

Anti-Semitism was forbidden as a matter of official Soviet policy. Yes, Stalin was a rabid anti-Semite, but laws and men don't always match.

During late 1942—this I know from the history books—Hitler himself had issued an order calling for increased anti-partisan efforts in the newly conquered European nations that made up his Reich. The partisan activity was disrupting his war efforts, and to make matters worse, there were Jews who had escaped liquidation and were now fighting back. So there were efforts underway to put a stop to all that—newly formed *Einsatzgruppen* [mobile killing units]. The units were assisted by local collaborators—persons of the same national or ethnic background as the partisan fighters themselves, who were recruited by the Nazis and then sent to join the partisan groups and betray them.

Here is a craziness: it was an antipartisan effort by the Germans that "liberated" Tanya and myself from our particular hell of rape and abuse. But the "liberation" turned out to be brief.

A couple joined the group—a Russian soldier and his wife. They brought with them a rifle and some ammunition, and so they were treated with honor and given a tent. The partisans ordered us, the Jewish "sluts," to act as maids for the newcomer's wife. Whatever she needed, we were to provide—make her food, wash her clothes. She was the "queen" in the camp. We tried to please her as best as we could.

Then, about a week later, the couple told the commander of our group, Sorokin, that they knew a farm where retreating Russian soldiers had buried a lot of ammunition, and that they also knew the farmer who lived there. The commander liked the sound of that. He sent one of his partisans with the couple to bring back the ammunition. Well, the couple was spying for the Nazis. They killed the partisan who went along with them, and then they reported to the Nazis the location of our camp.

Tanya and I never really slept during the night, because we were tending the fire. At dawn, we started to hear a machine gun. The first shots we heard were the Germans killing the guard we had posted about one-half mile from the camp. Before I knew it, the bullets were coming from all sides, like a snowstorm. I heard screams, German voices calling, "Halt!"

Tanya and I started running almost immediately. We had been cooking up barley stew, and there was a ladle hanging from a tree branch just above us. A bullet hit the ladle and it shattered into pieces. That brought us to our feet. I thought to myself, "It was hell on earth here anyway." Somehow—once again—Tanya and I fled for our lives. I remember, just as we started, seeing our friend Sonia trying to wrap a bandage over the head of a Russian partisan who had just been hit. His head looked half-open and blood was pouring out.

Once we had gotten clear of the camp, we never thought about going back. We ran as long as we were able, until we could hear no more shots. At some point in our running I caught sight of Sonia again. She and her "husband" were also attempting to make their escape—in a different direction—from the camp. I had no time to stop and think about whether or not she would make it. In truth, I still expected that none of us, not Sonia, not Tanya, not myself, had long to live.

That day, after hours of running and hiding, Tanya and I crossed the Luze River and entered into the large wilderness region called the Nalibocka Forest. The wilderness was a natural haven for partisan activity. It was at that time that we met up with another Russian partisan group that called itself by the name of their army training—the *parachutzistn* [parachutists].

There was a wooden house along the bank of the Luze River that belonged to a Belorussian farmer who made a side-living ferrying people. That's where we first met the *parachutzistn.*

We had come up to the farmer hoping to get some food, and it was only then that we saw the *parachutzistn,* who were sitting there drinking vodka like crazy. The farmer warned us in a whisper, "Listen, they're very mean and very drunk. If you can get away from them, run. I don't know if they'll let you come out of this meeting alive." There were about a dozen *parachutzistn*—they were in dirty uniforms, and their eyes took in Tanya and me as if we were cattle or worse.

We tried to explain to the *parachutzistn* how we had run away from the German ambush. We didn't know that the *parachutzistn* were the worst of all. It was a group that took special effort and pleasure in hunting down Jewish partisans. They had killed a group of fourteen boys from Jack's town of Mir—that I learned only later.

The *parachutzistn* were carrying a number of bottles of vodka and kept filling glasses for themselves and for us. They also offered us some food, but there were no polite preliminaries. They had no intention of letting us just walk away from them. They told us straight off, "Drink vodka and eat so that it will be easier for you to die. If you get drunk, you won't feel the bullets." Who could eat or drink? Who could swallow? I thought to myself, "I'm not going to get drunk. If I die, I want to know what I'm doing."

There was a bush behind Tanya and me. Instead of drinking the vodka, we kept secretly pouring it into the bush. I must have poured out ten glasses. We watched them drink, and they thought that we were as drunk as we could be. But in fact they were so drunk that they couldn't tell what our condition was. The river had started to freeze up a little. When it got to be evening, they told us to run. They said, "Okay, now it's time to get rid of you." We ran to the river; they were shooting and I was waiting for the bullets to hit.

I don't know whether they weren't really trying to kill us or whether they were just too drunk to hit us. It was kind of dark, and that might have affected their aim. But we ran across the river—the thin ice was cracking under our boots. I kept yelling to Tanya, out of panic, as we ran, "Are you bleeding? Can you keep moving?" But neither of us was hit. We crossed the river and ran back into the woods. Why not the woods? By now it felt natural. We were nothing but hunted animals.

Late the next day we found another Belorussian farm. The farmer said, "I can't keep you for long. But you can stay overnight in this barn." It had big bales of hay, and so we cuddled up and waited for morning. During the night we decided that we had both had enough of the partisans—of the entire business. I told Tanya, "Let's go back to the Stolpce ghetto.

We'll find a floor in a house to sleep on until the Germans discover us."

I thought I might as well die like a human being—in a house, the way I used to live. We were cold, full of lice, miserable, hungry. It was nothing but a prolonged death. A bullet would have been a good thing!

The next morning, while we were still sleeping in the barn, they came in. They found us . . . the *parachutzistn*. They started yelling, "You Jewish sluts! We thought we got rid of you! You're still here!"

I was sure they would kill us. But they were very drunk and finally they fell asleep.

At that point, Tanya and I crawled away and started walking toward Stolpce. Let the Germans shoot us, that's it. There was no more fight left in us. Stolpce was where my family had lived, and to die in Stolpce would be to join them in a sense, in spirit.

Tanya agreed with me. We were both ready to die. We even walked for a time by way of open roads—an invitation to death. At last, we came to the outskirts of the village of Luze, maybe twenty miles from Stolpce.

There was a farmhouse. We decided to knock on the door. Let the farmer kill us, let anyone kill us. As it happened, the man who lived there was a Belorussian who worked as a forester and had once supplied lumber to my father's factories. He said to me, "I know you. You're Schleiff's daughter." I said, "Yeah." He said, "Come in. I'll give you some food."

So we went into the house, and he gave us some hot soup. He asked where we were going and told us that we looked terrible. I said to him, "We've been wandering in misery for a month. We can't find a Russian partisan group that will let us live. Now we're heading back to the ghetto." I didn't go into detail.

He said, "Wait! Don't be silly. See the little hill over there, near the woods? There are some Jewish boys and girls living there in an underground bunker. They'll probably help you. Don't go back to Stolpce!"

I wasn't very taken with that advice. We wanted to die. We

were still in our two left boots each, sitting in ripped clothes that left us virtually undressed. The forester cut some blankets in half for us to use as shawls. As we were eating, he pointed out the window and said, "You see over there! Some of the Jewish kids are on their way somewhere. I'll go call them." He knew them because they had come to his house before for food.

Two of these Jewish partisans came back with the forester. A girl and a boy. The girl had gone to high school with me! She was from Mir—her name was Fania. She was a bright girl and had always been very pretty and sure of herself. She had a rifle and was wearing a jacket and boots. We looked at each other and said, "Oh my God!"

I had already mentally and physically given up. And she was saying, "You know, there's a guy with another Jewish partisan group near here. . . . Izik Sutin. Remember him? He's looking for you." I thought, "Oh great! What should this boy whom I barely knew once upon a time want from me?" She went on, "His group has a bunker not far from here. When they built their bunker, Izik swore to everyone that you would be coming, and that he would save a place in it for you!" I thought either she was crazy or I was crazy. I didn't even remember what Izik looked like.

Fania said, "Come on! I'll take you there."

I looked at Tanya and Tanya looked at me.

I should say something at this point that somehow I skipped before. Before we had arrived at the forester's house, Tanya and I were walking down the road that led to Stolpce.

Like Jack says, certain things you can't explain. Maybe there is something, some power. . . .

We were heading toward the ghetto. All of a sudden an old man came out of the woods. He had a salt-and-pepper beard, was dressed in a worn jacket and hat, and walked bent over with the help of a stick. I don't know where he came from. He said, "Get off the road and run into the woods. A convoy of German police cars is coming in a couple of minutes. Run away!"

So we ran into the woods and lay down. Within five minutes maybe twenty-five cars and trucks came—German police and troops. Our lives, which we had felt ready to surrender, were saved. When it came down to it, we hid rather than be shot. But who was the old man? I had never seen him before. And as soon as he spoke he disappeared into the woods again!

It was soon after this that we found the forester's house and got in touch with the Jewish partisans. And now Fania was telling me about Jack and offering to take me to his bunker.

Tanya looked at me and asked, "Do you still want to go back to the Stolpce ghetto?"

I said, "Well, we can always do that." I saw Fania with her boots, her jacket, and her rifle. She looked good. I thought, "Maybe there is hope. Maybe with Jews we won't go through such misery." So Tanya and I agreed to give it a try. We went with Fania. At the edge of the forest, she told us to wait—she would go and tell Jack that I was there.

There I was, with two left boots, the blanket around me, lice in my head, dirty, smelly. Ready for the garbage pile.

Within fifteen minutes, Fania came back with a guy in a big sheepskin coat. He had a mustache, a fur hat, a rifle. I thought, "Who is this?" He looked like a wild man from the woods.

It was Jack. Even when he told me who he was, I could barely recognize him. And he was saying that I could come with him to his bunker. Beyond the fact that I was surprised he was there in front of me, a survivor, I felt no emotion as he made his offer. I was dead inside, exhausted. It was a relief to see Jews who actually looked like human beings—who had food to eat and clothing to wear. But basically my feeling was, "If you have a hole that I can lie down in and sleep, fine. That's all I can do."

There was no room in Jack's bunker for Tanya, but there was a Belorussian farmer nearby named Petrovich. His family came from Russia, he was a friend of the Jewish partisans, and we were told that he would give Tanya shelter. Tanya agreed to this.

So I went with Jack to the bunker, and Fania took Tanya to Petrovich.

VI

Courtship in the Woods

JACK

At once I invited Rochelle to come join us in my bunker. She hardly knew what to think, I'm sure. Still, she accepted. It wasn't that she was so taken with the sight of me. But where else did she have to go?

There wasn't room enough for Tanya, but I promised to find a place for her as well, and I did the best that I could. Petrovich, the Belorussian farmer to whom I sent her, was very good to the Jewish partisans. If we needed medication, he would go to town and get it for us. But the Russian partisans, who were also active in this Nalibocka Forest, were convinced that Petrovich was a double agent pretending to help the partisan cause but secretly informing to the Germans. I could never verify whether it was true or not.

Tanya came to visit us at the bunker after she had lived with Petrovich a couple of weeks, to see Rochelle and to let us know how things were going. Tanya explained to us that there were Petrovich and his three sons—their mother was no more—and that she had to satisfy all four of them as a wife. Otherwise, they were nice to her. She had enough to eat, a warm house in which to sleep. She went back to Petrovich's that same day. Given the kind of hell we were living in, it was the best refuge she had.

Some time later, we found out that Tanya had become pregnant. The father was one of the members of the Petrovich family—precisely which one was unclear. But the baby was never born. The Russian partisans decided to take revenge on Petrovich for his alleged betrayals. So one night they surrounded his house and burned it down—burned everyone in it alive. Maybe Petrovich was too good to the Jews and the Russians hated him for it. I heard later that Tanya had begged the Russians to let her go because she was Jewish and not an informant—and also because she was pregnant. Even if the Russians genuinely suspected Petrovich, they could have let a pregnant woman go. But they killed all of them. So that was Tanya's fate.

You can imagine the reaction of my fellow group members when I brought Rochelle back to our bunker. They couldn't begin to believe it at first. And Rochelle had her own difficulties believing me. Yes, Fania had told her how I had saved a place for her. But when I revealed to her the story of my dream and how I had been waiting for her, she was sure I was bluffing. It was just a fantasy to win her over, to get her to have sex with me. That is what she believed until she talked to the other members of the group and they confirmed that what I was telling her was true.

Even if the whole story had made half-sense, it would have been difficult for Rochelle to accept. At the time she came to us, she had just gone through a period of terrible suffering. How could she accept the fact that a strange man in the woods was waiting for her arrival and offering his love?

I can't say that the other members of my group were very thrilled by her arrival. But they had no choice. I was the leader, and they felt they needed me to keep their food supply secure. Thank God there was a space that had been prepared for her—without that space, the complaints would really have been overwhelming.

ROCHELLE

My mental state, as I went with Jack to his bunker, was that it was easier and better to die than to suffer further cold and humiliation. My expectations were low, my emotions were non-existent. I was thinking to myself, "Well, we'll see what will happen here!"

The other members of the group did confirm that Jack had predicted my arrival. But even so, I didn't really accept it as true. How could he know that I was alive? What kind of dream could prophesy to him to wait for me in the middle of the wilderness? I thought that the other group members were reciting the whole business only because Jack had told them to, to make me feel more welcome.

But welcome I never felt. To those other members I was another mouth to feed. And I was a woman. It was the men who went off on the farm raids to get the food. The women were waiting behind to be fed. So now there was one more woman waiting on a little bed of six small trees.

Living with their feelings toward me was bad enough. What made it worse was that I had never lived under the ground before—I wasn't used to the bunker as the others were. When Tanya and I had been roaming around, we had slept out in the open or occasionally in barns. It was miserable, but I was like an animal in the woods—I had gotten used to living in the fresh, open air.

The first time I entered Jack's bunker, it was through a hole in the ground with a square cover. You slid into the bunker. Inside it was very dark. And with twelve or so people inside there, you can imagine the air . . . so stale. Almost at once I got so sick to my stomach that I thought I would pass out. I had to get back outside immediately, just to catch my breath. The stench was terrible. None of the group members bathed—there was no way to do so in the cold weather. All of them were full of lice and vermin. Eventually I learned to stand it, but in the first days I was sick continually, nauseated and fainting, running in and out of the bunker just to keep from vomiting in their midst.

The members of Jack's group saw this and said to him, "See what you've got on your hands? Not only another person to feed, but she's probably been raped and is now pregnant to boot!" Jack's little group was half men and half women, but the men and the women alike spoke that way about me.

None of them came up to me and asked me personally if I was pregnant. All of this was said behind my back. But of course these accusations began to reach me—I would overhear comments, and I could see that they were trying to torment Jack with their charges.

I knew that I wasn't pregnant. But I thought that, in a way, they were right. Who needed me there? That was my state of mind.

JACK

They would pester me about Rochelle being pregnant. I kept telling them that it wasn't any of their business and that it didn't matter—I would take responsibility for everything, however matters stood.

ROCHELLE

Jack was also very forceful in making a moral case for me to stay. He would say, "If Rochelle is pregnant, that's all the more reason to keep her with us and give her shelter. That's what she needs—shelter and someone to care for her."

That was the nicest thing anyone could have said to me at that time. Of course, I had no idea how to take it, because I could not really believe it. I would think to myself, "There is something wrong with this guy." All I had been hearing for a year or more was "Jewish whore" this and "Jewish slut" that. And now Jack, who as far as I was concerned didn't know me from Adam, was saying he would take care of me.

Jack was an effective leader of that group. He knew how to smooth things out, to keep the morale up. So he would add that—if worse came to worse, and a baby was actually born in the bunker—he knew a Belorussian farmer who would take my baby and raise it.

JACK

This was the same Kurluta family that had helped me in the past. Because of our background together, I knew I could trust this particular family.

I should say that both the farmer and his wife liked me very much—they considered me as the son they had never had. If I had been willing to marry one of their three daughters—all in their late teens to early twenties—they would have been delighted. I had a very nice relationship with their daughters. I would sometimes spend nights in the barn with them.

Courtship in the Woods

ROCHELLE

The family loved Jack. It didn't bother them that he made love to their daughters. They approved completely, and it didn't happen only in the barn. They had a small farmhouse, and all of the family shared a single bedroom—the parents in one bed, the three daughters in another. Jack was sleeping with the daughters right in front of the parents and they didn't care. In part it had to do with the atmosphere of the war—the attitude toward sex changed for a lot of people, because life itself was so uncertain.

At the time, of course, I had no idea that Jack had been having his little affairs. He didn't talk to me about them. If he had, it wouldn't have mattered to me. I didn't care, I wouldn't have felt jealous.

Clearly, the Kurluta family was not particularly jealous either, because one night—we never really left the bunker, except at night—Jack suddenly said to me, "Let's go. I'll introduce you to this family. I've let them know you'll be coming." So I said all right.

I don't know to this day how Jack found his way so well in the dark woods. He moved in and out of the trees and branches like a rabbit, and I followed him as best I could. Somehow, we arrived at the house. It was the middle of the night, but they let him in when they heard his knock.

Well, they had prepared a feast for us. Blinis, fried salt pork with onions, even a little jar of honey to bring back with us to the bunker. And I should mention that Jack introduced me to them that night as his wife!

All I could think to myself was, "I don't know what's going on." I still had no emotions. My body was not responding, my mind was not responding. None of it seemed to be happening to me. None of it made sense. We returned home through the woods in the hour before dawn. I was in a daze.

I remember one thing about the end of that night. There was fresh, shining snow on the ground, and we were carrying that tiny jar of honey that the Kurlutas had given us—a tremendous gift. When we returned to the bunker, we decided to see what it would taste like to drizzle some of the honey on the snow. So Jack went in and fetched a small dish, and then we sat outside together and tried it. Fantastic! The most delicious thing I can remember eating in all of the war years. We sat and ate and we couldn't get enough—I think we ate the whole jar of honey that night with the snow.

Maybe twenty years later, when we were living in America, I remembered that night and how delicious the snow and honey had tasted. It was a snowy winter night and I went outside our house and scooped up some of the newly fallen snow into a bowl and poured some honey on it. It tasted awful! A sticky frozen mess that melted into water. Nothing like the heavenly pleasure I had remembered. But that night we must have been so desperate for something cool and sweet and refreshing. Anything that enhanced the flavor in your mouth . . . sweet or salty . . . was wonderful.

Within our group, I was considered Jack's woman even though nothing romantic was happening between us. All the same, none of the other men in the group would have dared approach me. But I could see how, with the other men and women, relationships would develop as a result of being together, talking about the past, sometimes softly singing Yiddish songs to lift our spirits.

In general, in the partisan groups, the men were always looking for a woman because there were more men and a shortage of women. Affairs would arise now and then—very seldom were serious feelings involved. It was an atmosphere of "Live today, and die tomorrow, so make the best of it while you can."

Jack was very nice to me the first weeks I was in his bunker. He gave me a pair of pants without rips and tears, and a real pair of boots to replace my two left army boots. I remember he also gave me, as my first clean shirt after all my experiences, the top part of his own pajamas, which had been part of the little bundle Jack had carried with him when he escaped from the Mir ghetto. That pajama top was the nicest thing I had to wear during my first days in the bunker. With that top and boots that fit my feet, I was suddenly fancy . . . all ready for the wedding!

Courtship in the Woods

He wasn't physically insistent, but he was definitely in love with me. After a month or so, he did try to be more affectionate, to kiss and hug me. And I thought, "Aha! This is it. All that sweetness and protectiveness toward me was just a prelude for sex! Men just want to use you." But I was wrong.

JACK

The relationships between the men and the women in the bunker had no fixed pattern. There were unattached men and women. And there were married couples—husbands and wives who had gotten married before the war and had escaped to the woods together.

Sex meant something different in the conditions in which we were living. It was a way to feel some kind of pleasure and to forget the misery for a while. But what you would call a romantic atmosphere did not usually exist. When you hear the stories of Jews who lived in partisan groups, you hear of couples forming, but often they were for the sake of survival through the war years only—more convenient than committed.

With Rochelle, I felt differently. Sex was not the issue then. I never pressed her on that—it wasn't what mattered to me. A couple of times I tried very gently to get close, but when I saw the effect it had on her I stopped altogether. But I felt in my heart that she was the woman destined for me. It was that sense of things that guided me in the first weeks we were together.

I wanted to do something special for her—to get her some decent clothes to replace the pajama top, to make her feel that life in the bunker could be bearable.

One of the Jewish guys in our group was named Liss. He had grown up in the region and knew all of the farm families very well. Well, he had told us in the past about a little community called Piesochna in which there were several well-to-do farms, many of which had sons serving in the Polish police. The Polish police were the right-hand agents for the Germans, and so to strike back at their homes was very tempting, given what had happened to our own families. We had already conducted a number of raids in this area, as often as twice a week.

I figured that in one of the rich farms in that community I could find decent clothing for Rochelle and also bring back some good food to celebrate her arrival. So we went, four of us, including Liss. We all carried pistols and rifles, and in addition I had a pair of binoculars I had taken on one of the previous farm raids.

Things went very badly. About a half mile or so before we reached the farm we had in mind, the police opened fire. We were, at that point, in a fairly open area of fields and small stands of trees. The heavy woods in which we lived were roughly a mile off, so we were definitely in a tough position. It couldn't have been that they knew our specific plans for that evening. But, as I said, we had often before been their uninvited guests, and they probably decided that it was worth watching out for us for a number of nights in a row, figuring that we would show up eventually.

When the police opened fire, Liss, who was two feet away from me, was killed right away. So I and the other two guys began to make a retreat. We were running, running, then dropping and shooting back from time to time to make sure they weren't following us too closely. Slowly, slowly we managed to lose them and to make our way back to the woods. Once we got back to the woods we weren't afraid anymore . . . it felt like home. We knew the police wouldn't dare follow us into the woods so long as we were armed. We could have been behind any bush, picking them off.

Still, we all felt very worn out and afraid—our adrenaline was draining away. So we rested for twenty minutes or so and then made the final walk back to our bunker—without Liss, lucky to be alive ourselves.

When we made it back, I sat down in my place in the bunker, not yet ready or able to sleep. I lit a small piece of wood just to have some added light. It was then that I looked at the coat I was wearing—a long sheepskin coat. There were two bullet holes in it! Ankle-height, low holes. If either of those bullets had hit my legs, I would have fallen, been captured, probably tortured, and certainly killed. And then I saw what had happened to the binoculars I had been wearing on a strap over my chest. The metal frame had been split in the middle, between the two glasses. My binoculars had blocked a bullet that otherwise would have killed me.

Somehow none of the three bullets hit me, even though they came as close as they possibly could. Wouldn't that be considered a miracle? In the days that followed, I would think about the dream I'd had about Rochelle's coming, and about the holes made by the bullets that had missed me. It gave me a kind of confidence that someone was watching over me and guiding me in the right direction. Since then, to this day, I have the feeling that someone is watching.

When Rochelle saw the bullet holes, she started telling me that I shouldn't take any more risks like that. She wanted me to be more careful.

ROCHELLE
He was overdoing it. It was almost a game with him.

JACK
It made me happy that Rochelle at least cared enough to worry about the risks I was taking. But other than showing concern, she was still very much keeping her distance during that time. The dream remained for her an unbelievable fantasy, no more.

I thought about what she said about risks, and for a couple of weeks we didn't conduct any major raids.

But then we found out about a very large farm a mile or so outside of Mir—a rich spread, an estate—where the family had three sons and two daughters, and all three of the sons had joined the Polish police force and were actively helping the Germans to identify and kill Jews. To raid an estate like that—with its three collaborating sons in the police—would be a satisfying revenge. We figured that we could make such a large food haul from that one estate that it would reduce the need for making smaller raids so frequently—twice or three times a week, as we usually did. We could lay in a supply that might last a month or more.

We discussed it within our own group. Our advantage was that we were, by this stage, well-supplied with pistols and rifles and hand grenades and even some automatic weapons. But we understood that we needed more men on the raid than our own usual small contingent of five or six. Not far from our bunker were some other small Jewish underground shelters. We talked over our plans for the raid with two other small groups and finally we reached an agreement—each of the three groups would send four men. We would take as much in the way of food, clothing, and supplies as we could carry and split it evenly between the three groups. If we didn't have enough room to store it all, we would give it to certain friendly farmers to store for us. It was late November or early December, and we could feel the brunt of the winter coming on. Extra food and clothing would be especially welcome at that time.

We set out early on a very snowy and stormy evening—we had waited for the worst weather possible to cover our movements as thoroughly as possible. The march took us three hours. When we drew close, we sent three men ahead to scout out the farmhouse. When they came within thirty yards or so, a couple of dogs started to bark. They quieted the dogs with food, as we had planned, and then we all picked up our pace, first surrounding the house and then breaking into it.

There were about seven people at home, the old parents and some of the daughters and maybe some servants as well. Immediately they started crying and begging. We held our rifles on them and told them that we knew about the three sons who had joined the police. We asked them if they knew how many Jews their sons had killed.

Some of the other guys started to search the house and they found some Jewish ritual plates, candlesticks, and Torah ornaments, plated with silver and gold. There was also, I remember, a silver ritual cup designed for the Passover seder [festival meal]. Finding these things made us really mad.

We opened up the trapdoor to the cellar and found down there a number of big barrels full of food—salted pork, ham, sausages, honey, bread, and more. We hauled all of the food out of the cellar, then herded all of the residents of the house back down in there. We told them to sit there quietly or else we would kill them and burn the entire place down. We also pushed their watchdogs in there, to make sure there would be no more barking that night. We then covered up the trapdoor with some very heavy furniture to make sure they would not escape too quickly and call for help.

Meanwhile, three of our men, whose families had been in the meat business, found a small number of calves and sheep. They were experienced enough to quickly herd the livestock and bind their feet to make it easier to take them along.

Then we had to figure out how to carry all of the food away. We solved the problem by finding two hauling sleds alongside their barn. We hitched two horses to each of these, then loaded them up with the livestock and the barrels. We packed in some Christmas baked goods we found—cookies and cakes. We also took lots of warm clothing and some cooking utensils and tools—any useful things we could find. Even with the four horses and the two sleds, that was all we could handle at one time.

Before we left, we debated amongst ourselves as to whether to burn the place down or not. The deciding factor against it was that, if we set fire to the house, the flames and smoke might be seen by the German and Polish police forces in Mir. So we decided not to bother with it. But one of the men found some large canisters filled with kerosene and emptied them all around the house, on the rugs, furniture, and woodwork. He was hoping that the residents might set fire to the house themselves, once they managed to push open the trapdoor and then attempted to light some lamps in the house, which we had left totally dark.

We managed to transport the loaded sleds most of the way back to our bunkers. Obviously, we could not drive up all the way with them, as we would have been leaving tracks that could have been easily followed. So some distance away, we simply let loose the horses, knowing that they would go back to their owners rather than stay in our part of the wilderness. Before we did that, we thought of giving the horses to some of the farmers we knew who had helped us. But then we figured that the danger of the horses being traced—they were branded and clearly belonged to the estate we had raided—was too great. None of our friendly farmers would have wanted to take the risk.

As for the farmers, we couldn't always be sure which of them really were genuinely friendly to us. For example, we left the calves and sheep we had taken with a farmer named Petrovich—the same one who had taken in Tanya. As I told you, the Russian partisans were convinced he was a police spy and later killed him and Tanya and his sons and burned down his house. I cannot say if they were right, but that was a risk you took with any civilian you decided to trust. But Petrovich took care of our livestock and we all benefited from that—we came back later for some meat, and Petrovich himself ate well from that hoard, as we had invited him to do.

A few days later, though, our group heard from some other farmers who had gone into Mir that the Germans were really outraged at what had happened. The thought of Jews carrying on a raid so close to their headquarters really infuriated them. If they had caught me at that point, they would have cut me into little pieces.

There was talk of an all-out intensive search for the Jewish partisans who had pulled it off. So we were afraid, for a while, that there would be a sweep through the woods that might mean the worst for our group and some of the others as well. But at that time we had some luck on our side, for a change. The winter storm continued on through the day after the raid. The wind was blowing like crazy and it must have covered up all of the footsteps and sleigh tracks. Because we were left in peace in the weeks that followed.

I remember that from the raid I brought back for Rochelle a pretty blue blouse and lots of other clothing—anything I could find that I thought would be nice for her. She accepted the clothing. And I think she was relieved that nothing had happened to me on the raid. But still, she was uncomfortable with my feelings for her. They made no sense to her. She was still frozen inside from all that had happened to her—which at the time I could only guess at, since she was absolutely unwilling to talk enough to give me any details.

I knew that things were difficult, and that Rochelle would need time. But what happened next I did not expect.

One day, in December, Rochelle left the bunker for what she said was a walk. But then she didn't come back. It was getting dark, and we thought maybe she had gotten lost. One of us went to check with a nearby group as to whether they had seen her. The news came back to me that Rochelle had decided to leave my bunker and to join that group instead. She figured that I would somehow try to stop her if she told me directly, and so she slipped out casually, taking only the clothes she was wearing.

The other group consisted mainly of a number of young boys in their teens, as well as an older woman in her forties and her son, who was only ten. It was not as well organized a fighting and raiding force as our group. Plus we had both a doctor and a pharmacist with us then. But the next day, when I went over to talk to Rochelle to try to find out why she had left us, she told me that she felt more comfortable in that group. She liked it there and she was going to stay there.

I left Rochelle and returned to my own bunker. I was disappointed, but not only disappointed. I felt disgusted and angry as well. The worst thing, from my point of view, was that Rochelle had left without telling me, without even saying good-bye. The men in my group really let me have it in the days that followed. They would say, "You see what happens? You treated that woman like a queen. And now she craps on you and leaves you!"

During those first days, my attitude was if that was the way Rochelle wanted it, the hell with it! I made up my mind to do nothing more—just to let her go. The others in the group wouldn't leave me alone, though. They made constant jokes, teasing me that Rochelle had left me for a group made up of little boys.

ROCHELLE

I made up my mind to run away because I became convinced that, even though Jack was gentle and respectful toward me, eventually it would come down to having sex with him in order to survive. I didn't want sex on any terms, and the fact that Jack was declaring his love to me didn't make it any sweeter. I wanted no part of love either.

I became aware of another group living not far from us in their own bunker. A bunch of young boys, and then an older woman, Gittel, and her little son. And the fact that the other boys were so young was a positive factor for me. I wasn't afraid of the sexual advances of a bunch of immature twelve- and fourteen-year-olds. I'd just give them one kick in the head and that would be the end of any love affairs they had in mind.

Another positive was the presence of Gittel acting as the "mother" for the group as a whole. It had the atmosphere of a little orphanage in the woods, and it was difficult for Gittel to keep up with all the demands upon her. I had talked with some of the younger boys a few times, and they assured me that I would be very welcome in their group because it was so hard for Gittel to keep up with all the cooking and camp work that she had to do. That set me thinking about how ideal it would be for me to work with Gittel, help her peel potatoes and all the rest, and get away from the love and attention business that Jack had in mind.

So I made arrangements in advance with the boys to come over to their bunker on a set day. They had talked it over with Gittel and she was happy with the idea. So when the day came I left. I didn't say a word to Jack or to anyone in his group. I didn't say thank you or give any reasons why. I picked myself up and walked over to the other bunker.

Gittel was really like a mother to me, very kind. I helped her cook for the boys. One of our common meals was a dish we called *palnitzes,* a kind of flour-and-water cake baked over the fire. I had peace of mind . . . no one was going to make advances on me. I had a job to do, and that was it.

One thing I remember from this time was that on the day I had left Jack's bunker for the new group, I was wearing a blouse and a pair of boots that Jack had gotten for me from the raid on the large estate outside Mir. The blouse and the boots were of high quality. A couple of days after I left—Jack had already paid his visit and gone back—one of the guys from Jack's

group, his name was Maryan, came over to my ne[
and said, "Izik wants his boots and his blouse back."

JACK

That was a lie. I never said that. He probably just wanted them for himself.

ROCHELLE

At the time, however, I believed that Maryan was speaking the truth. It fit my attitude about men to believe it. If you don't sleep with them, they take back the boots, the clothes, and everything else! It made me so angry that my answer to Maryan was, "That's too bad. I'm keeping my stuff!"

Maryan also told me that in the days since I had seen him, Jack had become very sick, with a high fever. He also said that Jack was depressed and wanted to shoot himself.

JACK

Yes, that was true. I was very disappointed. What had come to me in the dream was a vision of helping and loving Rochelle that gave my life in the woods a meaning. When that vision was lost, the purpose of going on seemed lost as well.

ROCHELLE

What made it even worse was the embarrassment he felt at being made fun of and treated like a schlemiel [fool]. He had done everything he could for me. He tried to insist that his group treat me nicely. And I just ran away, leaving him with his hurt feelings and a group that was mocking him constantly.

It got to me when I learned that Jack had actually fallen ill and wanted to end his life. I didn't know how to handle that. But I didn't go to visit him. I tried instead to put it out of my mind. I didn't enjoy the thought of his misery, and I didn't want to see him in the midst of it. But I was not going to go back.

Three weeks or so passed. I became used to the rhythm of things in my new group. We always cooked at night, for the reason that Jack has explained—in the day the smoke would have brought the Germans right to our bunker. The water stank just as it did in Jack's bunker—we were less than a mile away and situated on the same swampland.

JACK

For my part, after a few days, the desire to kill myself started to fade away. Instead, I made up my mind to see to it that Rochelle came back to our group. Again I had a sense that, maybe, just maybe, it still was our destiny to be together. After all, she had found her way to my bunker against all odds. Why couldn't the separation be overcome as well?

I went over to her new bunker to talk to her again. They had a little chimney hole in their cover, just as we did. Somehow I had learned that she would be doing the cooking that night, so I figured out that I could talk to her through that little chimney hole while she worked.

ROCHELLE

Jack was embarrassed to come inside the bunker and talk to me. It wasn't me he feared so much as the other members of my group—the teenage boys—who were sure to make fun of him if they saw him face-to-face. These boys came from lower-class backgrounds, and they knew of the Schleiff family and its wealth before the war. So for them, having Rochelle Schleiff come to stay with them was a catch . . . a trophy. The fact that I had left Izik Sutin, who had a price set on his head by the Germans, just added to their sense of prestige and triumph. The boys were very nice to me, but they would have been perfectly prepared to rub it into Jack's face.

So one night, as I'm sitting and cooking our flour-and-water soup, all of a sudden I hear a soft voice coming through our little chimney hole. At first I was scared to death because I thought the Germans had discovered us. But then I recognized Jack's voice. He started talking to me. His attitude was that he was just checking in to see how I was doing. It was clear, by the fact that he was coming at all, that he liked me and missed me and was no longer angry with me. But he was careful not to put any pressure on the situation.

Courtship in the Woods

JACK

I wanted her to see that I hadn't lost interest. I was afraid that, without those visits, she would assume that I was still upset and depressed and wanted nothing to do with her.

ROCHELLE

He came by a few times like that. I began to enjoy his visits while I sat and peeled potatoes. It was just friendly, casual talk, but it began to connect me to him. Little by little, I saw that Jack was a nice human being. It was more than sex. He really cared.

Our talks became more and more friendly and full of feeling. One time, both groups thought that our locations had been spotted by some unfriendly farmers. So we all abandoned our bunkers and ran away on foot into the woods. Jack came to find me, and we went on a separate walk together. Even while we were hiding for our lives, we kept on talking!

It was the beginning of our real courtship. The visits back and forth by Jack continued for three or so weeks—just talking through the chimney. Once or twice, as things grew closer between us, he even came down into the bunker to sit beside me as I cooked. He wasn't so worried anymore about being teased.

Gittel noticed what was going on, and she liked Jack. She said to me one day, "Listen, don't get me wrong, I'm glad that you're here in our group. You make it easier for me. You're a nice girl, and I hear that you come from a nice family. So I'll tell you something—you must be crazy to leave Izik and come instead to live with me and these boys. Izik is a fine young man. These boys here are *proste* [common] . . . not your caliber of people. Everybody knows that he wanted you and waited for you, and it's obvious he's going to be good to you. If I were you, I would go back to him. You have no future here. At least with Jack you can help each other."

Gittel really worked on me that night. But I was like a scared deer, still on the run. I couldn't respond to her when she spoke these words.

This was how it was as the New Year of 1943 approached.

JACK

By now, I was determined to have Rochelle back. I saw what there could be between us. Even the members of my group, for all that they liked to tease me about it, could see how stupid it was for Rochelle and me to be apart.

So about three days before New Year's Eve, I came up with a plan and instructed my group in how we would carry it out. I demanded their full cooperation—if they refused, I would leave with my father Julius and we would join another group. They recognized that my skill at planning and leading raids was important to their survival, so they went along with me.

My plan was this: We still had lots of food left from our raid on the wealthy Polish estate. So we would invite Rochelle's group to come to our bunker for a little New Year's Eve celebration. Actually, for safety's sake, to avoid being spotted by Polish farmers out late for the occasion, we planned to begin it well after midnight. But the spirit of the thing was the same. We had everything arranged—we planned for exactly where every member of her group would sit. Rochelle, of course, would be sitting next to me, in her old place. And at the end of the night, when it was time for them to leave, we would tell them that Rochelle wasn't coming with them. We weren't going to let her leave.

Well, they all came on schedule—all the boys that is. Gittel didn't come along for some reason. And for a while there we had a real party.

ROCHELLE

Believe it or not, there we were in a hole underground and we celebrated. We were young . . . we sang songs. It sounds so bizarre now that I couldn't imagine it if I hadn't been there myself. We had lived through another year.

JACK

After the main meal was over, I took Rochelle aside and told her in advance of our plans for keeping her with us when the party came to an end. I told her, "You're going to stay here with me." I meant it. But at the same time, I had already sensed, by the way my visits with her had been progressing, that staying with me was what Rochelle wanted as well. If I hadn't believed this, I never would have gone ahead with the plan. If she had said "no" to me that night, I would have let her go.

As it happened, Rochelle didn't say anything directly at first about her own feelings, one way or the other. What she did say was, "Well, my boys won't be too happy about this. They depend on me. I have my chores to do there." My answer was, "We weren't too happy when you left us. So this time let them be unhappy in return."

It was getting late, time for the boys to go back to their bunker. They were saying their good-byes, but then they noticed that Rochelle wasn't moving. We then pushed her into a corner of our bunker and surrounded her. They soon understood what was happening. At that point they became very angry, demanding to take Rochelle back with them. I remember that one of those boys, named Ephraim, reached for his rifle and threatened to use it if we didn't let Rochelle go. But we were prepared for that, and while Ephraim alone was holding his weapon, all of the men in my group had their rifles trained on the boys.

ROCHELLE

I was a prisoner of war!

JACK

I told them that if there was any trouble, we would shoot them all at once. This left Ephraim frozen and the rest of them frightened. Then Rochelle spoke up. She told them she wanted to stay, so they left peacefully for their bunker.

ROCHELLE

What I remember is that the boys asked me, "Are you going?" And that I didn't say anything. I just sat and watched. Not out of indifference, but out of confusion and a kind of frozen panic. Ephraim threatened with his rifle to take me back to their camp where I belonged.

have said something to try to avoid any bloodshed.
thank God nobody did any shooting. And I stayed
h Jack.

⌐⌐⌐ ⌐ .vant to stay? I can say that I did, yes. But it wasn't a
great romantic moment. It was hard for me. When Jack first
told me his plans that night, I thought about what Gittel had
said. Then I figured, "Okay, I'll stay here. Maybe she's right."
It wasn't that I was in love with him. But he really did want to
help and be good to me. That was as much as I could expect.

But in the weeks that followed, things developed gradually.
It wasn't sex right away. We were talking together more and
more, building a trust and a feeling for each other. Maybe the
seeds of that were planted a month earlier, before I had run
away to Gittel's bunker. When Jack had come back from that
raid with the bullet holes in his coat and the split binoculars, I
had a strong sense of how sad I would have been if he had died.
I had found a friend, and I could have lost him that night.

It was during the winter of 1943, after the New Year's Eve
showdown, that I progressed beyond feelings of friendship and
gratitude and moved toward a love for him.

One form that took was to worry constantly that he would
be killed leading one of his raids. Jack could be very reckless.
It was still a kind of game to him. It diminished his anger, his
fear, and his grief. He would make raids even when we still
had an adequate food supply. I began to insist that he make no
raids that were not absolutely necessary. And I tried to keep
him away from farms that were close to the towns—and to the
police. I began holding him back, in short.

Then he saw I really had begun to care about him. And from
there things evolved into a genuine love affair.

JACK

Even before that New Year's Eve, I was constantly thinking . . .
what would happen if Rochelle decided to stay with Gittel's
group? Or what if I had turned stubborn after she first ran
away and had refused to try to get her back? Even now I sometimes wonder . . . what would have become of us?

Of course, our lives would have been completely different.

Courtship in the Woods

Who knows if we would have survived without each other. If we had, we would have married different people and had different children. But I don't think that Rochelle could have survived had she stayed in Gittel's group with the boys.

ROCHELLE

That's so. I would have died somehow.

JACK

They were not a good bet to succeed in the partisan way of life. At the least, Rochelle would have ended up with a man she did not care to be with, just for the sake of survival and protection. And I, on the other hand, would have been very disappointed and depressed. I would have taken even greater risks than I had before, and eventually I would have gotten killed somewhere.

ROCHELLE

A woman couldn't survive alone in the long run during that time. Without Jack, I would have gone back to Stolpce to be killed by the Germans, or I would have wound up with some man . . . probably not even a Jew. There were not many women in the woods, and ultimately you needed protection. Either you let anyone have you, or you had just one who protected you from the others. That was the truth of it. But it did change somewhat as the war went on and two large Jewish partisan *atrads* [fighting groups] formed in our region—those led by Simcha Zorin and by the Bielski brothers. Within those groups there was a community framework in which a woman could survive without a male companion and protector. But early on, when there were only the small groups, a girl was bound to have constant trouble on her own.

As the years in the woods went on, a lot of people used to say to me, "We know you're not going to be together when all this is over. This is just for wartime." That was the case for most of the couples that formed at the time. As soon as the war was over, maybe 80 percent of the couples we knew split up right away. That was true whether or not the boy was Jewish. Survival and convenience did not translate well into peacetime. And the conditions of the war made the normal sorts of commitments impossible.

Pregnancy was the kiss of death. No one wanted you to join their group if you were pregnant, and the chances of you and the baby both surviving delivery were virtually zero. You had to be careful. Pulling out was the main means of protection, along with forms of sex in which there was no penetration at all. Some of the couples had babies during the war, but always it was by accident. One of the girls in a nearby bunker gave birth during that winter. As soon as the baby was born she placed it on a rag outside on the snow so that it would die right away and not suffer. That girl at least had a normal delivery. What if there had been complications? Certain death for both the girl and her baby.

So there was a great deal of cynicism and a great deal of pain. Most couples were only using each other, without feeling.

But Jack and I helped each other as much as we could. It took a while for us to get to know each other—two strangers put together into a hole. But we lived through so many terrible and dangerous moments together. We felt like two soldiers on the front lines. It was a crazy setting for any kind of love. But you grow closer each time you live through moments of hell like those. You have that in common with the other person and with no one else. And you had no idea of what would happen tomorrow.

We didn't expect to survive. But we hoped we would and we thought how nice it would be. Once we started to fall in love, we blended so well, it was as if we were one person. We were very afraid that one of us would die. It would have been terrible, like the death of a spouse, not just someone you slept with through the war. To this day, even though we were not formally married until after the war, we celebrate our wedding anniversaries starting from 31 December 1942.

Lazar Schleiff

Cila Schleiff

The Schleiff sisters and their friends. Rochelle and Sofka are standing in dark dresses in back; Miriam is directly in front of them.

Julius and Sarah Sutin with their son Jack.

Jack as a schoolboy.

*Jack in his partisan uniform—
photo taken just after the liberation in 1944.*

*Photo of Jack taken for identification purposes
by Soviet authorities circa 1944.*

Jack at his desk as administrator of the Nei Freimann displaced persons (DP) camp in Germany.

Rochelle in the kitchen of the Nei Freimann camp house.

Jack and Rochelle together in their Nei Freimann camp house.

Jack and Rochelle with baby Cecilia.

*Crayon drawing by Julius Sutin—this and subsequent drawings
all circa 1947–1949. None of the drawings were titled by the artist.*

Crayon drawing by Julius Sutin.

Crayon drawing by Julius Sutin.

Crayon drawing by Julius Sutin.

Crayon drawing by Julius Sutin.

This photo of the Sutin family appeared in the
St. Paul Dispatch, *22 September 1949.*

The Sutin family circa 1960:
Julius and Jack in front; Larry, Rochelle, and Cecilia in back.

VII

From the Bunker to the Atrad

JACK

It was a joy for me to see, as the weeks went on, that Rochelle began to seem more relaxed and happy. Before, when we had sung songs during the night, she would only sit and listen. But then she herself began to sing Polish songs, Russian songs, and also Yiddish songs like "Oifun Pripichok" and "Papirosun."

She got me to be more careful on the raids. As we fell more and more in love, I thought more and more about living.

ROCHELLE

It was in every sense a real love affair. But then you may wonder how a love affair is conducted when the two of you are living like wild animals in a hole in the ground with ten other people.

A normal mind—a mind that has always lived in a safe and comfortable civilized state—can never understand what it was like. I don't know myself how to explain. It was very cramped and crowded in the bunker. If you moved to the left or to the right, everyone else had to move from the left to the right. There was no privacy, no intimacy ... none. What was happening around us I cannot say. It was pitch dark at night. You could hear people moving. But there was no verbal expression. It was like a silent movie. For us, those conditions meant that in the bunker itself we hugged each other, we petted, we kissed ... and no more. It wasn't like having a normal sexual relationship and making love when you wanted to.

Once, I remember, we paid a return visit to the Kurluta family, to whom Jack had introduced me as his wife some two months before. I had been so shocked by his statement then. But this time, we did behave like newlyweds, and the family fed us and treated us beautifully. And on the way there, in the woods, we had stopped and made love.

But private moments like that were few and far between.

There was an activity, I remember, that took up a lot of our time that winter, in common with the other members of the group. It was removing the parasites from our bodies. On sunny days, we used to take turns slipping out of the bunker hole, taking off our clothes, and squeezing off the lice, which we were all full of. One of those, a breed that dug into our skin and fattened on our blood, we called *mandavoshkes*. They would get into your pubic hair, under your armpits, around your eyes. Only when you sat naked in the outdoor light could you see fully what was happening to your body. One day, I recall, I woke up and sensed that my eyelids were heavy. I put my fingers up to feel and there were little black bumps all along my eyelashes. I went outside, taking with me a straight pin and a tiny mirror that we all shared. I poked these out one by one, but had a hard time holding my hand steady because I was so revulsed by the fact that what I was poking at was my own filthy body. My fingers, my hands . . . everything was itching.

Once I tried hard to get rid of them from my clothing. My basic daily outfit was Jack's pajama top, a pair of men's pants, and some boots. There was no brassiere or underwear. The basic way to rid your clothes of lice was to hold them close to the fire until the little creatures overheated and jumped off. But one time I was determined to go further than that. I took the shirt and the pants and boiled up a pail full of melted snow and threw these clothes in the boiling water. Then I hung the clothes up outside on a nearby tree branch. They were quickly frozen stiff, like icicles. So then I took them back into the bunker, thinking that they would be free of vermin at least for a little while. But when they defrosted near the fire, I could see the trains of tiny white lice still crawling over the fabric! It was impossible, but it was happening before my eyes.

All of us, that winter, took turns killing the lice, the worms, and God knows whatever else we found on ourselves. Those who had somehow paired up would help each other out with backsides and hard-to-reach spots.

I helped not only Jack but Julius as well—I treated him as if he were my own father. I would wash him, scrape the lice from him. Julius was a very calm and patient man. He had the ability to be almost oblivious to the physical conditions in which he was forced to live. That was remarkable enough, given what those conditions were, and especially so for a man who was already in his late fifties. I remember that he often wore a hat with a little visor, and that the lice were parading around on that visor like cars on a highway. Big ones! I would watch him for a while and then ask, "Doesn't it bother you?" He would shrug and say, *"Beist mir nit"* ["They don't bite me"]. That would exasperate me, so I would grab his hat off his head and shake it, to show him how many lice would fly off from even one shake. Finally, seeing this, he would take a piece of wood and scrape the rest of the lice off this hat. That was the way he was. He didn't clean himself—he didn't feel the itching the way the rest of us did. One of the reasons I was willing to clean him was that I figured that, if I didn't, the lice would jump from him onto us after we had already cleaned ourselves.

But not everyone retained a sense of family. Most did, but there were terrible exceptions: Jack and I had personal knowledge of one of those. It involved a mother and a daughter who ran away from the Mir ghetto at the same time that Jack did. What happened to them shows how family bonds could break down terribly under the weight of hardship. The daughter was maybe seventeen, and her mother was somewhere in her forties—an age that seemed very old to the Jewish youth who were hiding out in the forest. Well, the daughter found a young group who was willing to accept her but not her mother. I should mention that this daughter also had a boyfriend who was a son of a bitch, as bad a character as she was. I say she was bad because what she told her mother at that point was that she, the daughter, had a chance to survive and that the mother was only a burden to her. One of the members of her group had a small bottle of poison, and as a solution to the difficult situation the daughter convinced the mother to drink the poison! The mother didn't want to, but her daughter basically forced it upon her as the only way out. It went from worse to worse—the poison didn't take right away, it wasn't strong enough. The mother suffered for a whole day before she went—gasping, suffocating, thrashing. They watched and waited a whole day for her to die.

Any attempt to hold onto traditional family bonds was difficult, given the conditions that were faced by the early small groups. Everyone was desperate, fearful of being found out, trapped, tortured, killed. There were cases we heard of, in a few of the bunkers, where mothers had escaped with young children—toddlers and a bit older—who would make noise or cry too persistently. The others would demand that something drastic be done, and when the mothers refused to suffocate their own offspring, the others would grab and kill the child!

Julius acted as a father both to Jack and to me and took care of us in his own ways. Because of his age, his most frequently assigned job in the partisan groups was to keep the fire fueled and going at night. Sometimes he would take a few raw potatoes from the food supply and stick them under the hot ashes to bake. He wasn't supposed to do that . . . it was like stealing. But he would do it so that he could wake Jack and me—his *kinderlach* [children]—in the middle of night and give us a little extra food. Julius was always very sweet and protective to me because he had seen how unhappy his *zunele* [affectionate term for son] was during the time I ran away.

That was how we lived in the first months together. But Jack and I did not have much time to get used to any sort of rhythm of life in the bunker. Because in March 1943, our location—as well as that of the other two Jewish bunkers in the Miranke region—was discovered by the Germans. Who knows how? Maybe one of the farmers in the vicinity saw the smoke from our cooking fire.

JACK

There had been pressure on the Germans to do something about the Jewish partisan activity. I won't say it was their first priority, but it mattered to them because they wanted to win the trust of the local Polish population and establish confidence in the stability of their rule.

Don't forget, we were basically living off the local Polish farmers. If we didn't raid their houses, we would go into their fields and dig up their beets, potatoes, or whatever else they were planting. Also, many of the farm families—as well as other members of the local Polish population—had husbands or sons who were now serving in the Polish police. None of those families wanted living Jewish witnesses who might someday testify as to how they had cooperated with the Germans. Even though the progress of the war at that time seemed to be favoring the Germans, the Russians might return and rule Poland again someday—as happened, in fact, in 1944. If the Soviet regime was reinstalled, those who had collaborated with the Germans could expect to pay dearly.

So all of those families were on the lookout for Jewish partisans. And even farmers who had no strong feelings about Jews one way or the other were intimidated by the Germans. They were afraid that if they helped us—or even if they seemed merely to be withholding information as to our whereabouts— they would be burned out and killed by the Germans and their Polish henchmen. So we were in danger of being spotted and informed upon from all sides. If we heard the sound of sawing nearby us in the woods, we were terrified, for it meant that a Pole stocking up on firewood might have seen us.

ROCHELLE

One day there was an ambush. We heard shooting all around us. One of the nearby bunkers was completely caught unaware— the Germans dropped a grenade down their entry hole and they were all killed at once. Exactly our own worst nightmare. Thank God we were spared that. But they advanced toward the two remaining bunkers—ours and Gittel's—lobbing hand grenades and firing steadily with their machine guns.

All of us in our bunker ran. There was nothing else we could do, taken by surprise like that. We took nothing with us but our weapons and the clothes on our back. We ran deeper into the wilderness, into the Nalibocka Forest, which despite its name contained large stretches of pure swampland. Into that swampland they did not follow us. We were afraid to go back to our hole or to any other dry portion of the Miranke woods. There might be other German sweeps. So in the swamp we stayed.

It was still winter, but from March through May we slept outside. It was freezing! Our beds—trees and branches to lift us off the snow and the muck—were all we had to keep us off the swampy ground. Food was a terrible problem. When the German and Polish police drove us out of the Miranke woods, they made sure to kill off any animals or livestock—horses, cows, rabbits—in the region that we might be able to steal and live on. A kind of scorched-earth policy. But they didn't reckon with our desperation and our hunger. At night we used to go out and find the dead carcasses in the woods or on the outskirts of the swamp. In most cases they had been lying there for days, maybe even a week or more. And we would cut slabs of rotting flesh off those carcasses and stuff our pockets with them. Then we would go back to our camp in the swamp and chew on this meat, getting ourselves to swallow as much as we could.

And no one got sick from the food—the mushrooms were not poisonous, and the germs and bacteria in the dead carcasses were not strong enough.

JACK
We must have been fated to live.

ROCHELLE
For the first few days of our hiding in the swamp, before we constructed pallets from trees and branches, we were often standing in water. There were leeches that would attach themselves in clusters to our legs, which were already swollen from the water.

During that time I developed a terrible pain in one of my legs . . . from the moisture and the cold. Maybe a nerve became inflamed. To move at all I had to hop on one leg. When, in May, we heard nothing more of German patrols, we left the deeper swamp area and returned to the more solid ground of the woods. But we were still outside, and cold, and miserable. Who would have thought that I would ever have missed the bunker?

What made our situation even more difficult was that we had no way of knowing what was happening with the war in a wider context. We had little idea of what was happening with the German offensive in Russia, for example. Later, when news reached us through some Polish farmers of the defeat of the German army at Stalingrad [in late 1942], we felt a little hope that maybe, maybe. . . .

But during that winter of 1943, as we hid in our swamp, we could only suppose that the Germans were marching in triumph toward Moscow and that the Nazis would be ruling Poland and Russia without any effective opposition. It was difficult to see any long-term possibilities other than death at German hands. Even if we made it back to dry land, how long could we expect to live by stealing food from mainly hostile farms?

On the other hand, there were terrible things that we did not know that would have made us feel even worse. We did not know at the time about the concentration camps. It was a secret that the Germans kept carefully hidden from the Jews, so as to keep as much hope in the minds of the remaining ghetto Jews as they could, and thereby reduce the likelihood of desperate resistance. What we thought at that time was that all the Jews were being killed the way our families had been killed . . . town by town, through shootings at mass graves. We also had no idea how many Jews had survived. For all we knew, the groups in the Nalibocka Forest were the only survivors. Not many parts of Poland had a wilderness equal in size to this—it could have been that we were uniquely fortunate. But we were Jews who were still alive, and that was something. It was enough, at least, to push us from one day to the next.

In May 1943, after a springtime with no major German activity in the area, we decided to risk leaving the swamp for a higher woodland site. At that point we had only nine in our group. We kept far away from our old bunker site. That time, instead of digging underground, we built little huts out of branches that were meant to be very temporary. Our plan was that we would change our location constantly, and in that way reduce the risk of being informed upon and ambushed. This was strictly a warm-weather tactic. For the coming winter, we figured that we would have to construct a new bunker due to the cold. Looking back, I can see that the plan was not a very good one. The part of the Miranke woods that we were in then was a relatively confined one—we could have been easily surrounded. As we were stealing food from the local farmers regularly, the danger of being spotted was especially high. Even if we had built a bunker, I doubt we could have survived the winter.

In our wanderings, we found a few other small Jewish groups, and that was a bit of an encouragement to us. But from those groups we also heard terrible news about the ongoing liquidations of the Polish ghettos.

ROCHELLE

Things didn't always go smoothly for us with the other Jewish groups. People were desperate, and that made some of them behave badly.

For example, Jack had been carrying with him all that time in the woods a small diamond necklace that had belonged to his mother. It had great emotional importance to him. And we also saw it as a means of buying food or ammunition if things reached a point of absolute emergency. During the spring we decided that it was too risky to be constantly carrying the necklace. So we put it in a little box and buried it under a tree, making a little mark on the tree that Jack and Julius and I alone would recognize.

But a Jew from another group, an older man named Moshe, spotted us while we were burying the box. Later he went back and dug the necklace up and kept it for himself. We found out, but when we confronted Moshe, he refused to give it back. He told us that he was an uncle to some young nephews whom he had to help support—and so he needed the necklace more than we did. That was his defense. Moshe hid it in a different place so that we could not grab it from him. Moshe wasn't afraid because he knew what kind of a person Jack was—Jack wouldn't kill him in cold blood for a necklace. So the necklace was gone, and we never got it back.

JACK

As the summer went on, it became obvious that we would have to come up with a better plan for survival through the winter and after. We were small in number, without a safe home base, without options in terms of any kind of military action aside from desperate food raids in the middle of the night.

Our problems were not only with the German troops and the Polish police. The Russian partisans who shared the woodlands with us could not bring themselves to let us alone. In the very large Russian partisan groups, the officers in command did try to maintain the official Soviet policy of non-discrimination toward Jews. But there were always individual Russians who would hate the Jews who had managed to survive in the woods. If our boys from the bunker went out for food at night, and they ran into a small band of Russian partisans, those partisans would take their food and kill them. While that was happening, the Russians would also complain that the Jewish partisans only stole food and never fought with the Germans. We were in tiny groups—and not military groups, but ones that included men and women, older and younger people, even sons and daughters taking care of their parents, as I was taking care of Julius. We were barely surviving, and the Germans, Poles, and Russians alike were our enemies. Where were our allies? Many of my friends were killed not by the Germans or by the Poles but by our supposed allies the Russian partisans. They killed fourteen boys from my hometown of Mir in a single day.

One day, in the woods, we ran into a young Russian Jew who gave us some news. He told us about a large Jewish partisan *atrad* that consisted of roughly 80 percent Jews from Minsk [a large western Russian city not far from the Polish border] and 20 percent Jews who had escaped from various

Polish town ghettos. They were located deep in the Nalibocka Forest. There were no farmers or little towns in that vicinity—no one to observe your movements.

The Nalibocka Forest was a massive exception to the open farmland that was most common in eastern Poland. Its dense wilderness allowed for a more large-scale partisan organization such as the *atrad*. In fact, we learned that there were not only two Jewish *atrads* operating in this wilderness, but also a dozen or so Russian partisan *atrads*. Approximately 15,000 to 20,000 partisans all told. One of the Jewish *atrads* was led by the Bielski brothers—Jewish brothers from eastern Poland. But the *atrad* we were told about by the young Russian Jew was led by Simcha Zorin, a robust middle-aged man with a large reddish mustache. There were some 300 Jews in that *atrad*—a distinct and real Jewish fighting force. That was exciting news, both for what it meant in terms of our own possible survival, and for what it meant about the survival of at least a small remnant of the Jews in the region.

Zorin had been a Jewish officer in the Soviet army, and so he had actually received formal military training in organization and tactics. He had organized the decision making of the *atrad* to include a chief of staff and other military-type leaders. Those persons had considerable power. When they told you to go out on a food raid, you went, no matter how you felt about it. It was a very regimented form of life as compared to the small group structures we were used to. But on the other hand, there would be a chance to go on missions that could have a real impact—missions that would involve enough men so that you would have a real chance in battle if you ran into a force of Germans or Poles. A larger group would also mean that we could reduce the risk of being killed one by one by the Russians.

The young man we met was a member of Zorin's *atrad*. He invited eight or so of us to come along with him and see what it was like. If we wanted to join, we could. If not, we could remain on our own. We walked for miles and miles into the most dense part of the Nalibocka Forest until we reached the camp of Zorin's *atrad*. It took us two full days. It seemed to us that the Germans and Poles would never venture that far. They could be trapped and ambushed too easily.

Of course, if we were to live so far from the farms in our own little group, the logistics of carrying out food raids would have become impossible. But, as the young man who guided us there explained, with a large-scale *atrad,* you could carry out a variety of raids in larger numbers. Different men could take turns, rather than the same ones risking their lives every night—and you could still maintain a safe and stable camp. There was another difference that the young man explained to us. In the winter, the *atrad* members did not have to live completely underground. They built shelters that were dug halfway into the earth, and then were completed with branches and even boards. Each of these shelters housed twenty-five to thirty people.

ROCHELLE
It was a major change—you lived less like an animal and more like a human.

JACK
We decided to join. It helped that there were some six or seven survivors from the Stolpce ghetto living in that *atrad*—some people we knew from before the war. And it felt safer to be with a large group. Personally, I felt relieved not to be so much in charge as I had been in the smaller groups. Now that Rochelle and I were together, I had something to live for. We were never optimistic, but we couldn't help but begin to hope that we could have a life together after the war. The *atrad* made that hope seem more real.

The population of the *atrad* was very mixed—young and old people, even some children. It was like a big family. And with 300 some people, you had a range of skills that was incredible, considering that we were living in the midst of the wilderness. There was a woman doctor from Russia. Though she rarely had the medical supplies she needed, her being there to give diagnoses and suggestions felt reassuring. There were tailors who could mend clothing, shoemakers who could keep boots intact. If a cow was brought in from a food raid, there were butchers who could make sausages from it. There was a big camp kitchen area in which someone was always in charge, overseeing a group that had to cook for 300 every day. My father Julius worked here. The younger men were the fighters and the raiders for the *atrad,* but men and women and children of all ages had chores and responsibilities. Everyone took a hand in the survival of the group as a whole.

There was a strict day-and-night security routine. We kept constant guard by way of six outposts located in different directions within a mile or two from the camp. We had passwords that everyone coming and going had to know. The guards at the outposts would shout, "Halt!" and would shoot if the password wasn't given. It was essential to keep out police spies. I and the other men were assigned guard duty every two days or so—in four-to-six hour shifts, sometimes in the morning, sometimes afternoon, sometimes at night. When we relieved one another, we had to say the password.

ROCHELLE

In the woods, I don't know of any cases in which Jews betrayed each other. No Jew would walk back alone into a German-held town and inform on partisan locations. Not after all the butchering. There were no illusions left about making deals with the Germans. When Jack and Julius and I first arrived at the *atrad,* the introduction from our guide was enough to establish that we were Jews and could be trusted. The problems with spies came in the mixed-population partisan groups— with Poles and Russians and Jews together. In those cases, again, it was not a Jew doing the informing. But the rumors constantly circulated that the Germans had sent Jews into the woods to join up with Russian partisan groups and then inform on their location or even poison their food. There was also the rumor—one that Tanya and I had lived with during our time with the Russian partisans—that Jewish girls with venereal disease had been sent by the Germans to sleep with the Russians. That was the poison that spread amongst the Russian partisans, even when their leaders were trying to keep to a less anti-Semitic policy.

From the Bunker to the Atrad

JACK

Another difference with the small groups—in them we fought and raided simply to survive. In the *atrad*, we not only went on missions for food, but we also, for example, placed mines under railroad lines that the Germans were using to transport their supplies to the Russian front. But the discipline of Zorin and his lower "officers"—for that is what they were, even if they did not all have formal commissions as did Zorin—was severe. They killed their own people who refused to obey. In exchange for greater security, we had placed our lives in the hands of Zorin and his officers.

ROCHELLE

Zorin was himself a loyal Communist, yet he managed to maintain the independence of that Jewish *atrad*, even though the Russian partisan groups would have preferred that Zorin be directly under their command. That was the official Soviet policy as issued by Comrade Stalin himself. Special officers were sent by the Soviets to join up with the Russian partisan groups in the Nalibocka Forest and to impose a disciplined unity on *all* partisan efforts. And there was Zorin with a group that was not at all organized on strict military lines. None of the Russian partisan groups allowed old people and children. Few of them allowed wives. A minority percentage of Zorin's *atrad* consisted of precisely these people. But Zorin was dedicated to saving lives. Because he was a charismatic man and a sincere Communist, he kept the Russians from controlling him. He deployed the fighting forces of the *atrad* in numerous joint missions with the Russians. But at the same time, he prevented the *atrad* from falling directly under Russian command—which would have meant constant and severe losses, as the Russians would have preferred to risk Jewish lives rather than their own. The *atrad* would have been decimated. So Zorin was no mean politician.

Zorin himself plainly enjoyed the power and privileges of being commander in chief of the *atrad*. He rode a beautiful palomino horse that had been taken during one of the raids. And, of course, though Zorin was in his late forties, he had taken a young girl as his "wife." She was from Minsk, maybe twenty years old at most.

You would be amazed how, even in that group of ragged Jews living in hiding, social classes and distinctions took on such life and power. There were the commanders, the fighters, the craftspeople, the washers, and the cleaners. But Zorin's woman was the queen. If fine clothes were brought back from a raid, they went to her. So even within our camp she was dressed in the height of fashion. She had her own horse that she rode alongside of Zorin and his palomino. They were the royal couple. They would ride by and we would wave and smile. We knew that our lives depended upon them. Zorin was a good commander and he took care to save the lives of as many Jews as he could. But *his* way was the way things went, and his woman had great power as well. If they wanted to get rid of you, they could send you on missions from which you would never come back.

The top echelon of officers in the camp was comprised exclusively of Zorin's fellow Russian Jews. His chief of staff was named Pressman. This Pressman had also taken a "wife" and he had a secure position of power because Zorin liked him. But Pressman wasn't too smart and he really didn't have the experience to make the decisions he was called upon to handle.

That was the reason Pressman came to rely heavily on the judgment of one of his assistants, a Jew from western Poland named Wertheim. Wertheim was in his midthirties. He and some of his family had escaped to Stolpce when the Germans first invaded in 1939. During the two years of Russian rule, his brother Manik had been dating a girlfriend of mine. Because of that, I was already very friendly with him. Wertheim took to Jack as well once he met him in the *atrad*.

I would say that Jack is alive today because of Wertheim. There were times when I would learn that the top officers were planning to send Jack out on a highly dangerous mission. I would go to Wertheim and beg him . . . tell him that Jack was sick. Some of the times he *was* sick, and sometimes he wasn't. Wertheim knew that I was often faking. But he would agree to keep Jack back in camp.

JACK

All this is true. But it is also true that I did go out on a number of armed missions and food raids. Rochelle could not keep me out of everything, and I would not have let her try. I wanted to live and be with her. But I also wanted to serve the *atrad* and to fight.

The main military focus was on selecting areas where we could get the food and clothing that would allow the *atrad* to survive. Sometimes we would plan raids specially to obtain medical supplies. The usual raiding group numbered twenty to twenty-five people. The groups had been smaller—four or five people—early on. But there was a terrible incident in which one of the groups had been murdered on the way back from a raid by Russian partisans, who then stole the sleighs filled with supplies. They let the Jewish boys do the work and then took their lives.

By the time I arrived, procedures had been worked out for encounters with Russian partisans. On first sighting them, we would immediately fan out into smaller groups, protecting whatever food or supplies we had taken, and we would show, by readying our weapons, that we were ready to fight back. That ended the problems. It wasn't worth it to the Russians to get into a fight with us on that scale.

ROCHELLE

There was another factor at work as well. Don't forget that we are talking about the summer of 1943. The Germans weren't doing so well on any of their fronts. We had at last a flicker of hope that they might be defeated and that the Russians might be coming back. For the Russian soldiers in partisan groups, it meant that they had to start thinking about what might happen to them if the returning Russian authorities learned that they had been killing off Jewish partisan fighters. As soldiers of the Soviet Union, they would have been subject to severe punishment. They knew that, and so they disciplined themselves and behaved better—more like military comrades and less like Jew-haters.

JACK

And they had good reason to behave like military comrades, because we were making a contribution by repeatedly blowing up the rail lines and the main highways with our mines and dynamite. That was weakening the German advance into the home country of the Russian partisans. The mines were not only blowing up trains and trucks with supplies—they also cost the Germans hundreds of casualties when their troop carriers were the target. Our good friend Simon Kagan, who had escaped from the Mir ghetto at the same time I did, had joined up with a Russian partisan unit. Simon was especially good at planting dynamite in the track beds and detonating—from his hiding place a short distance away—at just the right moment. He demolished plenty of trains. It took great skill and nerve.

Zorin and his commanders realized, just as the Russian partisans did, that the war was showing signs of turning against the Nazis at that point. They wanted it clearly understood that they had been helping the Russian effort against the Germans. It would not have been enough for them to say only that they had been saving Jewish lives.

ROCHELLE

During that first summer in the *atrad*, Jack developed a terrible infection that covered nearly his entire body. As best we could tell, it was partly due to the filth in which we all lived, and partly from malnutrition—nearly two consecutive years of eating very badly by that point.

There were boils from his feet to his neck and face, and especially on his legs and in his pubic area. They looked like big bumps, red and raw, and if you so much as touched them, yellow pus as thick as honey would run out of them. His body was a bundle of bones and pus.

JACK

I checked with our doctor in the *atrad* but she told me there was nothing she could do. She had no medications for a case like that. She thought it might disappear on its own. But I didn't see how it could disappear—it was all over me! The doctor also happened to mention that, if the infection should spread to my bloodstream, that would be the end of me.

Things were so bad that Jack could no longer physically bear to wear shoes. Instead he wrapped his feet in rags. The rags stuck to his boils, and so when he would take them off, the scabs would tear off and the pain and infection would become even worse. It was terrible with those rags, but the problem existed with any clothes Jack would try to wear. They stuck to him like glue. I thought that maybe exposing his body to the air might help to dry up the boils. But when we tried keeping him naked, all kinds of worms and bugs would start to feed on him.

It went on for three months and more. Jack was so sick— and so depressed. He was sick of himself! He told me at one point to go away, to stop bothering with him and trying to heal him. He said that he knew he was just making my life miserable, making the lives of others in the *atrad* miserable. He felt he couldn't take it anymore . . . he wanted to kill himself. So I took on the task of watching over him and not only trying to reduce the infection but also making sure that he did not end his own life.

There were others in the camp who were sick during that time, but none that were in such prolonged bad shape as Jack. I went to the chief of staff—not Wertheim but Pressman himself—and asked if Jack could be given better food. By that time Jack couldn't even walk. I kept him in the underground portion of one of the shelters, covered only with a thin blanket to reduce the sticking. I would give him part of my own meat and vegetable portions to try to build up his strength. But his depression grew worse and worse. I think that was the lowest Jack ever felt.

Nearly everyone felt sorry for him. But then there were others who were mean and vicious—including even so-called friends of Jack's. They would say to me, "Why are you futzing around with this guy? You're not married. He's not your responsibility. Why not just leave him?"

What a question. Not that it would have been difficult to ac-complish. All I would have had to do was to take my one extra pair of pants and move two bodies further away in the shelter.

But I would *never* have left him. By that time I loved him so deeply. I was just praying every night that he would survive!

JACK

I was thinking about suicide a lot of the time. My preference was to go out on a dangerous mission and get killed in action while killing some Germans in the process. But I couldn't even move around the camp very well, so a long march was out of the question. I would have to do it myself. There were two or three occasions when I felt 99 percent ready.

What stopped me from killing myself wasn't Rochelle—I thought she would have been better off without me. But I was worried about my father Julius—I couldn't expect Rochelle to stick with him after I was gone, and he might have suffered terribly without her to care for him. Even so, the thought of suicide did not leave my mind.

As for Rochelle, she was such a good and kind soul! She not only cared for me during that time, but another man in the *atrad* as well. He and his wife—their last name was Farfel, I remember. Well, he had a bad case of boils himself. Not as bad as mine, but terrible enough. And the boils needed to be squeezed out—they had black things in their centers—and cleaned. There was no fancy way to do this—no gloves, no anti-septic equipment. Someone had to do it by hand, with rags. That was how Rochelle worked with me as well.

ROCHELLE

Farfel's wife—she was a common-law wife, you would say, like I was to Jack—she couldn't bring herself to clean him. He was in great pain, so I went to him and helped him. I remember he was lying on his stomach . . . kind of an ugly guy. And I was squeezing, so that he could begin to heal. The man's father was alive and a member of the *atrad* as well. He worked in the kitchen like Julius did. He would watch what I was doing. Once he said to me, "Why couldn't my son have a wife like this?"

I thanked him for saying this. But I was not trying to make the other woman look bad. It was easier for me to help him than to watch him lie there in pain.

JACK

At last, we discovered the method to cure me. It was a case of trial and error. We tried every substance available to us in the woods. Finally, it proved to be very simple. Tar.

ROCHELLE

We would peel the bark from birch trees and then char it and cook it. That produced a thick black sap that we could apply to the open boils. I can't explain why, but the sap seemed to kill off the infection.

JACK

The birch tar was so thick that, after the infections started to clear up, it was a real problem to wash the tar off. And even after the tar came off, I had red circular spots on my legs for years. I still have some on my left leg . . . like old war wounds that have never really healed.

Looking back, I can see that this awful experience was, at the same time, a good test of our relationship. Another girl in Rochelle's place would have gone away. But she stuck with me and that proved that our love was very strong. I vowed to myself that if we survived I would protect and take care of her for all of our lives.

VIII

Nazi Assault on the Nalibocka Forest

ROCHELLE

In August 1943 there was an enormous invasion of the
Nalibocka Forest. It was a major operation ... tanks ... air-
planes ... soldiers and shooting all over. The entire *atrad* was
on the run. But we had no idea where to go.

We learned later that two German army divisions had been
involved, meaning close to 20,000 German troops. There was
also support from the Polish police. The entire Nalibocka Forest
was surrounded.

The Germans had made up their minds that the partisan
activity had to come to an end. It hurt them to have their
trains and trucks blown up. And it hurt them politically as
well, because the local Poles—whose farms were raided so
often—knew very well that the Nalibocka Forest wasn't under
German control. This made those Poles wonder how long the
Germans would hold on to the rest of Poland.

The goal in the big August attack was to encircle all of the
partisan groups in the forest and to kill them off once and for
all. The Germans had finally figured out, from all the spying
on our movements over time by the Polish farmers, where the
major *atrad* groups were encamped.

JACK

It was difficult for an *atrad* with a population like ours—so
many old people, so many women with children—to move
quickly and in a unified manner.

One thing worked in our favor—and in favor of all the other
atrads as well. When the Germans invaded the Nalibocka
Forest, they must have been very afraid of being ambushed

by one or more of the partisan units. And they should have been afraid—because that happened to them early on in their push. For that reason, the Germans didn't spread out as they invaded the forest. They kept to narrow column lines. That meant that we could see them—and hear them—coming from a distance and, if nothing else, know in which direction to run away.

As the Germans gained momentum, all of the commanders of the various *atrads* realized that retreat was their only real option—retreat to the centermost swamps of the Nalibocka wilderness. There was no way that a pitched battle could work in the partisans' favor—not against trained German divisions. And there was no possibility of unified resistance by all the *atrads*—the organization between the various camps wasn't that good.

So we ran. We left behind everything we had in the camps except for our weapons and some handfuls of food that we stuffed in our pockets.

ROCHELLE

We began by running away in the same direction. But in the swamplands there was very tall, coarse grass. And when we passed over it, there was an obvious beaten-down path that could not have been missed by the Germans.

I remember that, as the line of retreat spread out, there were five of us in a group—me, Jack, Julius, and another couple. And it hit me! All of a sudden I turned to the rest of them and—as if someone was instructing me in what to say—I told them, "This is no good! The Germans will track us down just by following this beaten path of grass. They are sure to go after the largest number of people that they can catch. They're not going to break off their advance to go after small handfuls of Jews. So let's leave this path and head off on our own."

They all agreed with me. So we went off to the right, straight into a thick and heavy part of the swamp. Very quickly the water came up to our chins. We stood in it and remained as still as we could. We had to hold onto each other, in a kind of human chain, to keep ourselves from slipping or sinking.

Soon we could hear machine guns, then loud voices shouting out in German. We were no more than two hundred feet away from their main line of advance. We couldn't make a noise or a movement . . . we couldn't allow the weeds to move. For a day and a night we were standing like that, because we could hear the noises and the shooting. We could see on one another's faces the leeches that were sucking on our chins. Below the waterline, they were sucking on our hands, legs, and feet as well. During the night we took turns waking one another up so that we wouldn't fall asleep and drown.

By the next morning, there was no more noise. We figured that the Germans had pushed far enough ahead for us to come out from the swamp water and stand on drier land. Our feet looked like elephant feet. Our clothing stank from mud and rot. We couldn't stand ourselves.

We took our clothing off to air it out and let it dry. We were naked and had nothing left to eat and only the swamp water to drink. For days we went on like that. Our big source of food was a dead horse that we scavenged—eating raw slices after scraping off the maggots. I remember watching Julius take one of these rotten raw slices and put it in his pocket to save for later.

Eventually we reached some higher ground that seemed quiet. There we managed to find cleaner water and also scavenged for blueberries and wild mushrooms. I remember we built a fire and I made a thin soup from water and the wild mushrooms. I remember that I used a fallen German helmet as a cooking pot. It was the first hot food we had eaten in a week or more. We had no idea if the mushrooms were poisonous or not. We thought we'd die of hunger if we didn't eat them, so we took the chance. No one died.

Our best meal of that time came when we spotted some rabbits and took the further chance of making noise by shooting them. We cooked up those rabbits immediately—a feast. We also found a dead chicken. It was the standard German strategy in hunting down partisan groups to kill off all livestock in the region. They burned some of the farms and even the villages down to the ground. That chicken was one of the victims, but it looked good to us. I cooked it up into a chicken soup. To the soup we added some beets and potatoes that we managed to find in a farmer's field on the edge of the forest. So that soup was thicker than the mushroom soup. But we had no salt, and the taste reminded me of castor oil . . . but it was delicious!

In that way we survived. And in that way most of the other partisans in the Nalibocka Forest survived as well. Ultimately, it was not a successful action for the Germans. They had the superior force, but we had a large wilderness with which we were familiar and in which there were many places to conceal ourselves. Terrible swampy places, yes, but they served their purpose. In a sense, the entire action was like one huge game of hide-and-seek. We would hear them go one way and then we would go the other.

That is not to say that many partisans, Jewish and Russian alike, did not lose their lives. But the vast majority survived. Even in our *atrad,* with women and children and the elderly, the majority survived in the end. The German losses outnumbered those of the partisan groups by maybe twenty to one.

JACK

The main brunt of the attack lasted for roughly two weeks. When everything was finally over, there were people scattered throughout the wilderness. Then everyone headed back to their own camps to regroup. During that time, we ran into partisans from lots of other groups. From them we found out that the overall attack had gone badly for the Germans.

There were even three or four German planes shot down. They were single pilot reconnaissance planes that flew low. Even with a regular rifle, if you shot in the right place, you could hit the pilot and bring the plane down.

We also heard stories of how some of the partisan groups had captured small numbers of German soldiers. They were hanging the soldiers by their feet.

What was most surprising to us was that, when we finally made it back to Zorin's camp, we found it intact. Nothing had been touched. Now if the Germans had found it, there is no question that they would have burned and demolished everything. So we were thinking to ourselves that if we had just stayed put, we would have avoided the Germans altogether. But who knew?

Zorin and his leadership group returned and organized the *atrad* for the coming of winter. We figured that the Germans would not be likely to launch such a large-scale attack again. It was now late 1943, and they were having major problems on their Russian front.

ROCHELLE

Now here is a story I have never before told *anyone* except for Jack.

The spring of 1944 was approaching. Liberation was close at hand—we knew that. Then there came what seemed to be very good news. A few of the partisans in Zorin's *atrad* had grown up in Stolpce and knew my family. They told me that they had run into my uncle Oscar. He was living on a Polish farm, passing as a Pole. He had taken up with a Polish woman, and living there with them was the woman's sister—she was what you call an old maid—and her brother and her brother's wife.

I knew that Oscar had escaped from the Stoplce ghetto before the final liquidations. Remember, he had been my father's partner in the family business, which was refined lumber products. Oscar had been the one to go out in the woods and do business with the Polish peasants and farmers. So he knew the woods and the people who lived in the region very well. In fact, he had been kind of a playboy, having affairs with a number of the farmers' daughters. When the Germans arrived, he would have known where to hide. But whatever kind of plans he made, he hadn't let the family in on them—he saved himself with not a word to the rest of us.

Still, it was very exciting to hear that a member of my family was still alive! The farm on which he was now living was several miles away from Zorin's camp—a long day's walk. But I made up my mind to pay Uncle Oscar a visit.

It was a dangerous trip. The Germans were on the run from the Russian front, but they still controlled the area and they still shot Jews on sight. I did not want Jack to come with me. He was definitely getting stronger, but the lingering effect of his boils was such that he would have made the trip more slow and more difficult than if I went on my own. Jack was not keen on my going, but he understood what it would mean to me to see someone from my family again.

I kept away from the roads, walking through the thickest woods as much as I could. It was a difficult walk, and I became very tired. But I kept thinking, "My uncle is alive! Maybe he'll be killed or I'll be killed before the Russian troops arrive. I must see him now, right away, before it is too late!"

Finally I arrived at his farm. Uncle Oscar was so glad to see me! He was in his late forties by now, but he still looked healthy and full of life. He had survived well on the farm through all of the misery, and I was happy about that.

He introduced me to the woman he was living with . . . her name was Antonina. She and her family had saved Oscar's life by hiding him. They welcomed me and offered me something to eat and drink. Then they left us alone so that my uncle and I could talk.

We decided to go out for a walk together. We were both pent-up with excitement at meeting again. Oscar was full of questions. He had escaped from the ghetto relatively early on and so he had never learned the details of what had happened to the rest of the family. I was his first source of information on those terrible matters.

We were walking around in the woods on the edge of the farm. It was very emotional and very nice to be with family again. He was crying and hugging me, calling me his *kind*— his child. It felt natural. After all, before the war, when we had last spent real time together, I had been only a little girl.

Then came the big surprise. We had gotten some distance from the house—and he started making sexual advances toward me! I don't mean fatherly love. He started kissing and hugging me. At first, I thought this was just more of his happiness in seeing me. But then I saw that he meant to go further.

I said to him, "What's the matter with you? Are you crazy?"

His reaction was to be angry at my lack of interest. I had already told him about Jack. So now he said to me, "What's the matter? You can sleep with that young man of yours. Am I worse than he is?" In other words, give *Oscar* a chance. Maybe he's even better. Can you believe that?

This was my uncle. And after all my emotional outpouring to him, after telling him all that I had gone through, he dried his eyes and wanted to have sex with me!

I had a hard time keeping him off me. He wasn't a Russian partisan—he wasn't going to beat me or rape me. But he kept pushing himself on me. I became very angry. I told him to get away from me and I made it clear that I would stand none of it.

It was a very awkward situation because it was already evening and I couldn't make it back to our camp. I had to spend the night in that farmhouse with Oscar and his Polish family. All through his advances in the woods, we both kept our voices down because neither one of us wanted to go through the embarrassment of being heard or spotted by them. And now, having fended him off, I had to walk back into the house with my uncle and act as if nothing had happened.

Somehow we pulled it off. My uncle was smooth as could be. He went to sleep with his Antonina and I shared a bed with her sister. At the crack of dawn I was up and saying good-bye. I was desperate to be on my way. Uncle Oscar kept insisting that I take along this or that, but I refused everything. I had lost all respect for him. It was a nightmare.

When I came back, I had to tell Jack what had happened. I thought about keeping it a secret, so as not to upset him. But when I came back, I must have looked shaken. Jack saw that something was wrong and I had to explain.

JACK

I brooded about that for a couple of weeks. Then I told Rochelle that I wanted to pay a visit to her uncle. I made most of the trip with a couple of other guys from the *atrad* who were off on another mission in the same vicinity. They would go off and complete that mission and then meet me back at that farm—so that we could all return together, for greater safety.

On the way I was thinking to myself that I would kill him. Could I have done that? I can no longer say at this point.

Maybe. I was so angry about what he had put her through. I was angry enough to think about murder, that much I can say.

I did not tell the other two men specifically about the plan, but I asked them to back me up if, when they returned to get me, there was any kind of trouble. I had no idea how Uncle Oscar would receive me. Maybe he would turn violent. Angry as I was, I was also, I must say, very curious as to what kind of a character he would turn out to be.

I had not given Oscar any notice that I was coming. But when I arrived, he was immediately very outgoing and friendly toward me. He acted as though nothing had happened. He showed no shame, no consciousness about it at all. He must have been faking—or maybe he just didn't care. But it was difficult for me to confront and kill a man who behaved in that way. I can't say for sure, but I don't believe he thought that I knew what he had done to Rochelle. He probably figured that Rochelle would have been ashamed to tell me. We talked about Rochelle and the rest of her family—how they had died.

The two men from the *atrad* came back for me, and I left with them. I never confronted Oscar. I decided to leave things as they were. On the way back to camp, I was very frustrated—my anger was still pent-up. But I said to myself that it wouldn't have helped Rochelle for me to murder the last of her family in all of Europe. There had been enough death, enough killing.

Meanwhile, even with continued good news from the Russian front, the war was not yet over for us. We still kept up our food raids and our demolitions of German supply lines. I was still going out regularly on guard-duty shifts on the perimeters of the *atrad.* If we had seen German troops during my shifts, our orders were to shoot at them, kill as many as we could. They were on the defensive, and we were to disrupt their retreat any way that we could.

But for the first time since the Germans had arrived in eastern Poland, we started to feel a real hope that they might be driven out and that we would be alive to see it happen.

Nazi Assault on the Nalibocka Forest

I followed all of the stories and rumors with incredible interest. We got our news mainly from other partisan groups. And our *atrad* had a radio that I had a chance to listen to occasionally. Some of the local farmers would tell any news they had heard to our food bands.

I knew that the Russian front was coming closer and closer to Poland. Our own partisan bands were skirmishing regularly with retreating German troops who were crossing through our region in disorder. Zorin sent out regular teams of men to watch the highways and crossroads and to ambush and kill as many of the German soldiers on the run as we could. That was good news in terms of the overall direction of the war, but at the same time it made our activities in the region all the more dangerous.

Jack and I had been through so much. And he was just starting to heal from those terrible skin boils that had covered him for months. So I thought to myself, "I've finally fixed him up and now he's going to go out and get killed in a raid!" Just when we could finally see the end in sight. Not that the Russians taking over again would be paradise, but it would be much better than the Germans. We would at least have a chance to lead a normal life together and not be shot on sight.

So I made up my mind that I would do everything I could to keep Jack alive. I told Jack that, even though he was getting better, he should pretend that he was still sick from the boils. He still looked terrible, with red marks and bumps and black tar all over him.

For my part, I would go to our friend Wertheim, who continued to have great influence in Zorin's leadership circle. I would beg him to realize that Jack was still sick, that they shouldn't push him into dangerous raids in which he couldn't keep up and would have no chance to survive. Once Jack was definitely on the list for a raid. I pleaded with Wertheim until he promised me that he would keep Jack back, which he did.

Once I even went to Zorin himself and started to cry. My

tears were sincere. I was afraid that Jack would be killed. And I wanted so much for him to live.

JACK

Again, the truth is that there were times when Rochelle kept me back from some raid or other action. But most of the time, once my boils had healed up, I was out there risking my life with the rest of the *atrad* fighters. That was the way I wanted it. I don't say that I was not sometimes conflicted—of course I wanted to live! But I still had the hunger to fight. It was not pleasant to watch my fellow fighters go off without me.

Then it was March 1944. One day we heard on our camp radio that the advancing front of the Red Army was only sixty miles away. A few days later there was even more exciting news—the Red Army had liberated our hometowns of Mir and Stolpce, as well as nearby Nieswierz. The Russian front was only thirty miles away.

It is impossible to imagine the happiness we experienced on hearing that, after nearly three years in the woods.

That evening, Rochelle and Julius and I sat around a campfire with some of our friends. We were still happy with the news, but the euphoria had worn away and we all somehow needed to take stock. We shared memories of our friends in the partisan groups who had been killed during shoot-outs with the enemy, who had risked and sometimes lost their lives during dynamiting raids to blow up the main German roads and rail lines. And we talked about the families we had lost.

For the older men and women in the camp, as well as some of the young children without parents, the news of our possible liberation was a tremendous joy—on first hearing. There were smiles on all their faces and they were embracing one another, shouting about going home at last. But by the next day, when I walked past their shelters and spoke with some of them, I could see that they had been doing some thinking. They had realized that they had no families to whom to return, that their homes would not be waiting for them, that their Polish neighbors would not be delighted to see them. They were remembering the dead, the parents and children they had loved.

Where were they to go? What were they to do?

A few days after the news of the liberation of Mir and Stolpce, we could hear the echoes of intensive shooting that was coming closer and closer. Our leader Zorin called a meeting of all the fighting partisans in the camp and said: "The German army is in retreat. Large numbers of German troops are trying to avoid the main roads, where they are being mowed down by strafing and bombing by the Soviet air force. So there will be many German soldiers coming our way through the woods."

Zorin laid out a plan for us whereby we would set up a series of ambushes on all sides of the retreating Germans, while still maintaining protection for our camp. We created six groups of fighters who took up various positions within a mile of the main campsite. By this point, we were well armed, with machine guns, automatic rifles, hand grenades.

Within a few hours, we could see several small groups of German soldiers walking slowly in our direction. They knew that there were partisans in the Nalibocka Forest, but they didn't know our locations.

When they came close, Zorin gave the order to open fire from all of our directions at once. Many German soldiers fell. Others managed to run away. We determined that there were twenty-one German casualties. Amongst those were several SS officers. We gathered up the fallen German arms and ammunition, regrouped and changed our locations. Then we waited.

It did not take long. The Germans opened fire in our direction. They had regrouped as well. What alternative did they have? They had to continue in our direction—the Red Army was on their rears.

Zorin ordered us not to return their gunfire. In that way he hoped to make them think that we had retreated. It also kept our positions secret until the last possible moment. After ten minutes or so, we saw that the Germans were slowly moving closer. There were more of them than before—more of their retreating comrades had joined them.

Finally we opened fire. It was a pitched fight. Several of our men were wounded, and Pressman, Zorin's second-in-command, lost his life. The casualties made us fight all the harder. A few of our fighters—very brave men—crawled forward with hand grenades and managed to eliminate some German machine gun nests that were causing us great problems. That enabled us to keep shifting our positions, to make the Germans think that we were greater in number.

At last, when the tide was clearly in our favor, Zorin called out to the German troops—it was in broken German, but he made himself understood—urging them to surrender. He told them that this time they were not dealing with defenseless Jews, but with armed Jewish partisans. Apparently that provoked the Germans to fight harder—because that was what they did. They must have understood that they could expect no mercy from Jewish partisans.

So the Germans kept up steady and intense firing. They had enough ammunition to continue for a while. We suffered more casualties. Zorin himself was badly wounded in the leg, but he continued on at his post, issuing orders.

Finally, about a dozen of our fighters managed to sneak up on the Germans from a different angle. The fighters opened up with their machine guns. That caused a panic amongst the German troops—they were convinced that they were surrounded. So they began to run for their lives in all directions, leaving all their heavy armaments behind. Some of them—a small number—did manage to get away. We didn't chase after them.

We took our wounded back to camp to be tended to by our doctor—a woman from Minsk named Katia. Her hands were busy that day. Later, some of our men surprised two German soldiers who had been hiding behind a bush in the vicinity, studying a map. Those Germans surrendered without any resistance and were taken back to camp for interrogation.

Zorin could not conduct the interrogation. He was in tremendous pain. Katia had given him what treatment she could, but she did not have adequate medications and supplies for such a seriously infected wound. If the Red Army did not arrive in time with a competent battle surgeon, Zorin was in danger of having his leg amputated to save his life.

The two captured soldiers were interviewed by some of the fighting group commanders, including myself. We learned that they were part of a group of some two hundred retreating German soldiers. The two soldiers had hoped to avoid any battles with partisans. They said that they had fired back at us only because they had no other choice—their superior officer had ordered them to do so.

They were very afraid of us. They were showing us pictures of their wives and children, looking for sympathy. Then we realized that these two Germans thought we were Russian partisans. So we explained the truth to them. We told them what the Germans had done to our families. When they heard that their faces turned white and they started to tremble.

They began to plead with us, insisting that they had had nothing to do with the atrocities. They had Jewish friends. One of them was in love with a Jewish woman whom he wanted to marry, but couldn't because of his wife. After a while they realized that they could not expect sympathy from us.

We received word from Zorin that he wanted them to be brought to his tent. He had rallied sufficiently to continue with the interrogation himself, with the help of a few of his senior staff members.

Meanwhile, we continued our search of the surrounding area, looking for any other enemy stragglers. In that way we found a small group of three German soldiers and two Polish policemen. They were moving slowly toward us, unarmed, and with their hands clasped behind their necks. When we searched them we could not find any documents. We handcuffed them to each other and some of our men took them back to our camp. The rest of us continued to search the area, until at last we felt certain that the remaining Germans had run off.

On our way back, we heard unfamiliar noises coming from the *atrad* campsite. They became louder the closer we approached.

When we arrived, a friend of mine filled me in on what had happened. Some of the *atrad* members who had been left behind in camp during the fighting—the older men, the women, the children—found out about the two German soldiers being interrogated by Zorin and his staff. Those people surrounded Zorin's tent and demanded that the Germans be brought outside for the purpose of facing severe punishment.

They were informed by Zorin that the interrogation had to be continued for the sake of obtaining information vital to the defense of the *atrad*. But the *atrad* members refused to leave the area, and began to shout out their desire for revenge.

At just about that time, the five new prisoners whom we had captured arrived at the camp. As soon as those prisoners were spotted, the shouting intensified. The angry *atrad* members immediately surrounded the new prisoners. Then the shouting drowned out everything. That was the noise we had heard as we approached our camp.

ROCHELLE

I was one of those shouting people.

We were so bitter, so full of anger. Remember that in all those years in the partisans, we never really had a chance to express that anger. Even when Jack or the other men fought during food raids or other missions, it was a distant kind of fighting—firing at the Germans and the Polish police, being fired back at. You didn't get a hold of them physically, confront them directly. And as a woman, I was never involved in any kind of fighting.

I still remembered my mother's last words as she was waiting to be taken to the grave, "Tell Rochelle to take *nekome*—revenge. Revenge!" I thought about that during the war, and I have thought about it ever since. And I always felt that I hadn't done as much as I could have—that I didn't put my life completely on the block in order to extract revenge. The instinct to survive was too strong.

JACK

Whatever I did in the war by way of fighting back—I always had Rochelle in mind as well.

ROCHELLE

Ultimately, what my mother asked for was an order I couldn't fulfill. Revenge for the death of my parents, my sisters—impossible. But I would tell myself that I was in the partisans—I helped with the maintenance of the *atrad,* I did what I could. I would reason with myself—I reason in this way now—that it would have been stupid to get myself killed in a desperate suicide mission. Surviving and starting up a new family, as Jack and I have done, was a greater revenge—the best of all.

But suddenly, there were the five prisoners brought in to our camp. For the first time in the entire war, personal revenge was possible for those of us standing there watching them arrive.

We didn't have either the physical capacity or the will to keep prisoners of war. Everybody was full of wild anger toward the Nazis and their Polish collaborators.

Everyone started beating them—with rifle butts, fists, boots. We beat them to mush. I remember that they were lying on the ground just barely breathing. And I . . . I don't think I could ever do it again . . . I came up to one of the German officers who had his legs spread. I started to kick him again and again in the groin. I was kicking and screaming, "For my mama! For my *tate* [daddy]! For my sisters!" I went on screaming out every name I could remember—all my relatives and friends who had been murdered. It was such a release! It was as if I had finally done what my mother had asked me to do.

It wasn't just me. The majority of the *atrad* members who were there participated. The Polish policemen might have received the most blows. We all knew that often the Polish collaborators had been crueller than the Germans. It felt like a mitzvah [righteous deed] for everyone to go in and give any of the prisoners a punch. To get the anger out at last.

When I think back, I'm not sorry for what I did. I don't think I could do it again now. But at that moment we were all so filled with anger, anxiety, bitterness. Seeing the enemy in our midst was all it took for us to explode. We had been forced to live like animals and for that moment we became animals.

It's also important to say that those emotions did not last in me. Maybe two weeks later, after the Russians liberated us, Jack and Julius and I were passing through a Polish town, looking for a place to sleep that night. And we walked by a house and there sitting in front of it was a group of unarmed and wounded German soldiers—so badly wounded they could no longer run or even move very well. They were under a very loose Soviet guard, awaiting their fate.

They were just sitting and looking at us. And I looked at them. Both Jack and I were still carrying pistols that had been given to us in Zorin's *atrad*. The advantage was all ours. But after leaving the woods for even a short while, I was becoming human again. Already I couldn't have done to these soldiers what I had done to the German prisoner in the *atrad*. That had been in the heat of battle, so to speak. I saw those Germans in front of us now as human beings, broken, wounded, hungry, and miserable. I thought, "They are just soldiers who were drafted and sent to the front—somebody's son or father." I not only could not kick them, I couldn't even say anything bad to them.

I didn't have it in my heart to give them something to eat or drink. I hadn't progressed that far yet. But I could walk by and ignore them without hurting them. And that was a big step forward!

JACK

As for the five prisoners in our camp, Zorin had tried to hold back the crowd that day. But he was helpless.

The other two German prisoners were ultimately released to the crowd as well, once their interrogation was completed. There was no way that we were going to keep them as prisoners of war. Zorin had seen what the mood of the *atrad* was.

The fate of the prisoners was crowded out of our minds once we took a tally of our own casualties. Six of our fighters had been killed, eleven wounded. We buried our dead and grieved that they had to die so close to the time of liberation.

Meanwhile, the news about Zorin's leg was not good. The Red Army was coming very close—according to the radio they were within a few miles—but even that would be too late. The infection was spreading rapidly. Amputation would be necessary. It could wait until the Red Army surgeons arrived. But there was no way that the leg could be saved.

Shortly after receiving that news, Zorin asked to be taken outside of his tent, so he could talk to the entire *atrad*.

His leg was heavily bandaged, and there were tears in his eyes even before he began to speak.

I wrote an account of his speech for a Yiddish newspaper [the *Landsberger Zeitung*] after the war, and I quote from it now, in an English translation I prepared myself:

> "Dear friends, we were together for a long time, and I was always proud of your heroic deeds and sacrifices. Together we have suffered, fought, cried, and shared good times."
>
> He wiped his tears, relaxed a few seconds, and continued—
> "In a few hours we will finally be liberated. We will disperse in different directions, forget each other, and probably never see each other again.
> "It looks like I will remain an invalid for the rest of my life. Please don't forget me. Please stay in close contact with me. You are my family."
>
> He could not continue. Tears covered his face, and all of us cried together.
>
> We realized that what he had said was the truth. Our future was uncertain. Who knew what would happen to us, or where we would build our new homes?

I am happy to be able to record his speech in this book, in honor of Simcha Zorin. It was true what he said—I never saw him again after the liberation. But I will always remember him as an unselfish savior of Jews during the war.

ROCHELLE

We all thought, as we listened to Zorin's speech, that liberation was only hours away. But that did not prove to be the case. There were a few days more of fighting before the Red Army arrived. Our men were constantly skirmishing with the Germans—right to the end. Some of them lost their lives.

I thought to myself, "This is no good." I could not let Jack be killed when we were so close to surviving.

So, in the final two days, I pleaded with Jack to follow a plan I had devised. I put a babushka on him and a blouse and a long skirt that covered up his legs. I told him to bend his head and hunch his shoulders and walk with difficulty, like an old woman. I disguised him because I did not want the other women to be resentful about Jack staying with me while their men went off to fight.

And Jack managed to look like an old woman. He was stooped, and moaning, and the other women never knew it was him.

It *saved* his life. That I know.

There was another man in Zorin's *atrad*. He had been a neighbor of mine in Stolpce, and he had escaped to the woods along with his son. Well, both the man and his son were killed in a final ambush with the Germans. They had lived through so much. . . . We were liberated within a day by the Russians.

JACK

Why did I agree to disguise myself in that way? To understand what I did, you have to understand this—Rochelle and I were madly in love. We had made it that far, through so many years of misery, and we had started to believe that we had a future. We were talking about one day living in a house together, having children . . . enormous plans and dreams.

Even so, if it had been left to me alone, I would have gone out and fought. But Rochelle was in tears, begging me not to. And my father Julius was the same way. My wife and my father wanted me to live. I could not stand to cause either one of them so great a pain as would have been the case had I died on the verge of our freedom.

This is the truth of the matter. It is the only explanation I can give.

There were terrible tragedies in those final two days. The Germans were literally running for their lives through the forest, heading west to their fatherland by any route they could find. Russian planes and artillery were pounding the main routes, so the German troops were disorganized and desperate—but still highly trained and heavily armed. There were constant risks, constant ambushes.

During the final days of the war, both Russian and Jewish partisan groups in the Nalibocka Forest captured some of the retreating German soldiers. But I don't think that any of the groups kept prisoners. For all of the groups, but especially for the Jewish partisans, the greatest interest was in capturing Gestapo and SS personnel. They were the specially trained killers, the ones who led and organized the butchering in the ghettos. They were often easy to identify because they had tattoed lightning bolts and other special symbols on their arms—out of pride at who they were and what they did. No one felt sorry for the SS men and they were usually beaten severely and then killed.

Finally, there came the day when one of our men came running into the *atrad* campsite with the news that the Red Army tanks were coming. We all made our way as fast as we could to the main highway, which was some two miles away. There we saw a steady stream of Russian tanks and troop trucks. They were heading west, chasing the Germans back to their borders.

We tried to make ourselves realize that we were free. As we watched the tanks pass, it began to sink in. Slowly.

We hardly knew what to say to each other. We hugged and laughed and cried.

IX

Under the Soviet Yoke Again

JACK

Once the Russian army took control of the region, we were able to move out of the wilderness.

There was no possibility of keeping the *atrad* together. Most of the Jews in the *atrad* were from Minsk or other towns just across the Russian border. And there were many Polish Jews like us as well, from various towns. Once the need to hide from the Germans had ended, almost everyone wanted to go back to their hometowns, wherever they were, and to find out what had happened to their families. There were also some men who wanted to join up with the Red Army, just so they could continue to fight the Germans.

Rochelle and Julius and I knew what had happened to our families. We weren't really sure where to go at first. All of a sudden we realized that we actually were survivors! But it took quite a while for it to really sink in that we were free again, that the Germans were no longer there to kill us on sight.

Ultimately, our plan was to head back to our hometowns of Mir and Stolpce, to see what was left there. But that would have meant a very long journey on foot. For the time being, we just wanted to find some kind of transportation that would take us out of the wilderness.

Then, one day, we saw that there were some empty Soviet army trucks that were heading east to Minsk. The trucks were going to load up with food and supplies there and then transport them back to the western front, which was pushing through Poland on the way to Germany. The drivers of the trucks allowed us, and other Jews as well, to hitch a ride to Minsk. We knew a couple there with a house—they had invited us to stay with them until we figured out what to do next.

During our drive to Minsk, the sides of the main roads were piled high with bodies of dead German soldiers. The Russians had been strafing the retreating German troops from fighter planes, then shoving their corpses to the side of the roads to allow their own troops to go through. From the heat of the sun the bodies had begun to bloat. Some of them looked like inflated balloons. There was a terrible odor. We had to cover our noses.

It was fine with me. The more corpses the better.

ROCHELLE

There were mountains of bodies, not just piles. Two or three stories high. The smell, the flies . . . it was terrible.

Soon after we arrived in Minsk, we learned that the Soviets were requesting that all males who had fought in partisan units were to report and register at an official Soviet office they had set up. We decided not to register immediately . . . to wait instead, and to see what the purpose was. That was a smart idea because we learned a few days later that the partisans who were registering were being told to report for immediate induction into the Soviet army. They were handed uniforms on the spot and sent straight off to the western front.

Seeing what their plans were for us, we decided that we should not stay in Minsk much longer, or in any part of the Soviet Union, for that matter. So we took to the roads again. We managed to get a ride on one of the Soviet supply trucks heading west. We had to switch trucks several times to get where we wanted to go, which was anywhere over the border into Poland. Finally, we wound up in a town called Iweniec.

We found an abandoned house that we could stay in. And by some strange chance that is beyond explanation it turned out that living across the street from us was Uncle Oscar and his Polish woman Antonina, along with the rest of her family. Antonina by that point lived as his legal wife under his real name, because Oscar no longer had to pose as a Pole.

Under the Soviet Yoke Again

So suddenly there was Uncle Oscar as my new neighbor.

We managed to keep things on a superficially friendly basis—it was very, "Hi, hello there, have a nice day." We couldn't completely avoid each other, because that would have seemed very suspicious to his wife, and I did not want to cause trouble.

He tried to be nice to me. He would give us some potatoes, flour, bread. He would bring the food over to us. I would never go to his house. His wife was a very jealous type, and she seemed to sense something, what I can't say, but she certainly didn't like having me around. That was all right with me. I avoided all situations that might leave Uncle Oscar and me alone together. I knew that I could never be close to that man again, or even respect him.

I later learned that Iweniec was just a temporary stopping place for Uncle Oscar and his wife. When the war was barely over, Oscar was already in the process of making himself a wealthy man again. As the Germans retreated and the Russians took over, there were a number of farms left abandoned in northern Poland, in the region that had been known as Prussia. The Poles or Belorussians who had owned them had been killed, or taken into slave labor—in some cases by the Nazis, in some cases by the Soviets—as political undesirables. Some of these farms had been run by wealthy Germans during the time of Nazi control.

So with all the untended farmland, it became a kind of grabbing game. Whoever came and settled down owned the land as a practical matter. That was the same for any livestock that had survived. Oscar was very smart. He found himself a large farm to begin with, one that had been German-run. It was located near the town of Ostroda. From that base, Uncle Oscar began to accumulate cattle.

His way of doing that was to bargain with the Russian soldiers who were handling the supply lines. As the Russian front progressed through western Poland toward Berlin, most of the cattle and other livestock in the conquered regions were being seized—as a matter of official Soviet policy—to be sent back to Russia, where there was severe famine. But there was a great deal of corruption in the process, and Uncle Oscar was good at handling the Russian soldiers in charge. He would provide them with a liberal supply of vodka, and in exchange they would give him not only cattle but horses and sheep as well. Uncle Oscar would also trade his vodka for Russian gold coins, which I'm sure he was burying in sacks somewhere on his farm.

The few weeks that we spent in Iweniec was the first time in nearly two years that I was sleeping regularly under the roof of a house. It was very difficult for me to adjust. For the first week, I felt like I was choking at night. I couldn't sleep in the house. I was like a caged animal—I had to go outside in the middle of the night to catch my breath. If I had been by myself, I would have slept on the ground outside instead of in the bedroom.

It was awkward for us in Iweniec, what with my uncle across the street. Also, both Jack and I were thinking that it was time to go back and see how things were in Stolpce and Mir. We decided to go back to Stolpce first—it was the town that Jack and Julius had lived in as well as myself. But for now, because travel was difficult and we weren't sure how smoothly things would go, we decided that it was best to leave Julius behind in Iweniec. So we rented him a small room and left him with a supply of food and told him that we would send for him as soon as we established ourselves somewhere.

And then we were off. Jack and I started walking by the main road. Even though the Russians had arrived, we still didn't feel completely safe out in the open. There were still small bands of retreating German soldiers who were trying to make it back to their own lines. If we had run into them, it would have been very bad for us. It took us one very long day to finish the walk. Jack developed some trouble on the walk. The skin on his legs was still tender, and the sweat and strain caused inflammation. We would stop and ask local farmers for a handful of flour to spread over the red and raw portions of his legs. It was miserable for him.

When we were getting close to Stolpce, we stopped at the house of two different Polish farmers whom I had known before all the troubles. Both had done business with my father and my father had good relationships with both of them—they behaved as friends, and my father trusted them. When the Germans began seizing our property, my father had stored in their houses much of our family furniture, along with my father's best clothing. The farmers had agreed, in exchange, to help our family if we ever needed help.

So I knocked on the door of the first farmer and we stood there, very tired and very hungry.

The farmer let us come inside the door for only a few minutes. I could see so many pieces of furniture that I remembered from growing up in my family. The farmer wasn't happy to see me. Immediately he began to cry to me that he barely had enough food to feed his own family. He and his family were standing there in front of my eyes and I could see that they were not going hungry. He gave us a small chunk of bread and told us that we had to go.

The second farmer—we knocked on his door as well. As that farmer looked at me, I could see that my arrival at his door had badly spooked him—it was as if he had seen the dead come alive. It was not a happy experience for him. I could see furniture from my family in his house as well. My sense was that, if he could have killed me then, he would have done so. I asked him to help us. We were on our way to Stolpce, we were hungry, could he offer us some soup, something warm, something cold? But he said he could give us nothing. He was hungry too, and so were his children. The Germans and the Russians had taken everything. Meanwhile, his house had a prosperous look and he had a prosperous belly. He told us to go away—he could spare nothing. Nothing.

I felt as if I wanted to kill him. But I also knew that the time was over for that. And there he was with his sons and his wife. And there were Jack and myself without anyone else who gave a damn that we were alive. For that matter, that farmer could probably have killed the two of us then and there and nobody would have known where to look for the bodies or even that we were gone. The Soviets weren't fully in control yet in Poland. It was a world without laws. You were on your own.

JACK

It was a very unpleasant experience.

But that was the way it was, as a general rule. Most Poles were not so happy to see the few Jewish survivors come back to their towns. Many of them had cooperated with the Germans and they didn't want Jews testifying to the new Soviet rulers. So they were made uncomfortable, even frightened, by us. The majority would pretend to be nice and friendly, but only on the surface. And the ones who had been entrusted with Jewish goods were, on the whole, unwilling to admit that any agreements had been reached. The survivors, like Rochelle, could fend for themselves. There was no way for her to prove anything or enforce any legal rights. Not in the chaos of that time.

When we finally arrived in Stolpce, we saw that not only had Rochelle's family house burned down—so had virtually the entire town. There was no place to stay. So we wound up sleeping outdoors again, with our boots as our pillows. The very next morning we started looking for transportation to Mir.

ROCHELLE

Coming back to Stolpce was very strange. When I had run away, there was still a town. Now we were standing on the edge of town and could see only a few houses and the river. It was hard to even recognize the streets. I had to strain to imagine the neighborhood and the house I had grown up in.

You remember a town, you remember your life, your family. And then you come back after years and there's nothing!

It wasn't like when a soldier comes back to his town and his people come out and tell him how glad they are to see him. No one was there to rejoice that we had come home. We were a nuisance, a burden.

The people I did see whom I recognized either pretended not to see me or shied away. We were witnesses to the tragedy. They would rather not have had any witnesses. But because of the Russians, they were afraid to be openly mean or hostile. So it wound up that they stayed away from us and we stayed away from them.

An empty feeling—that's finally what I remember about going

back to Stolpce. It was, in a way, more comfortable for us when we were living in Zorin's *atrad*. We had there a camaraderie—a sense of being part of the same group, the same people. In Stolpce, we weren't part of a family and we weren't a part of the town itself—what was left of it.

We went by foot to Mir.

There was one important side trip before we left for Mir, however. Remember that, when the Germans had first arrived in Stolpce, my family had run off to the nearby village of Kruglice, which was where one of my father's factories was located. During that time, my father had buried two glass jars, filled with Russian gold coins from the time of the czar, in places that he specially pointed out to me. So now we went back to Kruglice to dig up the two jars. If we could find them, it would give us an emergency fund to live on. Russian gold coins were illegal to possess, but they were the best possible money on the black market.

We managed to dig up those two jars, but we were afraid the whole time. Some of the locals saw me and remembered that I was the Jew Schleiff's daughter. They knew that I hadn't come back to Kruglice to recite memorial prayers for my father. They must have suspected that I was hoping to recover something. And I was sure that at least a few of the locals would be happy to rob or even murder refugee Jews. Who would have looked for us? So we tried to stay out of sight as much as possible, and we managed to dig up the jars in secret and hide them in one of our satchels.

On the way out of Kruglice, a local woodsman stepped out of the forest and started to come toward us on the road. He was carrying a long-handled axe on his shoulder. I was terrified. He stared at us but then he passed us by.

JACK

When we reached Mir, we discovered that a few dozen Jewish survivors had arrived there before us. Every few days some man or woman would show up from somewhere. There was a very small-scale Jewish community established, and that was very helpful.

We found a place to stay in a big house owned by a Jewish family—the Malishansky family. Rochelle and I took one of the rooms. In another room there were a few other survivors. The family was kind to us and we all shared meals together. Next door was another Jewish house that had survived the bombings. In that house lived my friend Simon Kagan, who had also escaped from the Mir ghetto, and who was a hero among the partisans for his demolition work on German railroads. Also living there was Simon's sister Sarah, a very kind woman with whom we became close.

There was a Polish family living in Mir—their last name was Talish. I was happy to see them again. And they were genuinely happy that I and my father had survived. I owe the Talish family a great deal. Back in 1941, when the Germans were setting up the Mir ghetto, the Talish house was located just across the street from our own assigned house in the ghetto. The Talishes would help to get us some extra food. And I was able to sneak across and store with them some photo albums of my family. And then, returning to Mir three years later, I was able to recover those albums. There were photographs of my mother. . . .

I introduced Rochelle to the Talishes and they took to her immediately. They often invited us over for a lunch or a dinner that summer of 1944. That was generous—they were not a wealthy family. They lived in a little house made of clay—a father, a mother, a son. We would sit and talk together.

There was a Catholic convent in Mir. My mother Sarah had given the nuns some of her furs and clothing to store. I went there and asked for these things. But the nuns explained that they had been forced to trade most of the furs and clothing to feed themselves during the Nazi occupation. They did still have a sealskin coat and a fox collar that they returned to me. The fox collar I still have—I also have a photograph of my mother wearing it. The nuns tried to be nice and friendly, but I didn't believe that they were happy to see me at their door.

Once we settled down in Mir, we arranged to bring Julius over to join us. He was still in Iweniec, waiting for word from us. Rochelle's uncle Oscar was helpful to us—maybe he was finally sorry for what he had done. We communicated with uncle Oscar and he arranged for a farmer with a truck to bring Julius to Mir. We were so grateful to see each other again.

But now that the Soviets were establishing firm rule over Poland, the old problem was facing us again: all former partisan fighters were being told to register for immediate service in the front lines of the Soviet army. We didn't want to run away again—and in any case there was nowhere left to run to. The war was still going on throughout most of Europe. Also, we enjoyed being part of a Jewish community here in Mir—a small one, but very precious to us after all the killing.

So I had to find a way to be excused from the Soviet draft. And having my father Julius with us suggested an answer. If you performed a vital civilian service, you would be excluded from military service. Dentistry was defined as vital. Good then—I would be a dentist. Why not? In wartime, no one expected you to have a diploma. My mother had been a dentist, my father had trained as a dental technician. I had a family right to claim I was a dentist—and there was no one left in Mir who knew that I wasn't except for my closest friends and family. In fact, there was no other dentist in all of Mir at that point—so I was filling a vacuum.

My father and I set up a dental practice in a room in our house. Because of my father's training, we at least had a general knowledge of how to make things look right. We didn't have a real drill, so we rigged up a drill made out of wooden parts except for the drill-point itself. We powered the drill with a foot-pump. We had no other dental tools. As for novocaine or any other anesthetic—we had none. But we let the Mir population know that we were dentists. Some of the farmers would come in and I would drill their teeth. I didn't have the slightest idea of what I was doing.

ROCHELLE

He was making holes in good teeth, he was making holes in bad teeth. He put on an act to stay alive. And yet somehow his patients were satisfied with his work.

JACK

After a short time, the Soviets moved me into a small building they fixed up for first aid and other medical services in Mir. There was a woman in charge of the building and I gave her a list of the equipment I needed to fully practice dentistry. She sent a requisition to Minsk and after a few weeks most of what I had asked for arrived. We were in business! Even so, I couldn't have carried on without my father. Julius was very creative. He made false teeth out of brass handles he would scavenge from the bombed-out houses in Mir. He found a machine in town with which he could flatten and shape the handles. You can imagine how well they fit in the mouths of our customers.

It began to circulate among the dozen or so Jewish houses in Mir that I was not really a dentist—so very soon my customers were exclusively Polish locals. I could remember that many of those locals had been highly enthusiastic when the ghetto had been created and all the misery followed. So when they came for my services, I would tell them, "Listen, this isn't Germany. I'm not obligated to work on you if you're not a Soviet official or soldier. So if you want my help, you bring me food." And so they started bringing bread, butter, honey, potatoes, now and then a chicken. For the first time in God knows how long we had plenty of food. We had enough to share with the others in our house.

To pull that off as I did, I had to be filled with bitter and angry memories. Because as a dentist I was a complete fake. But I remembered what I remembered. And when the people whom I knew had collaborated with the Nazis would be sitting in my chair squirming and screaming, I would think to myself, "If I could, I would drill off all your teeth!" With patients whom I didn't remember from those days, I just tried to do as little harm as I could.

But then, in the autumn of 1944, a genuine Russian dentist showed up in Mir to help with the medical center they were trying to establish. We were very frightened. I was sure that he would spot me as a fake immediately and report me to the authorities.

His name was Zenowey. He was a nice looking man, with

dark bushy hair and a round face. They put up a second dental chair for him just three feet away from my own. We would be working within constant sight of each other.

For the first day or two, while they were setting things up for him, we had a chance to get to know each other. Zenowey was an easy and outgoing person. He asked about how I had survived the war and I told him. He told me about his days in the Soviet army. He saw combat duty but had been wounded and was discharged and allowed to practice dentistry again.

Then the first patients for our newly expanded dental office began to arrive. Zenowey would take care of one, I would take care of another. I noticed that he kept glancing at me as I worked. I figured the end was near. But I didn't give up. I kept drilling and drilling and drilling. Zenowey didn't say anything. But I noticed that he was trying to work fast so that he would be free to take care of the majority of the patients who came through the door.

It went on for a week or so. Meanwhile, Zenowey and I were becoming close friends. We enjoyed talking to each other, sharing stories of the war. And I saw from the way he worked so hard that he had a good heart.

Finally, one day as we were sitting and talking, Zenowey took a look at me and suddenly burst out laughing.

I asked him what was the matter. I kept my face as serious as I could.

He said to me, "What a fine actor you are! You're as much a dentist as I am a carpenter!"

I couldn't try to lie to him—the truth was too obvious. So I confessed my situation to him. I told him that my mother had been a dentist and that Julius actually knew a thing or two from his technical training. I admitted that, because of all the killing in Mir, I couldn't feel too sorry for my patients. And most importantly, I explained that my choices were drill teeth or be sent to the front to die. And that I loved Rochelle and wanted to live and to start up a real life with her.

Well, Zenowey listened to all that. Then he told me that he had spotted me as a complete fraud within ten minutes of our working together—just as I had feared he would. But

Zenowey added, "Don't worry about it—it will be a secret be-tween us."

Zenowey started to give me some pointers on how to per-form a few basic dental procedures. He instructed me that if a patient came in for something beyond those procedures, I should just pretend to be busy with something else and let Zenowey take care of it. That was the kind of friend he was.

But I also knew that I could not keep pretending to be a dentist forever. So I was looking for a more secure position in the Mir medical center. Then one day a Russian official came in and announced that he wanted to organize a group to teach first aid in the schools and to adults in evening classes. It was being done all through Poland, because with so few trained doctors people needed to be taught how to care for themselves.

I had studied first aid in school. So I volunteered to help organize those classes. And I was genuinely good at doing the organizing—no more faking needed. I soon became the ad-ministrator for the first aid programs throughout the region, assigning classes to the few doctors and nurses we had. I even had the opportunity to give instructor jobs to friends like Simon Kagan.

In late 1944, there was very bloody and difficult fighting on the Russian front pushing into Germany. Everyone who had served with the partisans—even those like myself who hadn't officially registered—were being hunted out and sent to the front. So I began to understand that my days as a first aid administrator might be coming to an end if I didn't come up with a plan.

Again, I saw my opportunity by chance one day. A Russian army medical officer came to inspect the Mir medical center, He was now running the same kind of center in Baranowicze. I told Rochelle that we should try to make friends with the man because he could be very helpful to us. So we invited him to our home, entertained him with vodka, did everything we could to please him.

Things were going well, so toward the end of the evening I mentioned to the doctor that I was feeling kind of sick—I was having trouble breathing normally. I had been pretending through all of his inspection that I had a hacking cough. Now as the evening went on I was coughing even more. Finally the doctor suggested that I come to see him in Baranowicze for a medical exam.

What I was trying to do was convince him that I had tuberculosis, which would definitely keep me out of the military. I had one advantage here—at the time the Russians came to liberate us from the woods, I was still weak and skinny as a toothpick—my ribs stuck out. I had not gained much weight since. So I looked like a potential tuberculosis case. I could also sense that the medical officer was a foxy character—he suspected what I was up to, that I wanted to stay out of the army.

ROCHELLE

He was on the take. That's why he invited Jack to Baranowicze. Jack and I made the trip to Baranowicze together. We brought along not only vodka but also some Russian gold coins we had managed to dig up in Kruglice. Now vodka was one thing, but these Russian gold coins were very dangerous to possess— completely illegal. They were old, from czarist times, and all of them were to have been turned back to the Soviet government years before, after the Revolution. But they were a staple of black-market trading nearly thirty years later.

Aside from the risk of the gold coins, we were also afraid that the army doctor might try to take our bribe and then turn us in for attempted bribery. Who would take our word over his?

Very early on the day scheduled for Jack's examination— so early that the medical office was not yet open—I went to the home of the Russian army doctor. Jack wasn't with me. I had decided that, if I was going to be arrested for bribery, at least Jack wouldn't be there. He could say that he hadn't known what I was doing.

I knocked on the doctor's door. He had no idea that I was coming—he was still getting ready to go to work. I handed him some gold coins, which I explained were a present to him for writing down in his report that my husband had tuberculosis and couldn't serve in the army. I was very nervous. I figured that either he would slap my face and throw me out, or that everything would go well. He took the coins. He also mentioned that he wanted new curtains and a bedspread for his wife, and I told him I would find those for him that same day—and I did. Then he closed the door on me—no more conversation.

JACK

I showed up for my appointment at his office that day and he went through the motions of giving me a physical. Then he gave me a piece of paper and told me to take it to the army recruiting center in Mir. I did that, and they issued me a certificate saying that I was unfit for the Soviet army.

So that worry was over. I kept busy for a while longer organizing the first aid groups, while my friend Zenowey handled the dentistry.

ROCHELLE

While Jack was doing his dentistry work, I was keeping busy cooking and washing clothes. The Jews in the house lived together on a cooperative basis. We all used the same outhouse in the backyard. I remember one morning—it was a little chilly, so I put on a coat and started to walk to the outhouse. All of a sudden, something hit me in my behind. I weighed maybe ninety pounds then, and so I flew ten feet forward! It was a goat that had wandered into our backyard to graze—somehow I had offended the goat. I'm telling you, it hurt for a month! From then on, I kept a pot under the bed.

But the Russians decided that they had plans for me. Most of the young couples in Mir had already been separated—the men to the western front, the women serving in some kind of forced labor. So one day, late in the winter of 1944, an official came to my door and suggested that, since I was in good health and without children, I should prove my patriotism to mother Russia by volunteering to work for two years in a coal mine in Donbass, in southern Russia. It was a "friendly suggestion." But if you said no, you were considered unpatriotic and they took you to Donbass anyway.

Once the Soviets made that "friendly suggestion," we decided that it would be a good idea for us to move on.

Under the Soviet Yoke Again

JACK

That incident made us realize that our lives were never going to be our own as long as we lived under Soviet rule. Even though my organizing work was going well, we decided that there could be no future for us in Mir.

In the spring of 1945, the fall of Berlin was not far away. We decided that our best hope, strange as it seemed, would be to head in the direction of western Poland and Germany, where the Soviets had not yet established complete control. We hoped that eventually we could make it to a sector controlled by one of the Western Allies. Our plan after that was to try to emigrate to Palestine. At that time, isolated as we were, we had no idea of how difficult that was. We weren't aware of the exclusionary policies against Jewish immigration that had been established by the British mandate there.

ROCHELLE

There wasn't a state of Israel in existence then. We had no idea of the realities of life there. But it was a dream for us—to get away from the bad memories and to live among Jews.

JACK

"Go west, young man!" is the American saying. Well, we decided to go west. But it wasn't as easy as just packing up and going. As the Soviet rule in Poland became established, travel restrictions became more and more intensive. Train travel was no longer available to the civilian population. You had to have a work permit—proof that you were specifically being sent somewhere by Soviet edict—in order to board a train. That was all part of a desire on the part of the Soviets to keep the population in place—the beginnings of what would be called the Iron Curtain.

If we were going to move west, we would have to do it secretly. So we started to keep our eyes open for opportunities. Meanwhile, we began accumulating a supply of clothing and kitchen utensils and other basics that we kept packed and ready on short notice.

It was around that time I learned of a job opening in

Baranowicze. The Soviets needed help with organizing first aid groups there. I had developed a good reputation and so I applied for the position. They invited me to come for an interview and it went well—I was hired. It was a big job— Baranowicze was the largest city in the area, and all the major Soviet agencies had offices there. They would not only give me a salary but a house to live in as well. I asked them to write me up a letter confirming that I had been hired, so that I could show it to my employers and family in Mir. They did that for me. I already had plans to use the letter for my own purposes.

When I got back to Mir, I was allowed to take a week off and prepare for the move. I showed Zenowey my letter from the Baranowicze authorities. He would be taking over my first aid organizing duties in Mir. I explained to him that I couldn't turn down such an opportunity and that we would probably see each other again. But Zenowey was a smart man—I never could fool him! He suspected that I was planning an escape to the West, and that the whole Baranowicze business was a smoke screen. He said to me, "I don't think I'll ever see you again, and I'll miss you. Good-bye and good luck."

Thanks to my letter, Julius, Rochelle, and I could move out of Mir without suspicion. We hired a farmer with a horse and buggy, loaded up our possessions and rode to a little town called Horodej where there was a railroad station. From there we went by train to Baranowicze. When we arrived, I reported to my new office and asked for some time to find a place for us to live. They agreed. That gave me time to investigate transportation options for heading west, as Baranowicze was a railroad hub.

ROCHELLE

I remember that, just after we arrived in Baranowicze, we were walking down the street and there were radios in the shops blaring out the news that Roosevelt had just died. That was on 12 April 1945.

By that time I was pregnant. We were extremely happy. For years, hiding in the woods, we had hardly dared dream of surviving. And now we were going to have a family—our own family out of the ashes.

JACK

The fact that Rochelle was pregnant made me more determined than ever to get us out of the Soviet Union. After making lots of inquiries, I managed through some bribes to railroad workers to arrange for us to board a freight train heading for Lodz in western Poland, outside the Soviet sphere. There were maybe a dozen other people travelling in the same freight car with us. We were afraid that Russian soldiers might search the cars and discover us—it could have meant arrest and a terrible sentence, maybe even Siberia. But we decided to take the chance.

Our freight car smelled as if it had been used for livestock. They locked us in to reduce the chance that the car would be searched. And they told us to be very quiet when we reached the border between the Russian-held Poland and the western Polish region that was still independent—although it too would soon be taken over by Russia. At the border, the story they told the Russian guards was that the car was filled with building materials. Thank God things were still somewhat disorganized on the border—the Russians didn't search our car.

The train also stopped in Warsaw and Chenstochowa on the way to Lodz. One of the train workers whom we had bribed warned us not to even try to get off at Chenstochowa . . . because there were Poles there who watched the trains and would kill on sight any Jews who came out of the boxcars. There were many rumors circulating about boxcars being searched—not by the Soviets but by the local Poles—and Jews being pulled out and shot.

By chance, we happened to know one of the other Jewish couples on the freight car with us. Their names were Abram and Leah. They had also been in Zorin's *atrad,* although we hadn't spoken to them much.

We weren't carrying too much baggage, but one of our items was a wooden headboard. It had been given to us by our friends the Talish family in Mir. They had been kind enough to fix it up specially for us—they drilled a hole in it in which we could place some of the gold coins we had left. They left a wooden cap to place over the hole to make it look smooth.

Perhaps we talked about the headboard in a suspicious manner during the trip—telling Abram and Leah what sentimental value it had to us to explain why we would be taking a headboard along. Or perhaps we simply kept our eyes on it too much. But once we arrived in Lodz, we agreed to share a rented room with that couple—just to find a place to start out and minimize expenses. The five of us—my father, Rochelle, and I and the couple—shared floor space. After a few days in the room, we unscrewed the cap to get one of the coins to sell on the black market for food—and there were none left! We were stunned. But then we realized that it must have been that couple.

I confronted Abram and he admitted straight off that he had stolen the coins. He said he had a right to them.

ROCHELLE

It was like the man who stole Jack's mother's necklace when we were with the partisans. Abram claimed that he had an uncle, Ishke, who had worked for my father Lazar in one of my father's factories. And Ishke had always complained that he worked so hard and wasn't paid enough. So the gold coins that Abram had now stolen were supposed to make up for what had been done to Ishke. Who knew if the story was true or not?

As far as going to the police to complain, that was out of the question—because it was illegal to have Russian gold coins in the first place. And even though the Polish police in Lodz were supposed to be independent, we knew that word would reach the Soviets. There was nothing we could do.

JACK

I was full of rage. I wanted to strangle Abram. But Rochelle warned me that any kind of revenge would mean the risk of great trouble for us. I could go to jail if I harmed him. And if we even threatened too much, Abram could go to the police and turn us in as black-marketeers.

It was difficult to accept, but we decided to let the matter go. It was more important to keep ourselves alive and safe—because by the time we arrived in Lodz Rochelle was nearly seven months pregnant. The one step we did take was to immediately find a different room in which to live. We never saw them again.

ROCHELLE

We wound up staying in Lodz for roughly two months. There had been an office established by a Jewish relief committee that enabled survivors to obtain Polish citizen identification cards. The cards helped us walk down the street without worrying about being stopped by the police.

But it was still our goal to move further west. By now, Germany was a defeated nation that was being carved up into four territories controlled by the four major Allies—America, England, France, and the Soviet Union. Ideally, we wanted to make it to Berlin and, specifically, to the American sector of that city. We heard that in Berlin there were committees established to help refugee Jewish survivors. And we felt that things would be safest for us in the American sector.

But for the time being, given the stage of pregnancy I was in, we made up our minds to pass some time in Lodz. Julius put up a little sign outside on our building, "Dentist." Somehow he managed to get some basic equipment. A few customers would come in now and then. That was a way to get some money for food. And we still had a small stash of the gold coins left—fortunately we hadn't stored them all in the headboard. But now Jack kept them on his person at all times—sewn into his coat.

I was going into my eighth month of pregnancy, and one day we heard that in a Polish town to the south of Lodz—a town called Katowice—there was a big pogrom. All the surviving Jews in that town were killed by the local Poles. That was after the war was supposed to be over! And still the Jews were being killed—not just in Katowice, but in other towns in Poland as well—as if the Poles in those towns were trying to make up for what the Germans had missed. Nowhere else in

Europe did they kill Jews who had survived the Nazis and were trying to come home. Only in Poland did that happen.

When I heard the news, I was filled with panic. We still weren't safe! Katowice was no great distance away. We thought for sure that Lodz would be next. We were afraid to stay and at the same time we could not possibly leave—not without a travel permit, and not in my condition.

I remember that one night—it was in July—the rumor had reached us that the pogrom was going to happen. We barricaded the windows of our room. We pushed our bed against the door. We were shaking. That rumor proved to be false. But it did its damage. Because I went into premature labor that night.

At the time, I had no idea what was happening. All I knew was that I was in terrible pain. I didn't even know that those were contractions I was experiencing. I had never been pregnant before, and I had no mother, no nurse, to tell me what contractions felt like.

I didn't want to worry Jack, so I told him nothing about it. But as soon as it was dawn, I went to the office of the gynecologist I had seen on a couple of occasions since we arrived in Lodz. His office was maybe four, five blocks away, and it wasn't really an office, just a room in his house. He had a couple of beds and a handful of instruments and medications and that was it.

I startled him by coming so early. He gave me a quick exam and said, "You're dilated completely! You're going to have the baby within an hour!" He put me down on one of the beds and the baby came within an hour, just as he said.

By that time, Jack had woken up and noticed that I was gone. He figured out that I must have gone to the gynecologist. So Jack arrived at my bedside, but by that time I had already given birth. A baby boy. He was about seven and one-half months old. The doctor told me that the baby was basically healthy, but that he needed oxygen because he was premature. Without oxygen the baby would die. And the doctor had no oxygen.

The doctor then said to me, "The easiest way to do it is to put the baby near a window. It's cold near the window so he'll die faster." I wanted to see the baby. The doctor told me, "It's better if you don't see him. You won't remember him this way." He took the baby and put him near the window.

He was living and breathing a whole day, from morning to evening. At about five o'clock in the afternoon the doctor came to my bed and said, "He's turning blue, so he won't last long." Maybe a couple of hours later, the doctor came and told me that the baby had died.

Jack was as devastated as I was. He called someone from the local *Chevre Kaddishe*—the Jewish burial committee, like the one my father had served on in Mir. A Jewish man arrived, Jack gave him some money, and that man took our baby, covered him up with a little blanket, and promised that he would be buried in a Jewish cemetery. I remember I watched out the window as he carried the baby off, a little bundle under his arm.

I was thinking, "Wherever I go, I leave a grave behind." In Stolpce all of my closest family members were in graves. And then in Lodz, after only a couple of months, another grave. As soon as I could get up off that bed and walk, I told Jack, "We have to get out of here. We have to start heading west again."

But there was more medical treatment to go through first. My breasts had filled with milk. The doctor had no proper medications, so he took some very heavy cotton sheets and wrapped them like a bandage over my breasts. He wrapped them so tightly that I looked like a boy. He told me that it would take a few weeks for my milk to burn up, so to speak. I was to keep the bandage on and never remove it.

Finally, when after some weeks I took it off, I saw that the tissue in my breasts had broken down. I was scared: they didn't look like my breasts any longer.

JACK

I was working on how to get us all out of town. Finally I found out that the best route was through Sczeczin, a small town in eastern Germany. From there, we would have to figure out how to proceed further. We decided to travel there together with another couple we had met in Lodz—David and Nechama Garmizo. They were good people, and by combining our funds we could manage the bribe expenses better.

We made our move in August 1945. The man we bribed was both Jewish and an officer in the Soviet army. He sympathized with us, but he still wanted his payoff. He did get us all on a Soviet army truck with a canvas camouflage covering. Then he covered us up with boxes and boxes of supplies. And he told us that the truck would pass through a Soviet checkpoint and that if we made a sound we would all end up in Siberia or dead. We made it through safely.

In Sczeczin, we stayed only a few days, renting a room from a German family with a large house. Immediately we started checking out the possibilities for getting to Berlin. We were very frightened the whole time we were in Sczeczin—it was a mixed German and Polish population, and memories of the war were still very fresh with everyone. There were no smiling faces from the landlord's family, or from the people we passed as we walked through the streets.

Luckily, we very quickly arranged to get to Berlin, which was by now no more than a day's drive away. Again, we found a Russian army officer to bribe and the three of us were hidden on a supply truck—not as large as the last one, more like an oversized jeep with a canvas-covered storage bed.

We were very anxious to make it to the American sector of Berlin, because we had learned that there was a Jewish-American relief organization established there called HIAS [Hebrew Immigrant Aid Society]. There was also UNRRA [United Nations Relief and Rehabilitation Administration], which helped Jewish refugees. But mostly we wanted to reach a territory that was administered by Americans—not by Russians, Poles, or Germans.

All the same, we had no idea what to expect if we made it to Berlin. We knew only that we could have greater peace of mind in terms of our day-to-day safety. The past was weighing so heavily upon us that it was difficult to think about the future.

ROCHELLE

Everyone was telling us that getting to Israel was difficult if not impossible. The British wouldn't allow it. And the Western countries didn't want us either—there were very strict policies and quotas controlling immigration by Jewish survivors. So we were thinking to ourselves, "Are we just going to wind up sitting in a refugee camp in Germany? In the lion's den?"

JACK

The last border crossing into Berlin would be the most difficult of all. That was because Berlin was a highly contested area, carved up into sectors by the four major Allies, and so movement in and out of the city was under very careful scrutiny. But we had all taken so many chances since we first ran away from the German ghettos that we really weren't so frightened by this.

The ride was a very bumpy one. I remember that we were all packed together very tightly and were tossed up and down. There was a little piece of protuding metal in the frame just above my father's head. Julius kept hitting it and his skull began to bleed. He showed tremendous control—he never moaned or made so much as a sound, because we had been warned to keep absolute silence. We put a handkerchief on it to stop the bleeding. I was afraid that he had been seriously injured. But he came through all right.

At last we reached the final checkpoint leading into Berlin. The officer we had bribed knew just how to handle the guards. He handed them a bottle of vodka and told them that he was just transporting supplies. After a few minutes of conversation they waved him through.

After some more driving, the officer pulled the truck over to a corner and leaned in back to whisper to us. We were still in the Russian sector of Berlin. He couldn't take us all the way into the American sector, because he had no right to enter that sector. But the American sector was only a block away. That block was a no-man's-land, he said, disputed between Russia and America and sporadically patrolled by both. It was up to us to make it the rest of the way. He said to us, "Get out of this truck and run. If the Russians catch you, you'll know that it's Russian territory tonight! There's nothing more I can do for you. Run like hell!"

We grabbed the little baggage we had and we ran. We made

it past that block and a block or two more. We saw no one. It was nighttime, and Berlin was a badly bombed-out city. We saw a few standing buildings but many more that were nothing but rubble.

But even though we didn't know where the Americans were, we knew that we were in their sector at last. And that was a tremendous relief to us. For the first time, the war felt *really* over.

X

From Germany to America

ROCHELLE

We were definitely confused. Now that we were finally in the American sector of Berlin, we were lost!

It was made even more strange by the fact that Berlin was so badly bombed-out that in some directions you could see for miles.

But we kept walking and began running into people and asking directions. And after a few hours, we met someone with a car who knew his way around. The man gave us a ride to the building where HIAS carried on its operations.

When we went inside, we saw that there were maybe two hundred Jewish refugees from all over Europe. That was the temporary location where all the newcomers were being kept. There were four large rooms, with roughly fifty Jews to a room. Each person was given a cot, a blanket, and some canned food. There was also a little cafeteria where you could get something hot to eat or drink.

HIAS put us up that night. The next day it was explained to us that we would be transferred in a few days to a DP [Displaced Persons] camp somewhere in Germany. There had been several of those established in various locations throughout what would become West Germany. Every day the names of some of the Jewish refugees were called and they were taken off by trucks for resettlement in these DP camps.

Finally our names were called. We had been assigned at random to the DP camp in Feldafing. Our driver was a black man—the first black man we had ever seen. We didn't get a chance to talk much with him because he was up front in the cab with one of the male Jewish refugees for company. The rest of us sat in the back freight bed. It was a drive of two days, in September 1945. It was cold and drizzly most of the time. We covered ourselves with blankets.

Feldafing was a little community not far from Munich in southern Germany. It had been a German army-training center, and there was a cluster of seventy houses that had been built to house German army personnel and their families. Those houses were now being used for the DP camp, which had a Jewish refugee population of two hundred or more. In the room to which we were assigned, there were roughly thirty other people. We slept on bunks.

The camp was run jointly by HIAS and UNRRA. The UNRRA officials registered us and supplied us with food and clothing. They also asked us straight off if we had relatives anywhere in the Western world . . . places like the United States, Canada, Australia, South Africa. If so, they would make contact with those relatives for us and let them know where we were. The idea was that perhaps those relatives could help us economically or even make it possible for us to join them.

JACK

Julius had a brother, Louis, who had left Russia for Johannesburg, South Africa, well before World War II began. Louis sent us a few packages of food and a little bit of money. But Julius was not close to his brother, whom I never met. And we had no interest in going to live in South Africa.

We asked again about Israel, and again we were told that the British would never let us go there. They were trying to maintain peace with the surrounding Arab lands by forbidding further Jewish immigration.

As for America, we knew that Rochelle had some family in America—her Uncle Herman had gone to America before World War I. She had never met him and didn't know how to contact him.

So we stayed for a few months in Feldafing in a kind of limbo.

Then the authorities decided to close up the Feldafing camp and to transfer us to a new camp located in a suburb of Munich.

The new camp was called Nei Freimann. During the Third Reich, the camp—which was like a small town, with maybe two hundred houses—had been used to house SS officers and their families.

Nei Freimann was much nicer than Feldafing. The houses were nothing fancy—they had a small downstairs and a small upstairs that was a finished attic area. The houses were each shared by three Jewish families—each family had one room, with a common kitchen. There was also a small shared bathroom—the toilet was a wooden bench set up over a hole in the ground that we cleaned out twice a year.

Our address, I remember, was Tulinger Street, number eleven. It was our first real home in five years.

Rochelle and I lived in a small room downstairs, and Julius had his own even smaller room—almost a closet—next to ours. In the center of our bedroom were a table and chairs for dining. It was at that table that Julius made the crayon drawings, based on his wartime memories, that have been reproduced in this book.

There was a little front yard with a small plum tree and a small apple tree. In the backyard was a little barn filled with hay and old broken-down pieces of furniture. And next to the barn was a little garden, nicely fenced-in, with some vegetables and a few more fruit trees. In the summer months we could sit in the garden and relax in private. We even rigged up a little shower back there. The workings were very simple: we punched holes in a bucket, hung it up on a tree branch, and poured water through it with another solid bucket. We took turns. A wonderful luxury!

We were settled, but we would have been living on just the bare basics if we had depended strictly on HIAS and UNRRA. I decided to find a way to make some money for us. In the UNRRA supplies we received, American cigarettes were included. I didn't smoke, so I began to accumulate the cigarettes to trade on the black market, where they were much in demand. In that way I managed to obtain a very fine Leica camera, one that had been used during the war by the Luftwaffe for aerial surveillance. And I began to teach myself photography.

I managed also to obtain on the black market an enlarging machine, along with other equipment, so I could develop my own photographs in our little room.

I started by taking pictures of small children and of family groups to sell to the families. I was already writing news stories for a Jewish newspaper that had been started up especially for survivors living in German DP camps. It was called the *Landsberger Zeitung.* One of the great services it performed was to publish lists of names of survivors and their whereabouts, so that survivors could find their families, friends, and loved ones. For the paper I wrote eight or so articles— memoir essays—describing not only my experiences with the partisans, but also recounting acts of heroism by fellow fighters, such as my friend Simon Kagan. I soon arranged to start taking pictures for the newspaper as well. Soon I became their lead photographer and was assigned to major events like the visit of General Eisenhower to the Nei Freimann camp in 1946. Things went so well with the paper that, when one of its editors managed illicitly to emigrate to Israel to work on the Hebrew newspaper *HaBoker* [The Morning], he sent me an invitation to come to Israel to take on a reporter's job there. It was very flattering and exciting, but it meant nothing without a visa for myself, my wife, and my father. And that was still, as a practical matter, impossible.

By taking pictures for families and for the newspapers, I became quite well known within the Nei Freimann camp. But all the same, I was very surprised by what came out of all this familiarity. There was an election held to form a committee of refugee Jews who would work with UNRRA to help administer the camp. Some people put my name on the ballot. There were maybe a couple of dozen names in all. And I was elected as the leader of the committee! That I never expected.

I had a number of duties that were very satisfying. We organized day-care centers where mothers who needed to work could leave their children. And we set up schools in some of the houses, where small classes of children could get real attention from their teachers. We also managed to convince the American leaders working for UNRRA that, even though we had a doctor in the camp, he couldn't be of real help to us unless he received adequate medical supplies. That was accomplished. Finally, we established a nice series of cultural programs—regular film showings, and even occasional stage performances by Jewish American singers and performers who would come over to entertain us.

But the leadership position did not give me sufficient power to make all of the changes in the camp management that should have been made. For example, I was in charge of making sure that the supplies of clothing that came to Nei Freimann were distributed equally amongst all of the Jewish refugees. But throughout the system of clothing delivery and distribution, there were crooked dealings. Good clothing would be stolen overnight and then sold on the black market the very next day.

ROCHELLE

The situation was known to everyone. Officially, America was very good in sending clothing. As a practical matter, the good clothing seldom reached the people they were intended for—at least not without a high black-market price. That's why this little rhyming Yiddish song became popular in our camp:

> *Lebn zol America, in naches und in gedule.*
> *Vos zi hot unz ungeshiekt, onetzes afule!*
> [Long live America, through good times and through bad.
> What she has sent to us—a bounty of rags!]

JACK

The situation was the same with linens, towels, Hershey bars, cigarettes, or favorite foods like sugar, fresh milk, eggs, bread, or Spam and other canned meat. Those were somehow always unavailable—the truck hadn't arrived.

ROCHELLE

But there was always plenty of powdered milk, powdered eggs, peanut butter, and ketchup.

JACK

And if you went around the corner to the black market, there were all the items on sale that they had just told you hadn't arrived.

There was at least one definite benefit for us from my position as camp leader. I had been given a set of official stamps for use in creating identification documents for incoming refugees. That meant that I could make sure that Julius, Rochelle, and I had all the documentation we needed to live safely. It also meant that it was easy for me to arrange things for people whom we especially wanted to help. That was important, because we had found out that an aunt of Rochelle's, named Ronke, along with her daughter Sofka, had survived and were living in a DP camp in the English sector of West Germany.

It was a chance to reunite with real family, and so I not only arranged for documents, but also for Ronke and Sofka to move into a spare room in our house that had opened up when the former residents had managed to emigrate to the West. We all became very close to each other. It was an atmosphere we had thought we would never experience again. Now Rochelle and I each had some living family members. Later we became friends with a second surviving daughter of Ronke's, named Eva, and with her husband Sam as well. But they did not move to Nei Freimann.

But Rochelle went beyond family in her hospitality. She made our house the social center for all of Nei Freimann. Her reputation among the Jewish survivors was second to none. If you had just arrived in the camp, you were told that if you went to Mama Sutin's place you could get something to eat, to drink, even a place to sleep for the first night or two, until you got settled. Our guest bed was the dining-room table in our kitchen, which we covered with blankets.

Rochelle's most popular dish was pickled herring. It was delicious. People would crowd into our kitchen to get their servings.

ROCHELLE

I was pickling herring twice a week and I still couldn't keep up with the demand. It was a two-day process: washing the herring, soaking it, pickling it. The smell of the herring would fill our little house. With the pickled herring I would serve bread and butter—the bread was challah [Jewish egg bread] that I would bake several loaves at a time. I also baked sweet rolls. People would sit at our table and eat and thank me as if those were the finest delicacies in the world.

I enjoyed having family and friends to cook for. There was a man who arrived in Nei Freimann during that time who had lived down the block from me in Stolpce. His name was David Zuchowicki. Today he lives in Israel and we are still in contact. Back then he was a skinny survivor, a very warm and funny man. We became friends immediately. He was always declaring his love for me then, and he still does today—all in good fun. I remember that when David first arrived, the kitchen table was already taken for the night by another guest. So we took the door of our bedroom off its hinges, laid it flat on two chairs, and there was a cot for David.

It was a pleasure to feel so much a part of that new life of friends and family. But there was something that still felt missing inside of me.

After I had lost the baby in Lodz, I was so devastated. A child had been taken away who *belonged* to me—and I felt a tremendous need to replace him somehow. I couldn't wait to get pregnant again. I wasn't alone in that—most of the young Jewish couples around us in Nei Freimann were starting families. They wanted to begin a new generation, to affirm to themselves and to the world that some of the Jewish people had survived and would make new lives for themselves.

In June 1946, we succeeded. That was a great joy, but I was also very worried. I was afraid that it would happen again—that I would never give birth to a live baby.

The baby was due in early February. It was a comfort to me that this time I had my aunt Ronke living in our house. She talked to me and helped to make me feel ready.

During the time I was pregnant, a number of our close friends suggested to Jack and me that we conduct a real Jewish wedding ceremony to declare our love for each other. That wasn't a strict legal necessity for us. We had already obtained three different sets of papers—from the Soviets, the Poles, and the Germans—confirming that legally we were married. But the idea was that a Jewish ritual, as opposed to a civil ceremony, would carry with it more emotion and joy.

It sounded good to both of us, and so we made up a guest list and arranged for an orthodox Hungarian rabbi who was living in our camp to perform the ceremony. It happened in September 1946. I was pregnant, but it was still early enough along—four to five months—that I was not showing. Only a few of our friends knew that I was pregnant. The rabbi definitely did not know.

But a different problem arose which still makes me sad and angry to this day. I was wearing at this time a ring that my parents had given me on some small occasion—I can't even remember what at this point. It was not a fancy or expensive ring, just a little thing with a tiny sparkling stone of some kind. But it meant a great deal to me as a keepsake of my mother and my father. When the Germans were demanding all the Jewish jewelry in the Stolpce ghetto, I specially hid the ring in my brassiere. Once I was with the partisans, I wore it openly again. And I managed to keep it through all the rest of the war.

Well, the Hungarian rabbi who was going to marry us was strictly orthodox. And one of the essential orthodox requirements for a woman who is to marry is to be fully immersed in a *mikvah* [ritual bath]. The immersion is presided over by orthodox Jewish women. And fully means fully—a complete exposure of the skin to the water, with no barriers. The ring had been on my finger for years—and it was a child-sized ring to begin with. I couldn't get it off—it felt as if my finger had grown through and around it. So the rabbi sat me down and took some pliers and broke the ring off my finger so that I would be capable of full purification. He was very cold and matter-of-fact about it. He didn't seem to understand what the ring meant to me, even though I tried to explain. I didn't go so far as to physically resist—I wasn't going to get into a fistfight with the rabbi who was going to marry us!

The wedding ceremony itself, which took place under the

chupah [ritual tent-covering for the bride and groom as they recite their vows], was a very beautiful occasion. It allowed Jack and me to say aloud, before our surviving family members and friends, what we meant to each other.

But still, that episode in the *mikvah,* having my ring broken off my finger in the name of God, stays in my mind. I can see now how well it fitted in with what had become, by that time, my overall attitude toward the Jewish religion. Remember that I had grown up in a home in which the teachings of Judaism were presented as the teachings of God—Judaism and God were one for me. That changed fundamentally during the war. I wanted to marry Jack in a Jewish religious ceremony. I still felt very Jewish, very much a part of the Jewish people. But I could no longer accept that the views of the orthodox rabbis represented the will of God.

In particular, it angered me that, in response to the hatred and madness of the Nazi butchers, so many rabbis took the approach that submission, martyrdom, was the correct religious response. To martyr oneself was to perform a *kiddush ha-Shem* [a sanctification of the Holy Name]. I understand the principle here. The Talmud instructs us to bless God not only for the good on earth, but also for the evil. We are to accept—and love—creation as it is, as God created it. And we are required to behave in a manner consistent with this: to face hardships, and even martyrdom when necessary, is the essence of *kiddish ha-Shem.* So be it.

But those are not teachings that I could accept. I could not see death at the hands of the Nazis as a sanctification. It was a degradation, a horror. I wanted to live, I wanted my family to live.

That is not to say nothing was left of my faith in God. But insofar as I had faith, it was no longer in the God of the rabbis. A few weeks before she was killed, my mother—who had faced the truth that she had not long to live—said to me and my two sisters: "If any of you should survive this war, always know that I will be in Heaven as your protector. I will plead on your behalf with God or, if I cannot go so high as that, with any angel who will listen."

I have always remembered those words. During the war, I did not pray often. And when I did so, I did not pray to God. I could not. God as taught by the rabbis no longer made sense to me, given what was happening before my eyes. But I could pray to my mother Cila. What mother Mary is to Catholics, my own mother Cila is to me. I pray to her to this very day. When I have to undergo surgery, or when Jack or any of the children have a health or personal problem, or even when I am about to board an airplane—I pray to my mother. I have never had a definite response, but sometimes I think she hears me. And I still hope—I can't say I believe, but I *hope*—that when I die I will find my mother waiting for me in Heaven.

JACK

Like Rochelle, I also pray to my mother. In my case, I pray both to God *and* to my mother. It was the voice of my mother Sarah—it *had* to be her voice—that I heard in my dream in the late summer of 1942, the dream that told me Rochelle would be coming to my bunker in the woods. My faith in God was strengthened during the war, not weakened. I felt the horror, but I also felt a sense of being guided.

After the war, in Nei Freimann, I went to the synagogue on the major holidays. I still go, but I don't feel that I have to be in a synagogue in order to pray. And when I am in a synagogue, I don't usually pray with the words that are in the prayer book. I say my own silent prayers, sometimes with my eyes shut. I pray in Yiddish. To God and to my mother. Sometimes I feel as if there is a response.

Just like Rochelle, I hope that my mother is waiting for me in Heaven when I die. I hope that my father is waiting as well. But when I think about this, I think how can it be that a mother is waiting for her child in Heaven. Would this not go back generation after generation, until multitudes of mothers—all the souls of all the mothers who have ever lived—were doing nothing but waiting? Life has to go on, to have a progression.

Still, I hope to see my mother again. But as to what the after-life holds, or if there is an afterlife, no one knows.

But the feelings that both Rochelle and I have for our mothers, for our families, should help you understand what it meant for us to start a family of our own.

The day came for the delivery of our baby—9 February 1947. In the Nei Freimann DP camp, there was no ambulance or other medical vehicle available. We managed to find an American soldier with a jeep who would drive us to the hospital in Munich. It was winter, and snowing hard. When we arrived, it was evening and there were no doctors there, only a handful of nurses, who were also nuns, taking care of the entire hospital.

ROCHELLE

The soldier who drove to the hospital told us that the DP camp regulations required that Jack and Ronke return with him while I checked into the hospital alone. There was no way that I could telephone back to the camp to talk to them—we didn't have a phone in our house, and the official camp offices were closed overnight. So I would be completely alone until the next morning, when Jack would be able to return along with my cousin Sofka.

I started feeling intense contractions around ten o'clock that night. There were two nurses working in the maternity ward. Around me there were a number of German women in various stages of labor. Our beds were separated from each other by little hanging curtains. Whoever started to moan and scream the loudest got the attention of the nurses. They would either say that it wasn't time, in which case there was nothing more they could do—no pain medication—or else they would wheel you on your bed to the delivery room.

When my time came, I asked if there could be a doctor present, because memories of my last birth were still in my head. They told me that there was a standby doctor, not present in the hospital, who could be reached in case of extreme emergency. For any kind of normal birth, it was the nurses only.

They kept telling me, all during the final labor, to push as hard as I could. And believe me I did—I pushed so hard that the blood vessels in my face must have broken, because when

Jack arrived the next morning he told me that I looked like I had the measles.

Our daughter Cecilia was born at one A.M. If it was a girl, Jack and I had decided that we would name her after my mother Cila. So our Cecilia arrived—alive and, as much as they could tell, basically healthy. I was exhausted and sorelieved.

Soon afterward the nurses transferred us into a postdelivery area that was really just a room filled with a dozen or so cots, close together. The main instruction they gave me was to lie flat on my back and not to move for twenty-four hours. Otherwise, they warned me, my uterus wouldn't settle properly.

My baby fell asleep next to me. But suddenly, in the middle of the night, I felt something hot and warm between my legs. I touched there and it was thick with blood. I was terrified that I would bleed to death and that no nurse would hear me— because I didn't have the strength to yell, and I had been told not to move no matter what. It kept going through my mind that if something happened, my baby would have no mother.

But a nurse did come by, and when she examined me she explained that I was all right—the blood and tissue between my legs was only a piece of afterbirth that had not come out during the delivery. During the night it just slid out on its own. The nurse replaced the bloody sheet beneath me with a clean one, and that was it.

I stayed in that postdelivery room for a few days, mostly lying on my back. That was the standard procedure for new mothers back then. I kept looking around me at the other new mothers on their cots in the room. I had my visits from Jack, from Ronke and Sofka, but almost none of the other women had any visitors at all. They were young German girls who should have had friends and family in the city. I couldn't understand it.

Then, one morning, I saw that one of the German girls was preparing to go home. The nurse brought her baby over to her— and the girl started crying, pleading with the nurse to keep the baby, not to make her take it with her. She even tried to get away without the child. Finally, she left with her baby, but I was so confused that I asked the nurse what was going on.

She explained to me that many of the German girls in the ward had gotten pregnant by black American GIs. And in those days, just after the Nazi emphasis on racial purity, it was an absolute disgrace for German girls to bring mixed-race babies—*mischlings,* they were called—home to their families. They didn't want the babies. In fact, so many of the girls tried to sneak out of the hospital without them that they finally had to place guards on duty to prevent it. Otherwise, the hospital would have been left with more abandoned babies than it could have taken care of.

JACK

Having Aunt Ronke there when we brought Rochelle home was wonderful. She taught us the basics of child care—helped us with bathing, cleaning, and taking care of Cecilia when she got colds and other ailments, which was very often.

That was probably due to the fact that our house was drafty and it was the middle of winter. The only heating we had came from a single stove on the main floor. The camp gave us limited supplies of wood and coal and that was it. Much of the wood was wet, and so you had to blow on it until you burst to get it started. Meanwhile, the house would be filling with smoke. So you had to open the window to let out the smoke— and there went much of the warmth. We would heat up water on the stove to bathe Cecilia.

Once a week we would wash diapers. They weren't really diapers, just a bunch of cut-up rag strips, but we called them diapers anyway. The diapers were a special problem for us because they wouldn't dry well in the winter air, and also because there was an extreme shortage of them in our camp. A lot of the time Cecilia just had to go without diapers. We would keep her in a high chair with a hole we had cut in the seat. Underneath was a bucket. That was the best we could do.

Fortunately, I had an aunt in Israel named Pola. She had moved to Israel back in the twenties, before all the misery started in Europe. We found out how to contact her and she was so kind to us—delighted that we were alive and had a new baby. Even though she was herself in need—economic conditions were terrible in Israel at that point—she sent some packages of diapers and baby clothes that were a great help to us.

We also needed to get supplies of powdered baby food. There was a terrible shortage of that as well. But again, having American cigarettes to trade came in handy. I went all over Munich knocking on doors and bartering for baby food.

Somehow Cecilia came through all that. She was sick a lot, but she was also a beautiful and loving baby. And Rochelle and I were parents together, as we had dreamed of being.

Since we had a real family, we wanted to emigrate to the West all the more. We registered with the HIAS agency to go to Israel, as did most of the people living in Nei Freimann. But things still looked difficult in that direction.

But we did find out, through the UNRRA officers, the address of Rochelle's uncle Herman—her father's brother who had emigrated to America after World War I, when he was only fourteen years old. He was a contact for us in America, and having such a contact could make it much easier for us to emigrate there. I should add that there were some Jews in America who showed kindness by signing up as sponsors for refugee Jews to whom they were not related—although that was the exception and not the rule.

We started a correspondence with Uncle Herman, who was at that time living in Saint Paul, Minnesota. Eventually he agreed to sign some papers saying that he would be our sponsor. He would put us up when we first arrived and help us to find work as soon as possible.

ROCHELLE

During that time—the middle months of 1948—we received a very touching letter from Jack's aunt Pola in Israel. She would have been willing to be our sponsor to emigrate there. The British restrictions were suddenly no longer a problem, since Israel had declared its independence in May 1948.

Pola knew we were thinking of Israel and considering going there even if we did obtain a visa to America. So she wrote us to say that, much as she loved Jack and would have welcomed us all there as family, the conditions were so difficult that she had to advise us not to come. Israel was in a state of constant military tension with its neighbors. Jack would have been back in combat again. Jobs and food were scarce.

For our own good, Pola told us, we should forget about her feelings and go to America. We would have a better life there. And that is what we decided.

JACK

After months of waiting, our visas were approved to emigrate to America. But there was one final requirement—Julius, Rochelle, and I all had to be checked out by the CIA to make sure that we weren't criminals or Communists or otherwise unfit to become American citizens.

When we had first registered in the DP camps in Germany, we told the truth about our wartime experiences—that we had served in partisan units, including that of Zorin. Unfortunately, the Soviet influence over partisan efforts in Poland made the CIA suspicious of all partisans, including Jewish partisans, who applied to emigrate to America. The presumption was that if you were a partisan, then you were a Communist.

That was very difficult for us to deal with emotionally. We had fought against the Germans—as Jews—and it was being held against us. Fortunately, we were able to explain the truth of our situation to a sympathetic CIA officer. He assured us that there would be no problems for us, and he kept his word.

It was August 1949 when we got the good news that we could go. Immediately, we packed up our worthwhile belongings. Along with other Jewish refugees with visas, we would go together as a small group by train from Nei Freimann to Bremerhaven, a German port on the North Sea.

We were still worried that something would go wrong at the last minute. Our greatest concern was that Cecilia was not a very healthy baby. She had constant ear and throat infections and had troubles with digestion as well. We were afraid that some official might give us medical exams and then rule that an unhealthy baby like that could not emigrate to America—which of course would have meant that none of us would have gone.

There was a Jewish baby doctor in the Nei Freimann camp, but he didn't have an adequate supply of medications. So we tried to find a German doctor whom we could trust. It was not so easy for us, given what we had heard about the medical experimentation in the death camps.

Concerning those death camps, it has to be understood that, while we were in the woods with the partisans, neither Rochelle nor I—nor anyone else in our midst—knew the truth about the workings of those camps. We thought that Jews were being killed by localized mass murders of the ghetto populations, as had happened in Mir and Stolpce. There were rumors that reached us concerning the camps, but only rumors. It was while we were living in Lodz, after our liberation by the Soviets, that we started to hear the real stories, not only from Russian soldiers, but from some of the camp survivors as well. And then, in Nei Freimann, with so many Jewish refugees as our friends and neighbors, we heard many more stories of life in the camps. Survivors could talk most easily with fellow survivors. They knew that they would be believed and understood. What those Jews told us about what they had lived through made us realize that, compared to the camps, our life in the woods—terrible and difficult as it had been—was a great good fortune, a blessing.

ROCHELLE

At least, in the woods, we had a kind of freedom. We were hunted like animals, but we had succeeded in evading the Nazis, at least for the time being, and now and then we could fight back.

JACK

In Nei Freimann, one of the young men who worked with me in the administration office was a survivor of Auschwitz. He was a good looking man, and several of the refugee Jewish women in our DP camp were showing an obvious interest in him. But all of that changed when the news got out that there was no chance of starting up a family with that man.

He told me the story himself. He had been experimented

on in Auschwitz by the Nazi doctor Joseph Mengele. The history books record the butchery that Mengele called "medical research." The young man was castrated by Mengele. He could not bring himself to be with a woman, and was living in agony. The option open to Rochelle and to me—to start a new family, a new life—was closed for him.

But you can imagine how it made us feel about finding a German doctor for Cecilia.

Finally we did find a female German doctor whom we both felt we could trust. We asked her for some medication that could keep Cecilia's symptoms in check while we were travelling. She prescribed some pills and ear drops. She also told us that sometimes a change in climate . . . crossing the ocean to a new continent . . . could be very beneficial in chronic cases. And in that she proved to be right.

So we went by train to Bremerhaven with our group. We had to wait for some days for our ship to arrive. During that time we rented a room with a German family and kept Cecilia on the medication, trying to get her as healthy as possible for the voyage.

The embarkation date was 29 August 1949. We arrived at the dock expecting to see a big ship. We had been told that the name of the ship was the *General Taylor*, a U.S. Navy ship with a U.S. Navy crew—all of which sounded big to us. When we finally saw the *General Taylor*, we couldn't believe our eyes.

ROCHELLE

It was a little thing, little and old. In the past it had been used to transport ammunition and supplies, not people. When the ship sounded its horn and left port in the early morning, of course we were happy. But as soon as it was out on the open sea, it started rolling and shaking . . . like a toy on the water, not a ship!

JACK

It wasn't a passenger ship and so there were no passenger rooms with bunks. Instead, they set up four different areas within the baggage holds. There were folding cots and blankets provided for the passengers—about two hundred in all, with fifty or so in each sleeping area. There were not only Jews but also refugees from all over Eastern Europe. Meals were served in group shifts in a small galley.

By evening on the first day of the voyage, Rochelle and I were both very seasick. Julius was holding up fairly well.

ROCHELLE

Fairly well! It didn't bother him at all. He was the only one of us who didn't miss a meal the entire voyage. Jack and I basically stopped eating after our first meal on board. We were mostly lying on our cots. We were dizzy and could barely bring ourselves to move. When we did, we held on to the ship railings for dear life. And we were constantly throwing up.

I became so sick and dehydrated that I began to wonder if I would survive the voyage, which would be twelve days long. And then things took an even worse turn. Cecilia's ear infections acted up again—something about the voyage aggravated her illnesses, even with the medication.

I was too sick to take care of her. So it was left to Jack.

JACK

There was a naval officer who was serving as ship's doctor, and I was determined to see to it that Cecilia got the treatment she needed. But as it turned out the doctor had a very inadequate supply of medications and no real knowledge of how to treat a small child. What the doctor did do was to isolate Cecilia—who was two years old at the time—in the ship's infirmary. That was so she would not infect anyone else on board.

Cecilia was the only patient in the infirmary, which was no more than a small room with a couple of cots. And they told Rochelle and me that we couldn't visit her, not even for a few minutes at a time. Occasionally the ship's doctor would try to feed her, but otherwise she was just lying there, often crying from the pain in her ears and throat. It was terrible for us—we couldn't stand the thought of leaving our daughter alone like that. So I set my mind on trying to figure out a way of seeing her.

I found out that the ship was looking for volunteers from amongst the passengers to help with the mopping and cleaning. The usual reward was increased food rations, but that was not my motivation. I couldn't hold down the food they gave me. But I thought that by cleaning regularly I would find opportunities to clean in the infirmary. And that proved to be so.

The first time I came in, I was carrying a mop and a pail. When Cecilia saw me coming she started to cry, maybe out of surprise and happiness. I remember that they had dressed her in a man's pajama top. She was starting to speak and said to me in Yiddish, "*Tate* [Daddy] look! They gave me a shirt to wear just like yours!"

I was carrying with me the medication that the German doctor had prescribed, and I was giving it to her every time I visited. I also talked and cuddled with her, just trying to spend as much time with her as I could so she wouldn't feel alone and abandoned. That went on until we reached New York harbor. Each time I visited with Cecilia, I would tell Rochelle all about it—reassure her that her baby daughter was alive and well. Rochelle worried constantly that Cecilia might not live to see America.

ROCHELLE

I was lying there in my cot, so weak and dehydrated. It seemed like the voyage was going to last for a year.

Then I heard from the people around me that the ship wasn't moving anymore. And that if I went up on deck, I could see the Statue of Liberty.

So somehow I picked myself up and went up on deck. The ship was anchored and stable and the fresh air that I breathed in was the first fresh air for me in days. It was nighttime, but the Statue of Liberty was lit up, and all of the city of New York seemed to be lit up as well. An amazing sight! People talk about the Old World and the New World. From where I was standing on board ship, it really did look like a new world. A world on which the bombs had not dropped. A world in which you could live in peace.

The next morning—12 September 1949—the ship docked and they set up the gangplank for us. We thanked God for letting us off that ship. Finally we were in America!

JACK

It was like having lived with a noose around your neck for years—and then suddenly having that noose cut off and feeling free.

Happy as we were, we also were wondering, of course, what would happen to us in the new country. We didn't know a single word of English. We knew that we were heading for a place called Minnesota, but we had no real idea where that was or how things would be there. We *were* certain that it would take a long time for things to develop for us in that new land— and that was exactly the case.

That morning, in a kind of mental daze, we went through the station that had been set up to check in new immigrants. They checked our documents, stamped them, and then pointed to where our luggage was being unloaded. We were officially allowed into America.

No, we didn't have any idea what to expect. But at least we were away from Germany, away from Poland, away from our past, away from our misery. That in itself was a blessing.

XI

Life in America

ROCHELLE

We were picked up at the immigration center by Shirley and Larry Greenberg. Shirley was the daughter of my uncle Herman Schleiff. They were there to help us find the train to Saint Paul, which was leaving at four o'clock on the afternoon of our arrival. So we had barely arrived in New York harbor and we were immediately due to take a train ride across half of the American continent. It was a bit dizzying.

Shirley and Larry explained to us that we would have to change trains in Chicago, and that Uncle Herman and his wife Rose would be waiting for us at the Saint Paul train station when we arrived.

To pass the time until the train left, Shirley and Larry took us all to the home of some very wealthy Jewish friends of theirs. We had a nice luncheon. Then Cecilia had to go to the toilet, and our hostess showed us where the bathroom was and then showed me how to flush the toilet—she assumed that I had never seen a flush toilet. The same with the elevator in her building—she started to explain to me what it was, without even asking if I already knew, which of course I did.

At that point I realized that those American Jews thought we were like *their parents,* the Jews who arrived in America in the decades before World War I. Those Jews had been mainly rural shtetl-dwellers with no experience of city life. Julius, Jack, and I saw ourselves as intelligent and modern Europeans. But that was not the way we were treated, by and large, by the American Jews whom we met in our first years in America. We understood that they were not intending to hurt our feelings. But that was how it was, and at times it was a barrier.

We had been given a twenty-dollar bill for travel expenses. It was explained to us that it was a lot of money and that we should be careful with it. I didn't yet understand American currency. I tried to buy the cheapest things on the menu in the snack car on the train. I also tried to emulate the Americans around me who would leave a little tip with the waiter. To preserve our money, I thought I would tip with the smallest coin—the dime—which I assumed must be worth the least. So for one of our meals I left three dimes—which by the prices of 1949 made me a big-time tipper. I'm sure the waiter, who had been sizing up our immigrant clothing and the sick daughter on my lap, must have been very surprised by what was left for him.

Somehow we managed to change trains in Chicago without getting lost. But on the second day of our trip, as I looked out the window at the midwestern prairie and saw only trees and fields and rivers and lakes, I started to wonder where we were heading. Was there really a civilization located out here in the midst of all this empty land?

Uncle Herman and Aunt Rose were there to meet us when we arrived, and for our first month or so in America we were guests in their house. Early on Aunt Rose decided to call a reporter from the local newspaper, the *St. Paul Dispatch*, to interview us about our Holocaust experiences and our feelings about coming to America.

JACK

In that article I was quoted as saying that I hoped one day to write a book about what had happened to us. And now, forty-five years later, that is coming about.

ROCHELLE

The article appeared on the front page on 22 September 1949, along with a photograph of the four of us—Julius, Jack, Cecilia, and myself. Unfortunately, the reaction to that article—or at least the reaction that we personally encountered—was very negative and hateful. The article included the address of Herman and Rose's house, and immediately after it ran we started receiving nasty letters and phone calls complaining about dirty Jews being let into America when there wasn't enough to go around for real Americans. Those letters and calls were always anonymous. We kept one of the letters, as a kind of a reminder to ourselves of that experience.

JACK

A few weeks later, the Schleiffs found an apartment for us on the corner of Grand and Dale streets in Saint Paul.

During that time we met with a number of American Jews, and I have to say that it was extremely difficult to talk with them about the Holocaust. Not because we were unwilling or afraid to speak, but because they simply could not understand. Especially when I started to tell them about our time with the Jewish partisans; I had the feeling that they didn't believe what I was saying. Rochelle had the same sense as well. So we decided that we would stop talking about our experiences.

ROCHELLE

It just didn't register with them at all. The horror of it, the magnitude of it—we could talk and talk, but it didn't finally sink in. My uncle Herman asked me once about my parents and other close family members, "How do you know they were all killed? Maybe they're still living there."

There was nothing I could say, not after what I had seen and lived through for all those years.

It wasn't just talking about the Holocaust in particular that was difficult for me. I felt a real difference between myself and the American women of my same age—in their twenties— whom I met. They had sent their men off to the war, but the war hadn't come to the American mainland, to the American cities and streets. And so to me the women seemed like little children in terms of experience and maturity. They were very sheltered, giggly, easy-going . . . they had never been forced to survive under difficult conditions and they didn't know what life could be like. I felt more like their mother than their contemporary.

JACK

Meanwhile, I was looking as hard as I could to find work to support our family. My first job was with a local clothing manufacturer who asked me to work later in the evenings and on weekends. He saw that I was an ignorant immigrant ripe for the picking, and so he cheated me out of the overtime pay that was given to all the American workers who did what I did. When I found out about that I left there immediately.

Eventually, Uncle Herman found for me a job working on the loading dock for a Saint Paul department store called the Golden Rule. People were very nice to me there, even though my knowledge of English was weak early on. I worked hard, and I took the classes they offered in the after-work hours on sales and marketing and other business subjects. I was very interested in those, because I had a dream of starting my own business someday. I even managed to come up with some improvements to the loading operations that increased efficiency and saved the Golden Rule substantial money.

Uncle Herman also found a job for Julius during that time—working as a "spotter" on a graveyard shift in a dry cleaner's. Having the two paychecks was a big help. Julius was supposed to make sure that no stains had been left on the clothes ready for pick-up. He would work all through the night, and then come home and pitch in with housework and child care during the day as well. In our home life, Julius was not only a father to me, but to Rochelle as well. And she treated him with as much kindness as she would have her own living parent. That remained true through all the years to come.

ROCHELLE

In early 1951, I became pregnant with Larry. He was born on 12 October 1951. A gorgeous big boy. We named him Lawrence after my father Lazar and his middle name is Stanley, the closest we could come to Jack's mother Sarah. So with Cecilia named after my mother Cila, we had given our children the names of all three of our parents who had died. And after having lost a baby boy back in 1945, it was such a blessing to have again a chance to raise a boy.

But when I brought the new baby home, I was feeling weak. Unlike the situation with Cecilia in Germany, where my aunt Ronke was there to help, I felt more alone in Saint Paul. Jack and Julius were both working long hours. Cecilia, who was four and a half, was as good a baby sitter as she could be—she really helped, even though she was disappointed to have a brother instead of a sister. But winter was coming and it got very cold in our apartment at night—our landlord was not generous with the heat. And Larry was waking up and crying for bottles every two hours. I was running barefoot back and forth between the kitchen and the crib, filling the bottles and then washing them with boiling water.

I started to have a cough and for a month the cough went on and then got worse. Finally, one night I couldn't catch my breath—it was as if knives were being stabbed in my back. They called an ambulance and took me to the hospital. It turned out that I had double pneumonia. I was there for over a week. Jack had to take time off work—which meant a drop in pay we couldn't afford—to take care of the children. Because Julius was helping as well, Jack could pay me visits in the hospital. He would bring flowers, hug and kiss me, and sit by my bedside feeling very distraught, worrying that I wouldn't recover.

Finally I came back home. The first few days I had to hold on to the walls to walk from the bedroom to the kitchen, I was so dizzy. It was a horrible time, but somehow we lived through it.

Also during that period, the Korean War made it necessary for the U.S. government to begin drafting combat-age men. I was afraid that Jack would be drafted and killed and I would be left alone in a strange new country to take care of two children. But even beyond this, I thought that the Korean War would expand into a World War III. And I didn't want to bring a new baby into a time of world war.

I know I wasn't the only wife and mother in America frightened for her husband and her family during that time. But in my case, my anxieties were obviously aggravated by what I had been through during the last war. I was still having nightmares in my sleep—people would come for us, would start beating me, and I would run. Or they would take us away somewhere, even send us back to Europe. During the day, when I was awake, I had peace of mind that no one would come knocking at the door. But at night it was different.

Aside from those horrors, there were the daily difficulties of figuring out how things worked in America. Learning— and really understanding—the language was an ongoing difficulty. For example, I would take Cecilia to the doctor now and then—Julius would stay home and take care of baby Larry—and while I was waiting for the bus someone would start up a conversation with me. And I would have no idea what they were saying. So whatever they said, I would smile and say, "Yeah."

I felt dumb, as if I didn't belong. I couldn't read the newspaper, couldn't understand the radio, couldn't converse. For Jack, working at the Golden Rule helped him progress in English more quickly. I was at home where we spoke Yiddish. But it was hard both for Jack and for me. We used to go to the library and check out books in Polish and in Russian, just to keep our minds going.

That doesn't mean that we were nostalgic for Poland. We weren't. We were not like other immigrants to America, who had ties to the Old World and were sentimental about what they had left behind. How can you be nostalgic for a place where everyone you had known was either dead or had fled for their lives? Where Jewish life itself had been extinguished?

JACK
I wouldn't want to pay a visit there for even a day.

ROCHELLE
We weren't yet fully at home in America, but we felt safe. We were grateful for that, and for food on the table. The difficulties we faced were minor compared to what we had been through, but sometimes they could hurt deeply.

Cecilia was then at the age where she could go out in the neighborhood and play with the other children. But she spoke very little English, and spoke it with an accent. After all, she had been born in Germany. Her first words had been in Yiddish, and we still spoke Yiddish at home. The other kids would hear her accent and decide not to play with her. I remember that in her kindergarten class, the teacher explained to the class that Cecilia had just come over from Germany and didn't yet speak proper English. But that didn't help. They called her a Nazi because her accent sounded German to them. Cecilia used to come home and ask me, in Yiddish, what a Nazi was. I couldn't tell her then what Nazis really were. I said only that the children didn't like Germans because the Germans had started the war.

Occasionally the language misunderstandings could be funny as well. The check-out lady at the grocery store would always say, in a very smooth and routine way, every time I made a purchase, "Thanks a lot." This sounded to me like "Thanksalad," and I thought she was constantly asking me if I needed salad or why I wasn't buying more of it. Finally I asked her about that, and when it was cleared up we both had a good laugh.

The biggest boost in developing my language skills came from the classes that Julius, Jack, and I took in order to obtain our citizenship papers. Watching television also helped, though. I learned a lot of English from Milton Berle and Eddie Cantor—they were my home teachers!

We all became United States citizens in 1954. Becoming citizens made us all feel much more accepted, more at home, in this country.

JACK

I kept telling Rochelle all through those years that someday I would start a business and that I would do really well at it. But I didn't have the slightest idea what it would be. Still, I had the intuition that in the future something would happen.

ROCHELLE

For my part, I didn't believe him at all. I used to tell him that we had no formal American education, no degrees. We had no capital. And when Jack would talk about his business, it would usually be with the idea that he would be selling something.

And I couldn't at all see him as a salesman. He was a quiet man, kind of shy, not a backslapper. He couldn't even speak English that well. So I couldn't imagine him approaching a stranger and making a sale.

JACK

Finally, in 1957, after almost eight years at the Golden Rule, I quit to start my own gift business. I am proud to say that I accomplished a great deal during my years at the Golden Rule. I received promotions regularly—every six to eight months—and eventually became the assistant vice president of operations for the entire store. I learned a great deal about American business, and the people I worked for there were exceptionally good to me—a new immigrant.

Giving notice at a job where I was happy and accepted was a big decision. But I knew that it was the only way to have the future for my family that I wanted. In a way, living through the Holocaust helped give me the courage to make that decision. I could see that the worst that could happen was that my business would fail and I would have to find a new job. That didn't scare me so much—I had already gone through far worse. But most of my fellow American workers thought that I was crazy to take such a chance. They had calm lives, comfortable homes. They were content.

Before I left the Golden Rule, I decided that it would be appropriate to give notice personally to the president, Mr. Phillip Troy. I wanted to thank him personally for all that the company had done for me, and also to ask him for advice on how to start a business of my own. Mr. Troy wished me the best and assured me that I would succeed if I continued to work as hard as I had at the Golden Rule. He also gave me three key points of advice: (1) Always be fair and honest in dealings with customers; (2) Never make any promises that you cannot keep; and (3) Develop and maintain a top credit rating. I followed all three of those points through all the years to come.

All of this sounds very smooth. But don't misunderstand—it was far from easy for me to go off on my own. It's just that I knew I had to try. Still, not long afterwards I ended up in the hospital with what we thought was a heart attack. The symptoms were severe squeezes in my chest area. It turned out that it was a nervous panic attack—and I've had many more of them in the years since.

But the business developed. I named the company Rochelle's, Inc. This name was not only a way of expressing my love for Rochelle. It also reflected the reality that she worked by my side and helped to build it year after year. Without Rochelle as a partner and an emotional support, I could never have succeeded.

I got a start-up loan from an American friend and paid that friend back in full the very next year. Also, Uncle Herman helped me in obtaining some bank loans by co-signing my applications. I developed into a good salesman. I realized that there was no such thing as learning sales technique in a school classroom. You either had the talent or you didn't. I worked hard because I knew I had a family to support—and the talent developed.

ROCHELLE

People liked him because he was a nice, friendly man.

JACK

For the first fifteen years of the business, we had both wholesale and retail operations. The retail end was always the lesser part. We started out with a little store in a poor location. Uncle Herman helped us with the rent, but things were terribly slow. Rochelle was running the retail store while I worked on the wholesale accounts in a small office and warehouse space. I would sometimes work from eight in the morning to three at night.

But we were starting to see results. In 1957, we could afford to leave our apartment and to buy a house. It had a yard for the children to play in. It felt like a real home.

ROCHELLE

I felt awful about working in that store in those first years. Julius was helping by staying at home and watching the kids. But it was still terrible to be away from them. And we weren't making much money. So I was away from my family and sometimes there was eight dollars in gross sales for the day—nothing! And at night I would come home and cook and clean.

But we kept on. We had to. And finally, again with the help of Uncle Herman, we could afford a better location—the lobby of a major Minneapolis office building—and things got better.

As a matter of fact, I became quite a popular figure amongst our customers. We had lots of regulars who would come in for cards and gifts for all the occasions in their lives. They would confide their marital troubles to me, even their secret affairs. I talked with everyone. I had a strong accent, but somehow they not only understood me, they trusted me as well.

JACK

In December 1974, my father Julius died at the age of ninety. He had lived with us for all the years we had been in America. We never once considered putting him in a nursing home. And during all that time, Julius not only helped to raise our children but acted as the bookkeeper for my business. He kept handwritten ledgers in a beautiful script and he was always accurate.

The business grew to the point where I finally felt I had succeeded in making a good life for my family. We sold the retail store in 1973. But the wholesale continued—a line of imported gifts from around the world that I sold to stores all across America. I employed twelve travelling salespeople, as well as three employees who helped me run the large central warehouse in Minneapolis. Rochelle and I would personally fly to the Orient—Hong Kong, Thailand, Singapore, and other ports—to choose many of our gift lines. In order to better compete with other wholesalers, we also began to design our own giftware items and to arrange for their manufacture.

Rochelle made friends for us wherever she went. And somehow, we managed to come up with items that would appeal to American customers. That was something I had a talent for. Uncle Herman and Aunt Rose were always proud of what Rochelle and I managed to achieve together.

In 1991, I finally closed down the business and retired. I thought that I would miss it, that I would find too much time on my hands. But instead I am relieved to be rid of the worries.

ROCHELLE

Both Jack and I had come from well-to-do families, and we had both been reduced to garbage scroungers during the war. We knew how we wanted to live and what we wanted to give to our children. And we thought that we were smart enough, and our desire strong enough, so that we could do it.

In the way that we raised our children, we were more lenient than most American parents we knew. To have children was a miracle for us. We didn't let our parents down . . . their bloodline was living on. The Nazis had destroyed so many Jewish families, but some at least had survived!

We didn't keep our children on fixed allowances. We gave them as much money as we could—and we were proud that we could give so often. If they wanted to stay up until nine o'clock instead of eight o'clock, big deal! If they wanted to go to a movie, let them go to a movie. There were no regular chores that had to be finished to earn privileges. Let them enjoy themselves and be happy.

I remember that when I first came to this country, I would listen to the American women talk about their weddings and baby showers. They were always family occasions—all the family coming together. It made me so jealous, especially when I would see mothers and daughters together. I couldn't stand to be in their company. I felt that they had everything that I was supposed to have but never could. Where was my mother, my father, my sisters?

All the love that Jack and I had for our lost parents, our lost families, went into our children. At least our children would be normal, not deprived in the ways that we had been. Our kids wouldn't dress any worse, live any worse than American kids. It would all even out with our kids.

The years have passed. Cecilia graduated from the University of Minnesota, while Larry earned degrees from the University of Michigan and from Harvard Law School. We have been blessed now with three grandchildren, David, Danny, and Sarah. In America we have had a good life.

JACK

And so that is our story. We've told you what we can.

Just one thing I want to be sure about. That people who read this should understand how much I love Rochelle.

An Afterword on the "Second Generation"

LAWRENCE SUTIN

I have been asked by some readers of my parents' story if I could add a few thoughts about being a child of Holocaust survivors. The issue of the "second generation" seems to evoke interest, particularly with respect to the nature of the psychological, moral, and spiritual legacies bequeathed by Holocaust survivors to their children.

I shall try to address these legacies as best I can in my own case. But first I must make plain my abiding discomfort with the very terms "survivor" and "second generation."

There is a strong tendency, in writings on the Holocaust by historians, philosophers, psychologists, and other concerned observers, to speak of the Holocaust "survivor" as a single, generalizable category. These observers usually do take care to distinguish the different ways in which survival occurred and the different postwar adaptations made by survivors. But the impression persists that the Holocaust "survivor" is a *type* of humankind who can exemplify heroism, or tragedy, or trauma, or other.

To a limited extent, I too can accept the "survivor" as a type. In my "Preface" I wrote: "Death in the Holocaust was omnipresent; the millions of Jews who died and the small living remnant are One, but for the accidents of fate." It is fitting and honorable that the Holocaust be a subject for intensive historical inquiry. It is a ghastly but necessary task to lay out the facts of the Nazi genocide and the fates of those caught up within it. It is permissible to ask how those who survived managed to do so, given what they faced.

Yet it is an obscene mode of inquiry to seek out—by way of character analysis—the alleged underlying reasons as to why some "survivors" lived while so many were butchered. It is obscene because it leads to the passing of shallow moral and psychological judgments on persons and circumstances that are beyond the ken of those who pretend (it is always a pretense by those who were not themselves present) to judge. It is further obscene because it implies that there was some sort of survival-of-the-fittest "Nazi justice" at work in the fate of those who lived and those who died. The reality was a systematic plan of mass murder that made *all* Jews in Europe—survivors included—its victims.

It should also be realized that, in the aftermath of the Holocaust, the Jewish survivors have led anything but unitary lives. I have had the privilege of meeting many survivors over the years. They have not seemed anything "of a type" to me. Some of them loved life intensely, in spite of what they had experienced during the Holocaust. Some of them were plainly living out an enduring agony. Some wished to express their feelings and share their stories. Others would never broach the subject. I could list many further differences, but suffice it to say that they are human beings, that their lives have diverged from one another in ways that matter. In sum, the category of "survivor" only goes so far.

Here, of course, lies the value of Holocaust narratives told by the survivors themselves. These narratives confirm that, within the maelstrom of death, the lives lost or spared were *individual* lives that cannot be encompassed by the horrific statistic of "six million." It is through reading these narratives that we can comprehend—in a vital, albeit radically limited manner—what it might mean to be subject to the forces the Nazis unleashed. This effort at comprehension must lead us to ask pointedly unpleasant questions as to who we, as humans, really are and of what we are capable. It is ourselves, and not the survivors, whom we can most usefully subject to scrutiny.

Just as there is no fixed category of "survivor," so too there is no such thing as a unitary "second generation." At least one basic division has suggested itself to commentators on the children of survivors—those whose parents spoke of what had happened, and those who did not. In my "Preface," I allowed that I was grateful to be in the former category. I believe that it eased what would have been an omnipresent tension. But I do not wish to be seen as passing judgment upon those survivors who did not speak. Disclosure or silence by the parent (or parents) was a critical choice, no doubt, but I would not conclude that it was, in all or even most cases, determinative of the child's life to come.

Therefore I cannot write of Holocaust "survivors" and "children of survivors" (though at times I may betray the temptation), only of the relations between my parents and myself.

Nor can I hope to satisfy those readers for whom survivors and their children are a tantalizing diagnostic puzzle. Acquaintances who know of my parents' past sometimes ask what I think it "did" to me. Now and then they even offer prescriptive labels, such as "transferred trauma" and "survival syndrome." If I question the meaning and aptness of these labels, I run the risk of being adjudged as "in denial."

It was hardly avoidable, then, that I do some reading of my own in the available psychological literature on the "second generation." The necessity for such a literature—that is, the searing psychological struggles that too many children of survivors have undergone—is an agonizing one to consider. The Holocaust does not end with the lives of those who experienced it. I can testify to this. The responses of the children will differ, but a response there surely must be. The published studies display a greater methodological caution than is shown by the casual questioners in my life. Here is a representative quotation, which has the further merit of linking the pressures upon the "second generation" to a broader aspect of human existence:

> As anticipated, not all themes are present or dominant in each [second generation] case, yet there is a common base—a *survival complex*—that is transmitted to children. Most, if not all, developmental phases are tinged with issues of survival. Perhaps this complex is as universal to human nature as Freud

thought the Oedipus complex to be. Thus, it may become a source of either strength or pathology.*

Well, it certainly may. In my family, survival was not—is not—taken for granted. I did grow up hearing stories of hatred and murder. That hatred was directed not only at my parents, or at Jews of their generation, but against Jews of all times and places, against the fact of Jewish existence itself. Against me. Nazis and "neo-Nazis" (a marvelous term, this, implying that there has been some sort of progression in Nazi "thought," as opposed to the reality of an ongoing cultlike adherence to ignorant hate) and their sympathizers want me dead to this day. I am quite safe in America for the time being. But if you suddenly transport the members of my family and myself to Germany, or Poland, or Russia, or Latvia, or Lithuania—to name only the most prominent modern day locales in which neo-Nazi movements and sentiments are in rousing good health—then suddenly we are at risk. To me, these are plain facts.

As for the "survival complex" becoming "a source of either strength or pathology," that is true insofar as it goes, but the dichotomous structure is misleading. It may become a source of strength, *and* of fear, *and* of fury, *and* of anguish ("pathology"), *and* of many things more. My passion in working on this book was that the story of my parents would thereby survive—and that it give strength not only to myself, from my work on it, but also to my daughter, when someday she will read it with comprehension and wonder.

I will go on now to some memories of growing up within my family. Hereafter the reader will have to apply his or her own diagnostic analyses to the bare bones of my account.

My father and my mother were both acutely aware of what they had lived through. So was I. It was a pervasive fact of life in our home. My sister Cecilia, in a speech she delivered recently to her synagogue congregation, has accurately described the

---

* Judith S. Kestenberg, M.D., "Survivor-Parents and Their Children," in *Generations of the Holocaust,* Martin S. Bergmann and Milton E. Jucovy, eds. (Columbia University Press, New York, 1990), p. 102.

sense we both shared of growing up in a family decimated by death:

> When my friends visited their grandparents, aunts, uncles, and cousins, I would think of the relatives I never got to know—because they were brutally murdered in the prime of their lives. All the special relationships with my grandmothers, my aunts, my mother's father—all of these had been stolen from me.
>
> As I got older, I would hear my friends' parents look forward to school reunions, talk of old boyfriends and girlfriends, and the fun times they had in college. There was so much they hadn't experienced. I often wished that I could share my own happy times with them, that I could somehow give them back the years of fun and freedom that they had provided for me.
>
> I am so grateful that my own sons, David and Danny, have grandparents, and that they have been spared the emptiness I felt at their age.

But there *was* one elder relative who had survived, and whose presence in our home gave both to my sister and myself the sense of extended family that we craved. This was my grandfather Julius, who possessed as sweet a disposition as I have encountered in my lifetime.

My grandfather and I shared a bedroom, and he cared for us, in the role of a third parent, through our childhood and teenage years. He died when I was twenty-three. His preferred diet was a remarkable one for a man who lived to age ninety. He especially enjoyed butter-and-sugar sandwiches and pan-fried fatty meats. There were two ritual medications in his daily routine—a spoonful or two of Phillips' Milk of Magnesia, and a shot (or, now and then, two) of schnapps. The schnapps was always imbibed between four and five in the afternoon, and was accompanied by appreciative lip smacking. Julius did not otherwise consume alcohol, except for wine or cherry liqueur during our family festival meals for the major Jewish holidays.

In all our years of family intimacy, I cannot recall a single occasion in which my grandfather lost his temper. When he found it necessary, on rare occasions (the rarity due to his forebearance, rather than my goodness) to discipline me, it took the form of a gentle pleading. His face—with skin that stayed smooth through all his years—would grow slightly redder, but his smile, a relaxed and almost moony smile, would only grow broader. His discipline, as he saw it, was never intended to deny me anything—only to protect me. It worked very well, by and large. I loved him and hated to displease him. He did not—this is how I felt it—*deserve* to be disobeyed. I disobeyed often enough, nonetheless.

My grandfather did have a quiet stubborn streak. This showed itself most strikingly in his attitude toward the English language. In twenty-five years of living in America, he never learned to speak English—or, perhaps more accurately, he never consented to speak it. Yiddish was his language; he subscribed by mail to a Yiddish newspaper published in New York City, *The Jewish Daily Forward,* for which Isaac Bashevis Singer, amongst others, wrote. Julius certainly understood a bit of English, as he would watch American television now and then and would seem to comprehend at least some of the English-language conversations swirling around him.

But Yiddish was his true tongue. We all spoke it in our household, sometimes mixing in English here and there—my sister and I did this more often, as we were and are far less fluent in Yiddish. I should clarify that English became the dominant language in my family as we children grew older and my parents grew fluent in the speech of their new land. But when matters became serious or emotional, Yiddish was the means of communication. The choice to switch to it was not a conscious one—an automatic instinct, perhaps an instinct of survival, prevailed. Yiddish is an extraordinarily rich language with respect to personality types and states of mind. To speak in Yiddish is to philosophize whether you wish to or not. I am grateful to have some knowledge of it in my bones.

I have said that my grandfather was a "partial" exception to the awareness of the past—the Holocaust—that was so strong in my parents. I say "partial" because I know that the years left their mark on him. Quite literally, his world was destroyed. But he spoke of it so seldom, and so briefly when he did so, that I cannot in honesty tell you what feelings he had about it. All I can say is that the serenity of the last decades of his life—and, mind you, he never fell into senility—was a kind of miracle of practical wisdom. It puzzled even my parents, who would joke that they wished they could have some of that peace of mind for themselves. It can be summed up in a remark Julius would make when he was asked why he did not attend synagogue on Yom Kippur. Yom Kippur is the most sacred day of the Jewish year, a day of penitence during which God inscribes the names of all Jews in the respective Books of Life and of Death. Julius would say (in Yiddish, of course), "Well, maybe if I'm not there in the synagogue, where He can see me, God will forget altogether that I'm still alive." This approach, in my grandfather's case, worked wonderfully.

As for my parents, the Holocaust remained visible in them. There was a tension, a fierceness, a constant intensity of feeling they manifested that was different from the other American adults whom I met growing up, as teachers or as the parents of other friends.

This intensity frightened me. I knew, early on, the basic facts of their lives. Now and then there were Nazis in my dreams. The Nazis wanted to kill me. The indifferent world (and indifferent it *was* in the years before and during World War II, when much could have been done to save Jewish lives) was willing to let me die.

And yet, this fear was mingled with, even superseded by, a sense of pride and of hope. My parents had not only survived, but they had also fought back. That in itself was a rare and blessed opportunity in the hell of wartime Poland. But that was not all. Oh how we *loved,* as children, to hear my father tell of his dream of my mother, how she would come to him in the woods, how they would love each other and spend their lives together. The dream had the magic of a prophecy. Life, we children learned, could be filled with wonders, *actual* wonders, rare though they might be.

My parents love for us was so strong, so passionately held—utterly unconditional, in a sense. It would never be withdrawn, no matter what we did. In the aftermath of the Holocaust, family was sacred to my parents and—because of the impassioned way they cared for us—became so to my sister and to myself as well. Within the bonds of family we were secure. Our talk was free and open. We laughed a great deal. We could bring up any topics with our parents, and we could be assured that we would receive direct and honest responses. My sister has offered this apt and paradoxical summation, "My parents managed to give us a normal, happy life—even though they had probably forgotten what 'normal' was."

There were tacit conditions to this love from our parents—conditions that affected not the fact of their love, but the comfort and happiness (the Yiddish word *naches* covers the feeling of gratified love that I mean here) with which they could bestow it. These conditions ensued because the sacredness of family meant that all youthful signs of independence were viewed with a mixture of pride (my parents wanted their children to grow up strong and happy and sure of themselves) and trepidation (when family loyalty was threatened by autonomous decision making or—more terrifying still—outright adolescent rebellion and defiance).

My father is, but for rare occasions, a relatively silent man. He worked long days and nights to support us. Adore his children as he does, he was always tentative in playing games with us in our youth and is to this day more comfortable in showing physical affection to our mother. She is the polestar of his life. But for one brief and painful exception, he has never taken a trip without her—not in all the years of conducting his sales business. His tender name for her is *maisele*—mouse—which originated with my mother's love for cheese. *Maisele* is the name we grew up with—"Rochelle" was the signal of an awkward formality imposed by the presence of strangers.

My father is a patient man who is, at the same time, ravaged by nerves. The wisdom he has learned in the course of his life is at odds with the damage done to him during the years of hell. For all his considerable achievements as a businessman, he is singularly free of greed or self-importance. He recognizes that money is an important means of survival, but he is also aware that it is no indicator of character and no guarantor of genuine happiness. His generosity, not only to his family, but to his friends, to employees, and to charitable causes, is a constant of his character—it does not depend upon a rosy mood or a canny plea. He certainly can and does explode into rages. The cause here is almost always something that he has perceived as a threat—or an insufficient showing of respect—toward my mother. If, during my years of growing up, I disagreed with my mother on any matter of importance, my father would storm into the fray. Not only would he argue on her behalf—that was a given—but he would also express loud and outraged disbelief that I would dare to cause my mother pain. *Nothing* that I could want or believe was worth that, in his view.

My mother never seemed, to me, to require quite as much protection as my father felt she did. She is, like my father, an extremely intense person, and is capable of rages and silences of her own. But these are very rare. For the most part, my mother radiates joy within the intimate bounds of our family life. She is the igniter of the best of our times together—the determined one who brings up the topics that need discussion, the daring one who laughs and teases with the greatest glee. My mother has an exceedingly sharp and swift sense of humor. This never bothered me, but it certainly has startled some rigidly nice persons who have met her. My mother will say what she thinks, and she happens to find a great deal of human behavior misguided, deluded, or hypocritical. Her best lines are generally in Yiddish, a language that delights in earthiness, which means that—in English, out of context—they can sound cruder than they are.

For example, what does she think of my career as a writer? Because she loves me and fears for me, and because she knows that (1) writers usually make a precarious living; and that (2) most people don't give a damn about what writers have to say, though they may fervently pretend to do so, my mother communicates her feelings on my profession by describing it, with a Yiddish-Russian phrase, as resembling a *"philosof na iaitzach"*—a philosopher sitting and scratching his balls. Does this offend you? It shouldn't. It is a caricature, apt enough in many respects. In my own case, I see it not only as a challenge that I have accepted, but as a useful curative to the pretensions that abound as to the "writer's role" in society. And when, as I write this, I imagine my mother's face as she offers that description, I start to laugh. By the by, even though I have written this book on my mother's life, her opinion of writing as a livelihood remains unchanged. She said once to me, during the long course of our interviews, "Better you should find a subject that could make you some money." The rewards for this book are certainly not economic—trust me on that. And my mother knows this, and included in her seemingly callous statement is a sense of doubt that people will really take in what she has said in the narrative, a sense of respect for the work I have done, and a sense of concern that I not do it too often, lest my wife and child suffer financially.

Having detailed my mother's acerbity, I should add that most people who meet her adore her. They enjoy not only her humor but also her evident kindness. She is a gracious hostess and a sumptuous cook. To be invited to her home for a meal is to enjoy a feast of Jewish delicacies—kugel and kreplach, chopped liver and kasha varnishkes, gefilte fish and chicken soup with knaidlach, and on and on. Of course, true to the Jewish mother stereotype, she pushes the food hard, but this has become less frequent in recent years, as health consciousness has begun to overcome memories of starvation. People not only wolf down my mother's food, they confide in her—and not just close friends, but also the beautician who does her hair, the handymen who come to work on her house, the customers who loyally patronized her gift shop in downtown Minneapolis for so many years. The very joy and recklessness of her humor convinces people that here is a human being who will listen to them with understanding, without fixed prior judgment. And they are right. My mother has seen too much to judge too quickly or too harshly. Her standards of what is truly contemptible are very high—after all, they were set by the Nazis themselves.

It was obvious, both to my sister and to myself, that, in a converse sense, the standards of judgment to be applied to my parents as Holocaust survivors required special care. We knew this even as children. It was unmistakable, a task we were given, a means of expressing our love, and, at times, a trial to our souls. My sister described it this way in her speech:

> I have always had an exceptionally close relationship with my parents. I feel like I understand them and why they act and feel the way they do. And . . .
> —if they sometimes cry a little more than others, they're entitled;
> —if they sometimes worry a little more than others, they're entitled;
> —if they cling to their family a little more, they're entitled.
> There are many kinds of heroes in this world: military, athletic, political. But there are also heroes of the spirit. I think my parents, and other survivors like them, are heroes.

It is true that my sister and I saw our parents as heroic for having lived through what they did. It is also true that we understood why, at times, they were so tense, so clinging, so demanding of our love and loyalty. But neither the sense of their heroism nor any understanding we could muster could shield us from the recurrent buffeting of growing up as "American children" in a Holocaust survivor household. Many of our very typical problems—fitting in at school, getting along with our friends, discovering our identities as adolescents—were all but incomprehensible to our parents, given the Holocaust standards of pain and struggle against which, *reflexively,* they measured the complaints of their children. The refrain that we heard over and over again was, "If that is your biggest problem, you should kiss the ground in gratitude." Given how much of their own adolescence and young adulthood was stolen from them, is it any wonder that my parents were less than adept in acknowledging the angst of our growing up in the safety of a suburb?

There was, in my case, much pain and desperation that I could not share, for all their apparent willingness to listen. Their response to me was almost always blunted by the fact that what worried me seemed ridiculous to them. Of course, in retrospect, much of it seems ridiculous *to me* as well. But that isn't the point. Growing up *is* a ridiculous process, and it was little help for me to be constantly reminded that it could have been worse—much, much, much, much worse. That approach, in my case, amounted to pouring gasoline on the fire. I rebelled all the harder during my teenage years in the sixties, on the simple grounds that my options seemed either to be rebellion or engulfment by my parents' past. My sister was far more patient than I was in this regard.

I can recall one brief incident of mutual rage between my mother and me that gives a sense of how little was needed to touch deep emotions on both sides. I was eighteen or so at the time, and was sitting talking—arguing—with my mother in our family den. I was wearing worn jeans with a tear in the right knee—a style that has since become an enduring favorite amongst American adolescents. In sheer frustration at seeing me dressed as if I couldn't afford decent clothes—at seeing me ungrateful and defiant despite all that she had and could and yearned to provide for me—my mother crooked her finger in the rip and tore my pant leg straight down to my ankle, rendering it unwearable. We stared at each other. I ran out of the den, out of the door of the house. I have no memory of where I went or even if I was gone for long. I was furious, but my mother's point prevailed within me. My torn jeans were a mere costume of life experience. I would have nothing to offer my parents or myself until I had lived a life that was truly my own. And so I tried.

The simple fact of my growing older has healed many of the rifts of those times. I have made choices that my parents can understand only with difficulty. I have, often enough, paid the steep price of incurring their pain and their anger in exchange for becoming the person I have become. I do not suffer from the illusion that I was always right in what I did. But I do know that, had I not broken away when I did and as long as I did—I left home for college when I was sixteen and lived in places far from my parents until I was twenty-five—I could not have respected myself. I also know that had I not, in the years since, returned to my home city of Minneapolis and lived in proximity with them, I would have lost precious legacies: the pleasure of their company, the sustenance of their wisdom, and the recognition (one that comes to many of us, if we persist with our families) that the best of myself is rooted in the best of my parents.

Please understand that never, not even in the nine years of rebellion and exile, did I lose sight of the fact that my parents are remarkable persons—and not only because they had survived the Holocaust. Let one example suffice. In 1971, my father—by then well into middle age—was walking to his car in a shopping mall parking lot when he noticed that a large, agitated man was grappling with a younger woman and forcing her into a car. My father quietly came up behind the man and then, pretending that a pen in his coat pocket was a gun, stuck the point in the man's back and demanded that he raise his arms. The man obeyed. My father marched him into a nearby store, where a security guard was summoned to take over. The man was ultimately arrested and convicted, and the woman he had assaulted was spared the worst. My father's explanation for his action, which put his own life at risk, and could have brought chaos and agony unto his family, was that when he saw what was happening, he thought that it could have been his own daughter being forced into the car.

I would like to record a final memory as regards relations between survivors and their children. I offer it as a warning for those who would seek to understand either generation too quickly.

I remember my bar mitzvah. The American rabbi who presided did not know me or my family very well. This was understandable. We had not regularly attended his services. But still, a bar mitzvah was a rite of passage that mattered to me and to my parents. It was, all of us in the family felt, a happy occasion to come.

Well it came, and the rabbi—who knew that my parents were survivors—chose to focus, in his Sabbath morning sermon, on the tragedy of the Holocaust and the fact that so many of our family members could not be present because they had been murdered.

I was sitting up on the platform, to the left of the rabbi. As he spoke I watched my mother and my father cry while my grandfather (taking in as much English as he needed) looked anguished and my sister writhed in discomfort, not knowing how to console the adults around her.

Even as a thirteen-year-old, I knew that the rabbi meant well, and also that he was behaving very badly, without genuine understanding. For him, the Holocaust was an appropriate topic for a sermon—and the presence of my parents made for a convenient rallying cry to the American-born congregants "Never to forget!" For my family, its emphasis was a gratuitous and banal infliction of pain (as if we had need to be reminded of our dead!) on an occasion when we felt that simple joy was what we deserved.

There is, for both survivors and their children, a constant inner turmoil between what cannot be forgotten and what must be laid aside for the sake of life. There can be no final *stasis* here. Memory does not come and go according to our conscious wishes. And the needs of the living have an urgency all their own.

Which brings me to the "third generation," the children of the children. When I speak of the needs of the living, I speak first and foremost of them.

At the time I write this, my daughter Sarah—named for my father's mother Sarah—is three years old. I have already said that someday I want her to read this book, to take the lives of her grandparents into her own life, to understand that the world is capable of the Holocaust, to recognize that even good people suffer from a craving to ignore evil.

But I am also a fatuous parent. I want her to possess all of this knowledge without paying the price of pain. I will take care not to make the Holocaust the presence in her life that it was in mine. I will try to shield her from ever experiencing my struggles with memory.

I may fail in these aims.

But this I know. I will love her with the ferocity with which my parents loved me.

Notes and Acknowledgments

The writing and publication of this book has been blessed by the welcome and vital contributions of a number of persons. My parents and I would especially like to thank the following:

My sister, Cecilia Sutin Dobrin, prepared typed transcriptions of the extensive taped interviews. Beyond this, the emotional support that she and her husband Steven provided for this project was an invaluable motivating force.

My dear wife Mab read through several drafts of the book and fostered the process of recording the truth.

Our agent, Gloria Loomis, took on this project well knowing that it would prove to be a marketing challenge. Her dedication and enthusiasm were key factors in making the book a reality.

Two good friends, Randy Pink and Mary Logue, provided insightful advice that helped shape the structure of the book.

Scott Walker, the former director of Graywolf Press who acquired the book, showed his remarkable dedication by offering to read an early version of the manuscript even after he had moved on to new responsibilities. His incisive comments led to further interviews with my parents and a deepened final narrative.

Fiona McCrae, the new Graywolf Press director, has been a second great source of editorial support. Her comments on the "Afterword" were especially valuable.

Gordon Thomas, Graywolf associate director, offered a rare degree of kindness at a time when it was badly needed. Janna Rademacher, marketing manager, has been a pleasure to work with. Anne Czarniecki provided meticulous copyediting of the whole. Erik Saulitis made the taking of the back cover photo a joy.

My parents' memories are their own. In the course of my background preparations for the interviews, I read a good many volumes on the Holocaust. Two which proved especially helpful were by Nechama Tec, a historian and sociologist who has written extensively and excellently on the Holocaust in Poland. *In the Lion's Den: The Life of Oswald Rufeisen* (Oxford University Press, 1990) is a full-scale biography of the remarkable man of whom my father speaks in Chapters III and IV of this book. *Defiance: The Bielski Partisans* (Oxford University Press, 1993) recounts the history of a Jewish fighting group in the Nalibocka Forest led by the Bielski Brothers; my parents served in a similar but smaller group led by Simcha Zorin.

For the sake of serious researchers, I note two points as to which my parents offer information which differs from that presented by Tec. (1) My father understood, through rumors in the Mir ghetto underground, that Rufeisen would—if the underground members made a successful escape—thereafter lead the German police into an ambush waged by those same underground members. Rufeisen, who was interviewed extensively by Tec for *In the Lion's Den,* did not mention such an ambush, though he did recall that he planned to give the underground information as to subsequent Nazi police movements and, ultimately, to join the underground himself. The ambush rumor—believed by my father and at least some others in the Mir underground—may not have reflected Rufeisen's precise intentions. (2) In *Defiance,* Tec reports that the fighting group led by Simcha Zorin suffered "heavy losses" during the August 1943 Nazi assault on the Nalibocka Forest. My parents, who were both members of this group, recall that there were few losses (see Chapter VIII herein).

In the printed narrative, bracketed language [ ] indicates an explanatory insertion by the editor. In a few instances not designated, first-name pseudonyms were used for certain persons— all Jewish—who play secondary roles in the narrative.

Index

A

Abram, 165–166
Anti-Semitism, in Poland, 5–6, 9, 14–16, 30, 154, 208
Anti-Semitism, in Russia, 21, 80, 208
Antonina, 150–151
Auschwitz, 188

B

Baranowicze, 18–19, 27–28, 161, 164
Belorussia (White Russia), 1
Benienson, Rachel, 1
Bergmann, Martin S., 208
Beria, Lavrenti, 30
Berlin, 163, 167, 170–173
Bielski brothers, 107, 118
body weight, attitude toward in Poland, 19
Bremerhaven, 187, 189

C

Carpathian Mountains, 10
Charkow, University of, 1
Chevre Kaddishe (Brotherhood of the Kaddish), 6, 169
Chenstochowa, 165
CIA (Central Intelligence Agency), 187
Ciechocinek, 10
comsomoles (young Communist pioneer groups), 30

D

Dobrin, Daniel, 204, 209
Dobrin, David, 204, 209
Donbass, 162
dowry customs, 3–4
Druskeniki, 10

E

Einsatzgruppen (mobile killing units), 81
Ephraim, 105

F

Fania, 69, 85–86, 88
Feldafing DP camp, 173–174

G

Garmizo, David, 169–170
Garmizo, Nechama, 169–170
Garmizo, Pola, 186–187
General Taylor (U.S. Navy vessel), 189
Gittel, 100, 103–104, 106–107
Greenberg, Larry, 193
Greenberg, Shirley, 193

H

HaBoker (The Morning), 176
Hashomer Hatzair (Young Guard), 15, 52

Hein, Reinhold, 54, 57, 59–60
HIAS (Hebrew Immigrant Aid
    Society), 170, 173–175, 186
Hitler, Adolf, 81
Hitler-Stalin pact, 12
Horodej, 62, 164

I
Israel, 9–10, 16, 163, 171, 174, 176,
    186
Iweniec, 150–152

J
Jewish Daily Forward, 210
Jewish partisans: 61–68, 85–86,
    92–98, 107–108, 110–114,
    117–124, 129–130, 132–133,
    136–147, 149
Jucovy, Milton E., 208
Jude yellow star patches, 22, 37
Judenrat, Mir, 48, 55, 57
Judenrat, Stolpce, 37

K
Kagan, Sarah, 156
Kagan, Simon, 124, 156, 160, 176
Katia, 140
Katowice, 167–168
Kestenberg, Judith S., M.D., 208
KGB (Soviet secret police),
    24–25
Krieger, Eva, 178
Krieger, Sam, 178
Kruglice, 35, 155, 161
Kurluta family, 49–51, 61–62,
    90–91, 109

L
Landsberger Zeitung, 176
Leah, 165–166

Lenin, Vladimir, 2
Liss, 93–94
Lodz, 165–169, 179, 188
Luze, 84
Luze River, 82

M
Malishansky family, 156
Maryan, 101
Mengele, Joseph, 189
Minsk, 1–2, 33, 80, 117, 122,
    149–150
Mir, 13–14, 18–20, 21–23, 26,
    47–55, 57–60, 62, 69, 85, 95,
    111, 117, 139, 155–160, 188
Mir yeshiva, 13–14, 48
Mir *zamek* (Mirski Castle),
    51–52, 54–55, 57–60
Miranke, 65, 112, 116
Molotov, Vyacheslav, 30
Moshe, 116–117
Mottel, 72–74

N
Nalibocka Forest, 82, 113, 118,
    129–130
Nei Freimann DP camp,
    175–179, 182–183, 187–188
Niemen River, 35, 73–76
Nieswierz, 62–64

O
"Oifun Pripichok" (Yiddish
    song), 109
Ostroda, 151

P
Palestine, 9, 19–20
"Papirosun" (Yiddish song),
    109

parachutzistn (parachutists),
  82–84
Petrovich, 86–88
Piesochna, 93–94
politruks (Sovet political advisors), 30–31, 62–64
Prass, Ashke, 28
Pressman, 122, 125, 139–140
Prussia, 151
Puchowicze, 12

R

Rassenschande (race defilement),
  79
Resnik, Dov, 53
Rochelle's, Inc., 201–203
Roosevelt, Franklin Delano, 164
Rufeisen, Oswald 52–54, 57–61
Rubizewicze, 13
Russian (Soviet) partisans,
  34, 55, 57–58, 75–84, 87–88,
  117–118, 120–121, 123–124
Rydel, Ronke, 178–179, 184–185,
  197
Rydel, Sofka, 178, 184

S

St. Paul Dispatch, 194
Schekele, 42–43
Schleiff, Cila (born Benienson),
  1–11, 24, 29–31, 34–43, 44–45,
  181–182, 184, 203
Schleiff, Ethel, 3, 43
Schleiff, Herman, 9, 186,
  193–196, 201–202
Schleiff, Lazar, 2–12, 24–26,
  29–32, 34–37, 39–40, 43, 155,
  203
Schleiff, Miriam, 4–5, 11, 41,
  44–45, 203
Schleiff, Oscar, 2, 133–136,
  150–152, 156–157

Schleiff (Sutin), Rochelle: early
  religious training, 6–7;
  education, 8, 30–31; parental discipline, 10–11; early
  meetings with Jack, 28–30;
  first encounter with dead
  bodies, 35; solitary journey
  to Stolpce, 35–36; in Nazi
  forced labor group, 38–39,
  42–47; asks after fate of her
  dead father, 39–40; witnesses
  liquidation of Stolpce ghetto,
  44–47; mother urges her
  to take revenge, 47; shock
  over fate of family, 71–72;
  escapes from forced labor
  group, 72–76; abused while
  with Russian partisan group,
  77–82; abused by Russian
  parachutists, 82–84; arrives
  at Jack's bunker, 85–86;
  negative reception by Jewish
  partisans, 88–90; leaves Jack's
  group, 99–101; returns to
  Jack's group, 104–106; hides
  in swamp during winter
  1943, 114–115; pleads on Jack's
  behalf with Zorin *atrad*
  leaders, 122–123, 137–138,
  146; treats boils of Jack and
  another *atrad* member,
  126–127; intuition to evade
  German pursuit, 130–132;
  overtures by Uncle Oscar,
  133–136; takes and then refrains from revenge, 141–144;
  sees Uncle Oscar in Iweniec,
  150–152; return to Stolpce,
  152–155; bribes Soviet doctor to keep Jack out of army,
  161–162; becomes pregnant,
  164–165; miscarries while in
  Lodz, 167–169; smuggled into
  Berlin, 169–172; hostess in Nei

Freimann, 178–179; becomes pregnant again, 180; Jewish wedding ceremony with Jack, 180; religious beliefs and prayers to her mother, 181–182; gives birth to Cecilia, 183–186; voyage to America, 189–192; adjustment to life in America, 193–199; gives birth to Larry, 196–197; parenting Cecilia and Larry, 203, 211–216

Schleiff, Rose, 193–195, 202

Schleiff, Sofka, 4–5, 28, 30–31, 41–42, 44–45, 203

Sczeczin, 169–170

Singer, Isaac Bashevis, 210

Sonia, 79–80, 82

Sorokin, 77, 81

Srkin, 11

SS (Nazi secret police), 36–37, 39–40, 139, 147

Stalin, Josef, 2, 21, 23, 26, 30–31, 81, 121

Stanislawski, 59–60

Stolpce, 1, 4, 13, 18, 23, 27–30, 34–38, 44–47, 62, 83–86, 138–139, 146, 152–155, 180, 188

Sutin (Dobrin), Cecilia, 184–186, 188–191, 193–194, 197–199, 203, 208–209, 211–213, 217

Sutin, Isaac, 12

Sutin, Jack: early religious training, 14; education, 14–15, 18, 27–28; involvement with *Hashomer Hatzair,* 15–16; divorce by parents, 16–17; dating experiences, 18–19, 28–30; bar mitzvah, 19; plans to emigrate to Palestine, 19–20; early meetings with Rochelle, 28–30; returns to Mir after German invasion, 47–48; performs forced labor in Mir ghetto, 48–49; smuggles grenades into Mir ghetto, 54; escapes from Mir ghetto, 57–61; joins small Jewish partisan group, 61–62; raid on German police station, 63–64; becomes leader of small Jewish partisan group, 64–67; dreams that Rochelle will join him, 68–69; leads raid against Piesochna farm, 93–95; leads food raid outside Mir, 95–98; goes to visit Rochelle at new group, 101–103; plans for Rochelle's return, 104–106; hides in swamp during winter 1943, 114–115; fights with Zorin *atrad,* 123–124; develops severe boils, 124–127; contemplates Nazi defeat, 138–139; fights in ambush on retreating German troops, 139–141; transcribes Zorin's final speech to *atrad,* 144–145; disguises himself, 146; retrieves family photographs from Talish family, 156; practices "dentistry" under Soviets, 156–160; claims TB to stay out of Soviet army, 160–162; rage at theft of gold coins, 165–167; smuggled into Berlin, 169–172; journalist, photographer and chief administrator at Nei Freimann DP camp, 175–177; belief in God and memories of mother, 182–183; first hears truth of concentration camp atrocities, 188; voyage to America, 189–192; successful business career, 199–202; parenting Cecilia and Larry, 203, 211–216; heroic rescue of woman under attack, 216

Sutin, Julius, 12–14, 16–19,
    26–27, 47–51, 58–59, 111–112,
    120, 126, 146, 152, 156–158, 164,
    167, 171, 175, 187, 194, 196–197,
    202, 209–211, 217
Sutin, Lawrence, 196–197,
    203–204, 209–211, 215–218
Sutin, Louis, 174
Sutin, Miriam, 12
Sutin, Sarah (Jack's mother),
    13–14, 16–18, 26–27, 31, 47–50,
    182
Sutin, Sarah (granddaughter
    of Jack and Rochelle), 204,
    217–218

T
Talish family, 156, 165
Tanya, 72-88, 120
Troy, Phillip, 200
Turec, 62

U
United States of America, 9
UNRRA (United Nations Relief
    and Rehabilitation Adminis-
    tration), 170, 174–176, 186
Usik, 76–77

W
Warsaw, 1, 12–13, 165
Wertheim, 122, 125, 137

Z
Zarutsky, Dmitri, 46–47
Zenowey, 158–160, 162, 164
Zorin, Simcha, 107, 118, 121–122,
    137–142, 144–145
Zorin *atrad* (fighting group),
    117–124, 129–130, 132–133,
    136–147, 149, 165
Zuchowicki, David, 179

Jack and Rochelle Sutin have been married for over fifty years and have two children, Cecilia and Lawrence, and three grandchildren, David, Danny, and Sarah. They have lived in Minnesota since 1949.

Lawrence Sutin is the author of numerous works including *A Postcard Memoir* and the critically acclaimed *All Is Change: The Two-Thousand Year Journey of Buddhism to the West*. He lives in Minneapolis, and currently teaches at Hamline University.

The Sutin Family Today

Jack and Rochelle has been typeset in Minion Pro. Composition by BookMobile Design and Publishing Services, Minneapolis, Minnesota, and manufactured by Versa Press on acid-free paper.